CW01160964

Island Studies

Fifty Years of the Lundy Field Society

The Lundy Field Society

Published by
The Lundy Field Society

First Published 1997

ISBN 0 -9530532 -0 -2

© Lundy Field Society & individual contributors, 1997

Island Studies
Fifty Years of the Lundy Field Society

Edited by RA Irving, AJ Schofield & CJ Webster

Typeset, printed, bound & distributed by
The Lazarus Press
6 Grenville Street
Bideford
Devon EX39 2EA

This book is sold subject to the condition that it shall not, by way of trade or otherwise, be lent, re-sold, hired out or otherwise circulated without the publisher's prior consent being given in writing, in any form of binding or cover other than that in which it is published and without a similar condition being imposed on the subsequent purchaser.

Contents

Foreword	Robert Irving, John Schofield and Chris Webster	1
Why Study Islands?	John Schofield and Jennifer J George	5
The Origins and First Fifty Years of the Lundy Field Society	Chris Webster	15
Lundy's Lost Name	Charles Thomas	29
Rebels and Recluses: Lundy's history in context	Clive Harfield	39
The Geology of Lundy	Sandy Smith and Clive Roberts	59
The Archaeology of Lundy	Caroline Thackray	67
Marine Archaeology and Lundy	Philip Robertson and John Heath	77
The Buildings of Lundy	Julia Abel Smith	87
The Birds of Lundy	Tony Taylor	95
Wild Mammals of Lundy	Ian Linn	107
Animal Psychology and Behaviour	Hayley Randle	119
Lundy's Non-marine invertebrates	Tony Parsons	131
Botanical Studies	Elizabeth Hubbard	141
The Freshwater Habitats of Lundy	Jennifer J George	149
Marine Biological Research at Lundy	Keith Hiscock	165
Lundy's Marine Nature Reserve – a short history	Robert Irving and Paul Gilliland	185
Lundy Wardens	Emma Parkes	205
The Contributors		215
Constitution of The Lundy Field Society		219
Map of Lundy		222

List of Figures and Tables

Page

The Origins and First Fifty Years of the Lundy Field Society — Chris Webster
Fig. 1 Leslie Harvey, drawn by John Dyke in August 1957 16
Fig. 2 Graphs showing number of pages devoted to selected subjects 23

Rebels and Recluses: Lundy's history in context — Clive Harfield
Fig. 1 The death of William de Marisco 43
Fig. 2 Portrait of Martin Coles Harman 45
Fig. 3 Portrait of William Hudson Heaven, 1869 49
Fig. 4 View of Millcombe, taken between 1885 and 1897 51
Fig. 5 Sir Jack Hayward's visit to Lundy, 1969 53

The Geology of Lundy — Sandy Smith and Clive Roberts
Fig. 1 Central intrusive complexes of the British Tertiary Volcanic Province 62
Fig. 2 Magnetically mapped dykes on Lundy and outcropping dykes 64

The Archaeology of Lundy — Caroline Thackray
Fig. 1 Battery Cottages 72

Marine Archaeology and Lundy — Philip Robertson and John Heath
Fig. 1 Map of shipwrecks which have been surveyed by archaeologists 79
Fig. 2 Sketch of the Gull Rock site 82
Fig. 3 Isometric sketch of the PS Iona II 84

The Birds of Lundy — Tony Taylor
Fig. 1 Fulmar numbers (number of occupied nest sites) 98
Fig. 2 Kittiwake numbers (counts of breeding pairs) 100
Fig. 3 Movements of willow warblers to and from Lundy from within the British Isles 104

Animal Pychology and Behaviour — Hayley Randle

Fig. 1 Definitions associated with the process of Evolution — 122
Fig. 2 The Influence of 'Organism Variables' on Learning — 124

The Freshwater Habitats of Lundy — Jennifer J George

Table 1 Relative abundance of plant species in Pondsbury — 152
Table 2 Macroinvertebrates in the Bottom Sediments — 154
Table 3 Relative abundance (Domin scale) of plant species at the four ponds — 156
Table 4 Species and numbers of macroinvertebrates (four ponds) — 158
Fig. 1 Location of streams (after Long 1993a) — 159
Table 5 Summary of macroinvertebrate sampling data from the streams — 160

Marine biological research at Lundy — Keith Hiscock

Fig. 1 Zonation on an exposed granite shore — 167
Fig. 2 Zonation on a sheltered slate shore — 168
Fig. 3 Zonation on underwater rocks — 171
Fig. 4 Sediment fauna from the east coast of Lundy — 174

Lundy's Marine Nature Reserve – a short history — Robert Irving and Paul Gilliland

Table 1 Reasons for the establishment of a marine nature reserve — 187
Table 2 Marine nature reserve's code of conduct — 190
Fig. 1 The seaward boundary of the voluntary marine nature reserve — 193
Table 3 Reasons for and against becoming a statutory marine nature reserve — 195
Fig. 2 Administrative structure for the management of the MNR — 197
Fig. 3 Guide produced for use on the snorkel trail — 199
Table 4 Recent developments in interpretation and promotion — 201

Lundy Wardens — Emma Parkes

Fig. 1 Lundy Field Society quarters in the Old Light, 1948 — 206
Fig. 2 David and Mary Lee arriving at the Landing Bay, June 1950 — 208
Fig. 3 Peter Davis, warden 1951-1953 — 210
Fig. 4 Barbara Whitaker (warden 1954-1957) — 212
Fig. 5 Tree planting and maintenance in Millcombe Valley — 214

List of Plates

(Between pages 128 & 129)

The Geology of Lundy — S Smith and C Roberts
Plate 1   Metamorphosed sedimentary rocks
Plate 2   The Lundy Granite
Plate 3   Dykes intrude the Lundy granite

The Archaeology of Lundy — Caroline Thackray
Plate 4   Prehistoric hut circle at North End
Plate 5   Keith Gardner

Marine Archaeology — P Robertson and J Heath
Plate 6   Diver with recording slate
Plate 7   Stepway on the MV Robert

The Birds of Lundy — A M Taylor
Plate 8   Puffin in Jenny's Cove
Plate 9   Three breeding guillimots
Plate 10   Whitethroat
Plate 11   Veery: a North American species
Plate 12   Manx shearwater

Wild Mammals of Lundy — Ian Linn
Plate 13   Pigmy shrew *Sorex minutus*
Plate 14   Black rat *Rattus rattus*
Plate 15   Brown rat *Rattus norvegicus*
Plate 16   Feral goats *Capra hircus*
Plate 17   Soay sheep *Ovis Orientalis*
Plate 18   Sika deer *Cervus nippon*

Non-marine Invertebrates — Tony Parsons
Plate 19	*Cteniopus sulphureus*
Plate 20	Damselfly *Calopteryx virgo*
Plate 21	Green hairstreak *Callophrys rubi*
Plate 22	Ichneumon *Eniscospilus ramidulus*

Botanical Studies — Elizabeth Hubbard
Plate 23	Lundy cabbage *Coincya wrightii*
Plate 24	Flowers of the Lundy cabbage
Plate 25	Flowers of the balm-leaved figwort
Plate 26	Bog asphodel
Plate 27	Heath spotted orchid
Plate 28	Bog pimpernel *Anagallis tenella*
Plate 29	Carpet of thrift

Freshwater Habitats of Lundy — Jennifer J George
Plate 30	View of Pondsbury in August 1979
Plate 31	The Rocket Pole pond
Plate 32	View of the larger pond at Quarter Wall
Plate 33	The Quarry Pool in June 1996

Marine Biological Research — Keith Hiscock
Plate 34	A ballan wrasse
Plate 35	Animal dominated rocks
Plate 36	A concentration of rare species
Plate 37	Community off the Hen and Chickens

Marine Nature Reserve – R Irving and P Gilliland
Plate 38	The Zoning Scheme (revised version 1995)
Plate 39	Key to Zoning Scheme

Lundy Wardens – Emma Parkes
Plate 40	Snorkelling

For Peter Cole and Tony Langham

Foreword

Lundy is a small island, composed largely of granite, set in the approaches to the Bristol Channel on the west side of mainland Britain. It has a striking appearance, its sheer cliffs rising on all sides to some 100m, but with its plateau sufficiently level and its resources sufficiently rich and diverse to have enabled settlement, subsistence and farming over a period of some 10,000 years. Although it appears from maps to lie relatively close to the mainland coast of north Devon, Lundy is, by British standards, an isolated island. Although often hard to believe, it can be an inhospitable place, once being described as, "so immured with rocks and impaled with beetle-browed cliffs, that there is no entrance but for friends".

Today Lundy has a considerable following with large numbers of people enthusiastic about and dedicated to the preservation of its character, not to mention its precious natural and historic resources. Some of the most dedicated and enthusiastic have over the years formed themselves into groups, clubs and societies: the Lundy Collectors Club; the Friends of Lundy; and the Lundy Field Society. Of these organisations the Lundy Field Society is the oldest, with its fiftieth anniversary passing in 1996.

Four years ago, the then Committee and Officers of the Lundy Field Society began to consider how its fiftieth anniversary might be celebrated, and one proposal, from the editors of this volume, was that a book should be produced, seeking to document and publicise the important work undertaken by the Field Society over that period. The proposal was warmly endorsed and this volume is the result. Our aim has been to cover fully the range of work undertaken on and around the island, and to address its worth both locally and more widely within each discipline. Much of this work has been undertaken by eminent scientists and academics and some is of national, even international, significance. With some disciplines, particularly those involving birds, mammals and archaeology, numerous projects have been undertaken over the years by various groups and individuals, and the authors here were asked to provide overviews covering aspects of this work. For those less familiar with Lundy, or those whose interests are perhaps specific and scientific, some general papers are included. Charles Thomas and Clive Harfield present some new perspectives on Lundy's history; John Schofield and Jennifer George offer some general thoughts on the significance of islands for the types of research documented in the papers which follow. There are also contributions documenting the history of the Field Society (the first "official" history to appear in print) and, to close, the role of the Lundy wardens. As well as the obvious emphasis on research, managing Lundy's natural and man-made resource is not forgotten: Robert Irving and Paul Gilliland provide insights into the setting up and management of the Marine Reserve, while Caroline Thackray and Julia Abel Smith discuss the archaeological sites and built environment respectively.

We are not aware of a comparable publication covering such a range of subject matter, and this has presented a significant challenge in editing this volume. Aware that many readers will be unfamiliar with the detail and some of the general issues raised in some of the papers, we have tried to ensure that all are written such that the lay reader can understand their content. We hope that has been achieved and apologise if any jargon has got through the net.

Many have helped in the production of this volume. We are of course grateful to the contributors for agreeing to help, for keeping tight to our brief, and for meeting deadlines. The committee members and officers of the Lundy Field Society (1992-6) gave advice and made helpful suggestions concerning the format and content of the volume: Jennifer George, the Society's current Chairman, and Ian Lovatt, its Treasurer, made notable contributions. We are most grateful to John Dyke for allowing us to reproduce his drawings. Thanks also to Peter Rothwell and Ann Westcott. Peter and Ann both gave advice and practical assistance throughout, while we are particularly grateful to Peter for providing the cover illustration. The production of this volume in its present form would not have been possible without financial assistance, and we are indebted to English Nature and the World Wide Fund for Nature for their support in this regard. Finally, it seems an opportune time to express thanks on behalf of the Field Society to the occupants and inhabitants of Lundy, the staff and crew of the MS *Oldenburg* and its predecessors, and, from 1969, the staff of the Landmark Trust at Shottesbrooke, for all their kind assistance with and support for all aspects of scientific research and fieldwork undertaken on Lundy over the years.

Anniversaries are opportunities for reflection and forward thinking. This volume concentrates on the former, documenting what we are proud to describe as our achievements over fifty years. We hope this volume does justice to those involved, and provides the necessary inspiration for another fifty years of achievement. Things do look good. The Annual Report, in which virtually all of the work undertaken on Lundy is documented, is receiving more contributions covering a wider range of subjects certainly than at any time over the past ten years, and perhaps ever. There are also some exciting (and potentially hugely significant) projects now in their early stages. We would be only too delighted if the equivalent volume in 2046 were to describe the achievements of the Field Society's first fifty years as comparatively insignificant compared to those of the second fifty.

Anniversaries are also occasions on which individual achievement is noted, and many references are made in the volume to some of those who helped shape the Society in its early years. When plans for the anniversary were first discussed four years ago, two long standing members of the Society took a prominent role, giving practical help and valuable advice; both fully supported the volume we proposed. It was especially sad, therefore, that both died before the plans came to fruition. Tony Langham (1928-95), perhaps the most quoted individual in the various bibliographies in this volume, and Peter Cole (1929-94), both Honorary Secretary and Vice President at various times, are greatly missed. It seems entirely appropriate that this volume should be dedicated to their memory.

                            Robert Irving
                            John Schofield
                            Chris Webster

                            November 1996

Millcombe House

Why Study Islands?

John Schofield and Jennifer J George

*Be not afeard: the isle is full of noises,
Sounds and sweet airs, that give delight
and hurt not.*
            (William Shakespeare: The Tempest)

Introduction

Islands have, for centuries, had a particular attraction, whether for achieving strategic objectives in a military campaign, for creative inspiration in literature and the arts, or for attaining personal contentment. They also have a significant role in both cultural history and the history of science. But when we think in these terms, we tend to visualise a particular type of place: small, isolated islands with sandy beaches backing onto woodland, and a rich flora and diverse fauna thriving under a hot equatorial sun. It is as well to emphasise the obvious: that not every island is such a paradise. Some islands are barren and inhospitable places; some are so large as to not have the feel of islands at all. Clearly the degree of islands' separation, and their size, vary considerably, while their position on the globe largely determines the nature of their ecology. Some islands are new, emerging in comparatively recent times as volcanoes, and some cease to exist as true islands, perhaps following the construction of bridges. Yet, despite the size range, and scale of their separation or isolation, most islands have something distinct about their ecology and the terrestrial communities they support. In this contribution, we will consider this background, providing a selection of the better known examples of island research by way of illustration.

The character of islands

Islands, and the opportunities they provide for seclusion and retreat, seem to have a particular poignance in the modern high tech world of the mobile phone and the World Wide Web (but it is interesting to note that the small communities on Shetland are now using the Internet to protect their sense of *community* [Spinney 1995]). That islands had similar appeal in the past is well recorded, with terms like 'magical' and 'irresistible' being frequently used in contemporary accounts and literature. Examples include the quotation from *The Tempest*, presented at the start of this chapter. In the context of Lundy, a similar message is conveyed by Felix Gade in a quotation from his autobiography:

"...In spite of the comparative primitiveness, inadequacy and even hardship of living on a very small, remote, windswept island, there is some indefinable attraction about such a place which lures one back...Sometimes I think it is purely and simply the

peace and quiet, which exists even when the elements are at their worst; or it may be the sense of freedom, the independence, the absence of the minor tyrannies of life in a large community; or it may be the challenge of wringing a livelihood on this bleak outpost in spite of the storm and tempest, drought and deluge. Then again, it could be that one's entity is more apparent amongst a small island community. Every single person has an importance, an individuality. Finally there is the island itself, which ingrains itself into one's very marrow; the beauty, the grandeur, the endurance, the solitude..." (1978,16).

A theme often presented in literary works is the formative effect of being marooned, and, as is well documented in fact and fiction, this cuts both ways – good in some cases, ill in others. The first of this genre was *Robinson Crusoe*, published in 1719, about a man shipwrecked on a desert island for 28 years. The possible effects of such isolation are discussed more fully below.

The seclusion islands provide also contributes to their appeal as natural research laboratories, the physical boundary acting as a constraint on regular movement. As is discussed elsewhere (Schofield in press), this seclusion or separation provides islands with certain characteristics, rendering them distinct from other types of location. First, there are the associated properties of security versus isolation, limitation of resources versus abundant availability of certain island products, and the sea as a barrier versus the sea as a means of communication (Blache 1950). Then there are the characteristics which make them units "that the mind can pick out and begin to comprehend" (MacArthur and Wilson 1967,3): relative isolation, limitation in space, limitation in or absence of resources, limitation in organic diversity, reduced interspecies competition, protection from outside competition (Fosberg 1965,5). However, to use 'anything with all of the above' as a definition risks oversimplification. In this sense, a quotation from D.H. Lawrence's short story *The Man Who Loved Islands*, first published in 1927, is useful in defining what, in terms of locations suited to the kinds of scientific research addressed in this volume, we mean by island: "An island, if it is big enough, is no better than a continent. It has to be really quite small before it feels like an island".

Island studies

As this contribution will demonstrate, islands of the type described above have been the subject of many aspects of research since at least the mid 19th century, and many individual islands are well known as a result; the Galápagos archipelago and finches for example are synonymous, as are Easter Island and the maoi, or giant statues. Many islands, however, less well known in their own right, have seen significant data collected which have contributed to broader research themes, such as the role of bird observatories in understanding migration; alternatively there are islands where research covering many disciplines is constantly underway, gradually changing our perceptions of animal or human behaviour, evolution and so on. Since the Lundy Field Society was founded in 1946, and through to around the mid 1950s, Lundy saw an emphasis on bird observation, not surprisingly given its origins. However, this has changed in more recent years, arguably from around 1956 (see Webster, this volume), since when a greater diversity of research has been undertaken. Some aspects of this research involve topics which are of considerable interest and worth, but for which Lundy's island status is of less relevance; others *require* islands to such an extent that other types of location will be unsuitable.

As the papers in this volume make clear, the cumulative results of fifty years of research on Lundy, building to some extent on previous work, has made a significant contribution to our understanding of many specific aspects of what come under the very general headings of ecology, and the history of human occupation. Important research has also been undertaken in other fields such as geology, and these are covered elsewhere in the volume. Here, we review just two of the main themes which make island research important, and which provide a framework within which the achievements of the Lundy Field Society, 1946-1996, can be better understood: evolutionary ecology and human occupation and adaptation.

Evolutionary ecology

Charles Darwin, at the beginning of his career, wrote: "The zoology of archipelagoes will be well worth examination". How true this was. From his observations and those of Alfred Russel Wallace in his studies of islands on the archipelago between Southeast Asia and Australia, the modern theory of evolution was born.

Both men were developing similar ideas on the origin of different species, but it was Darwin who in 1858 published his theory of Natural Selection that is now accepted by scientists. Simply, the theory says that a pair of animals or plants produce many more offspring than are needed to replace them, and that these offspring are not identical with one another; some are better fitted for survival than others, and these will have an advantage in the competition that occurs for food and shelter, finding a mate and so on. They will therefore survive and reproduce, and their favourable characteristics will pass into the next generation. If a species becomes isolated, as occurs on an island, then the gene pool of a population can become different from a similar population on the mainland and eventually a new species may evolve. These species are unlikely to leave the island habitat because of the surrounding ocean, and consequently, will not occur elsewhere in the world. Such species are said to be *endemic* to that island.

The study of the flora and fauna of islands provides an understanding not only of the process of evolution, but also an insight into how organisms colonise an island from the mainland, and subsequent adaptation of these organisms to a new and often different environment. Also, factors such as the numbers of organisms that can be supported on an island and the rate of extinction of a species can be quantified, and the development of the island flora and fauna into an integrated self-sustaining ecosystem can be studied. The emergence of an island from the ocean, such as Surtsey in the Atlantic in 1965, provides a unique opportunity for research into the development of animal and plant communities.

The very existence of a species on an island provides knowledge of colonisation and dispersal patterns. Oceans are effective barriers to distribution, except of course to birds and flying insects. However, some land animals may arrive on rafts of drifting debris, while the seeds and spores of plants can be carried by wind or travel attached to the bodies of birds and large insects. For example, it is thought that 60% of the indigenous flora of the Galápagos islands were brought in by birds, 30% by the wind, and 10% drifted in by sea. On large islands there is a tendency for plants and animals to lose the dispersal mechanism that brought them to the island in the first place; for example, plant seeds often lose their feathery tufts, insects become wingless, and birds have become flightless over a period of time. Examples include the kiwi of New Zealand and the dodo of Mauritius (now made extinct by man). The absence of predatory species on islands is often a contributing factor to this phenomenon.

Isolation is a major factor influencing the development of species on an island. As a result, islands have a high proportion of endemic forms. On the Galápagos islands about 34% of the terrestrial plants, 50% of the terrestrial animals and 25% of the marine flora and fauna surrounding the island are endemic. In the Hawaiian islands in the middle of the North Pacific ocean, over 90% of the flora are endemic. If islands are situated a long way from a continent, then often many groups of plants and animals may be absent; for example, on the Hawaiian islands there are no freshwater fish, no native amphibia, reptiles and mammals, except for one species of bat.

For an animal or plant to survive on an island it must be able to adapt to different conditions. A species that can utilise many kinds of food is therefore at an advantage, and a well-known example of such adaptive radiation is that of the finch population on the Galápagos islands (Weiner 1995). There are now thirteen different species of finch present, feeding on a variety of food - seeds, nuts, fruit, flowers and insects. On the mainland these niches are occupied by different bird species, but on the Galápagos the different finch species probably evolved from a seed-eating ancestor and were able to adapt to different ways of life due to lack of competition from other birds.

Another example can be found on the Hawaiian islands where members of the plant family *Lobeliaceae* have undergone extensive adaptive radiation (Carlquist

1965). There are now 150 species and varieties of lobeliads ranging from erect tree forms 9m tall to small soft-stemmed species. Linked to adaptive radiation of the lobeliads is the evolution of the nectar feeding bird, the honey-creeper (family *Drepanididae*), that has eleven endemic genera in the family, species of which now also feed on insects, seeds and nuts as well as plant nectar (Amadon 1950).

Life on islands is more hazardous than on the mainland. Islands, with their smaller and less diverse communities, are less stable than the mainland, and consequently are much more susceptible to environmental change. Furthermore, severe weather or catastrophe such as a volcanic eruption can cause species to become extinct; and there is little chance of the species returning to colonise when good conditions return as often happens on the mainland.

Islands and their ecology are thus of considerable importance in our understanding of biological processes and how life develops and functions. They provide a unique opportunity to study evolution as their isolation provides the ideal environment for rapid population change and adaptive radiation that cannot be seen so clearly on the mainland. The small-scale studies that can be attempted on islands often provide valuable information that can be used to interpret community and population structure on the larger continents.

Human occupation and adaptation

In a paper, now over twenty years old, the advantage of using islands as laboratories in the study of human cultural development, was explored by John Evans (1973). Amongst other things he noted the fact that natural scientists, arguably beginning with Charles Darwin, and anthropologists, such as Margaret Mead, were among the first to recognise their potential in these terms, and that archaeologists had been relatively slow to follow on. As with non-human populations, island life imposes restrictions on communication with groups living elsewhere, and this isolation makes it possible to study their development over long periods, unaffected by radical interference from outside. Two aspects of island research into human populations are considered here: first, islands can be used to study colonisation, the processes involved, the population size required for successful colonisation, and the likelihood of survival (adaptation, in other words); second, islands provide the opportunity for studying the tendency isolated communities have towards exaggerated development in some aspects of their culture.

Colonisation, and the minimum size of population required for this to be successful, was addressed by Stephen Black in 1978. Taking Polynesia as his study area, he used a computer simulation to assess the probability of success of small founding populations, concluding that a mixed group of ten individuals could survive under ordinary circumstances. In short, a canoe-load of voyagers may be sufficient for a successful colonisation (Black 1978,66), even taking into account the potentially damaging effects of inbreeding. This finding however appears to contradict the reality of life on both Pitcairn and Henderson, also in Polynesia, where Marshall Weisler's (1994) fieldwork has provided insights into human group dynamics with its portrait of a tiny population dying out under the social equivalent of solitary confinement. In both cases the populations, c.50 in the case of Henderson, hundreds on Pitcairn, died out at around AD 1600 following around 500 years of continuous occupation. As Weisler suggests, eventually no marriage partners could have remained who did not violate incest taboos, while the effects of inbreeding may have appeared before that. Another possibility might have been a climatic fluctuation driving the islanders to starvation. The population may equally have responded to the threat of extinction by murder and cannibalism, as is thought likely with California's Donner Party of pioneers (Grayson 1990). Or the islanders may have become insane from social deprivation, as happened to a Belgian Antarctic Expedition trapped by ice for over a year.

These are examples where populations failed to adapt under conditions of duress, specifically isolation. But isolation can have a positive effect in some cases. It can, as John Evans suggested in his 1973 paper, promote exaggerated development of some aspect of an island's culture. This is often ceremonial in nature, and the Easter Island maoi come into this category. It is also tempting to suggest the megalithic monuments of Orkney, and perhaps even the spectacular cliff castles of the Aran Islands as representatives of this exaggerated development. The study of these monuments, and of the communities who built them, will tell us how this process developed, when the exaggeration occurred, and why. In the case of the maoi, was it to 'advertise' the insularity of the island's communities, or was the sheer number of monuments indicative more of the competition which existed between island families or communities? But this physical manifestation may take another form: literature. On the Blaskets and the Aran Islands, off the south-west and west coasts of Ireland respectively, communities in the early twentieth century began to write down what had previously been passed by word-of-mouth: a wealth of folk tales, poems and songs reflective of their history and lifestyle over generations (Schofield in press), seemingly out of proportion to the size of community from which they derived. Works of a narrative anecdotal nature are particularly useful in telling us about the way of life among island communities before the advent of modern technology and communication. This is as close as we come to a direct ethnographic analogy for the prehistoric and early historic occupation of small islands. The works tell us about social organisation and politics, how decisions were made; they tell us about ordinary daily events, such as fishing trips, seal hunts, kelp gathering; they tell us about the hardships of island life and the advantages of sometimes being "a world apart", such as during the time of the Great War.

But the question remains, is this degree of creative achievement unusual? If so, why does isolation have this effect, and, assuming that it is not inevitable, under what circumstances might it arise? There are various possibilities: maybe it is the fact that "every single person has an importance, an individuality" (Gade 1978,16) and thus something to contribute. Or maybe it is as Rogers (1978,x) has suggested:

> "where life in general is limited and monotonous, its least detail is exalted into Drama: islanders who live in the shapeless shadow of poverty will always put a pattern of dignity and ceremony on it, in order to endure and redeem their existence".

Literature, such as that described here, is but one manifestation of the exaggerated development witnessed amongst some isolated communities. It also constitutes a cultural resource of immense importance in understanding how island communities survived, as well as documenting their decline (the Blaskets were finally abandoned in 1954). At the end of Tomas O'Crohan's book, *The Islandman*, first published in 1937, his perceptive remarks betray his awareness of the inevitable, but also demonstrate his knowledge that by writing down what was previously passed by word-of-mouth, he had done those who follow a great service:

> "One day there will be none left in the Blasket of all I have mentioned in this book, and none to remember them. I am thankful to God, who has given me the chance to preserve from forgetfulness those days which I have seen with my own eyes and have borne their burden, and that when I am gone, men will know what life was like in my time, and the neighbours that lived with me" (O'Crohan 1992,244).

Islands therefore have a particular part to play in understanding human occupation and adaptation, and that is reflected in the amount of research undertaken on islands around the world in recent years. Some sceptics continue to interpret this more in terms of the pleasant working conditions that islands provide; but there is a real significance in scientific terms, as the examples presented above demonstrate.

Conclusion

What we have presented in this contribution is nothing more than a background against which to place the papers which follow. Our intention has been to outline the significance islands have in scientific research generally, and to demonstrate the potential they have to address questions which are often either best addressed, or can only be addressed, by studying islands.

As we have said before, Lundy has been the subject of research covering a wide range of disciplines over many years, and this has been supported and, in many instances, undertaken by members of the Lundy Field Society. As well as providing some new insights into Lundy's history, the contributors to this volume have been asked to illustrate the range of work undertaken, the significance of the results within their subject generally, as well as providing an illustration of changing methods and objectives over a fifty year period. We think Lundy has a significance in these terms which justifies this treatment at the time of the Field Society's fiftieth anniversary; the papers presented provide the opportunity for you, the reader, to reach your own conclusion.

References

Amadon, D, 1950. The Hawaiian honey-creepers. *Bulletin of the American Museum of Natural History* 95, 151-262.

Blache, J, 1950. Les particularités géographiques des iles. *Bulletin de la Société de Géographie de Marseille* 65, 5-22.

Black, S, 1978. Polynesian outliers: a study in the survival of small populations. In I Hodder (ed), *Simulation studies in archaeology*, 63-76. Cambridge University Press.

Carlquist, S, 1965. *Island Life*. New York: Natural History Press.

Evans, J D, 1973. Islands as laboratories for the study of culture process. In A C Renfrew (ed), *The Explanation of Culture Change: Models in Prehistory*, 517-20. London: Duckworth.

Fosberg, F R, 1965. The island ecosystem. In F R Fosberg (ed), *Man's place in the island ecosystem*, 1-6. Honolulu: Bishop Museum Press.

Gade, F, 1978. *My Life on Lundy*. Privately published.

Grayson, D, 1990. Donner Party deaths: a demographic assessment. *Journal of Anthropological Research* 46, 223-242.

MacArthur, R J, & Wilson, E O, 1967. *The theory of island biogeography*. Princetown University Press.

O'Crohan, T, 1992. *The Islandman*. Oxford University Press. (Originally published by the Talbot Press, Dublin, 1937.)

Rogers, W R, 1978. Introduction to Sayers P, *An Old Woman's Reflections*. Oxford University Press.

Schofield, A J, in press. Exploring insularity: some thoughts on island archaeology. In M Patton and K Brown (eds), *Island Archaeology*. British Archaeology Reports.

Spinney, L, 1995. Electronic crofting. *New Scientist* 147, 30-33.

Weiner, J, 1995. *The Beak of the Finch: A story of evolution in our time*. Vintage.

Weisler, M, 1994. The settlement of marginal Polynesia: new evidence from Henderson Island. *Journal of Field Archaeology* 21, 83-102.

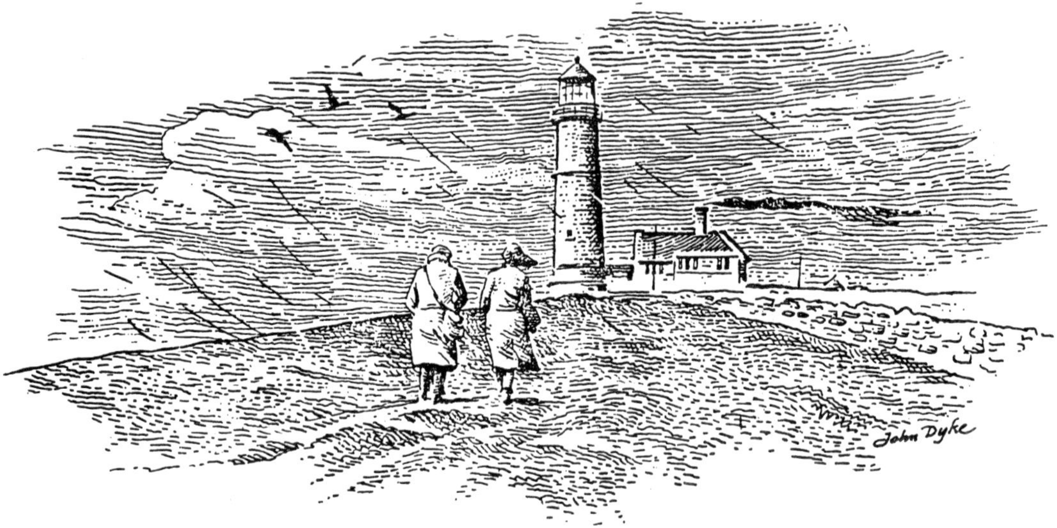
John Dyke

The Origins and First Fifty Years of the Lundy Field Society

Chris Webster

Origins

The Lundy Field Society was founded on 29th May 1946 but its origins can be traced to a meeting held the previous year on 8th December by the Devon Bird Watching and Preservation Society (DBW&PS). This meeting heard an interesting report of the development of the Pembrokeshire islands of Skomer and Skokholm as bird ringing stations. The speaker hoped that the study of bird migration undertaken before the war would be greatly extended and the DBW&PS was invited to support this work. In discussion of this proposal Leslie Harvey (Fig. 1), a lecturer in the Zoology Department of the University College of the South West (now Exeter University), "made a suggestion that consideration might be given to linking Lundy Island and the Scillies with the activities on the Pembrokeshire islands. ...the meeting decided later to explore its possibilities" (DBW&PS 1945). It is evident from subsequent events that they asked Harvey to investigate the situation on Lundy.

Harvey wrote to Martin Coles Harman (see Harfield, this vol. Fig. 2), the owner of Lundy, on 14th December 1945. Harman was a keen naturalist, who had published brief notes on ornithological topics (Harman 1943a, 1943b), but he was also extremely keen to preserve the independence of Lundy from the mainland authorities. His reply expressed interest in the project but...

"I have had some experience of the lengths to which Government Departments will go in trying to deprive one of one's birthright. I have had it said in Court by the Attorney General, (which the Court did not accept) that by virtue of the Wild Birds' Protection Act and its supposed application to Lundy, that Lundy had lost its independence; and I am very nervous of giving the mainland any handle."

(Harman 1946a)

Harvey responded:

"Thank you very much indeed for your reply to my enquiry about the possibility of establishing a bird station on Lundy. I am delighted to know that you are prepared to discuss the idea. I can readily understand your anxiety to preserve the integrity and independence of the island, and am quite sure that no member of the Devon Bird Watching Society or of the group associated with the Welsh project would wish to do anything to infringe this.

...

> *We shall be completely dependant on your goodwill, and it follows that you have the power to impose any terms you think fit."*
>
> (Harvey 1946a)

Harvey wrote again in March 1946 saying that he would like to put proposals to the DBW&PS meeting of 6th April which included: the erection of a Heligoland trap, the presence of biologists to operate the trap, ringing of nesting cliff-breeding birds, and periodic publication of progress reports and results. Harvey also expressed a personal interest in the study of other forms of wild life.

Harman replied, apologising that pressure of work had prevented him from replying to the previous letter, and continuing:

> *"What you desire to be done can be done provided your Society is prepared to agree to the following conditions:*
>
> *(a) A Lundy Bird-watching Committee to be formed which will have no other object but the Birds on <u>Lundy</u> [original underlined].*
>
> *(b) The said Committee to be formed at my suggestion herein made: I to be the first subscriber to its funds in the sum of £50 hereby promised.*
>
> *(c) The Committee men and those employed by them or associated with them to tell you that they will respect the Island's peculiar rights and privileges and see to it as far as they can that anyone they bring along does the same.*

Leslie Harvey, drawn by John Dyke in August 1957.

(d)   I or my successors to issue annually written invitations to the people whose names and addresses the Secretary of the Lundy Committee gives me, to visit the island and to land without fee. Anyone not able to produce such an invitation will be charged the usual 1/- [5p] landing fee and will be subject to the usual Black Listing if his or her presence is not desired.

The other aspects of the Island's wild life can, of course, be taken in the Committee's stride, but I want to avoid the Committee being a branch of anything else..."

(Harman 1946b)

Harvey was able to reply to this on the 29th thanking Harman for "your proposals [which] are so generous that I hesitate to demur from them" (Harvey 1946b). This was understandable as the £50 donation was a considerable sum at that time and, for instance, would provide half the annual salary for a warden (see below). Harvey did, however, ask for clarification of point (a) which appeared to preclude working with the Welsh group.

Harman responded that this was not his intention...

"All that I want to avoid is that, the Lundy Committee can be dictated to from 'on high' ...

It was for this reason and not because I want to interfere at all, that I suggested the matter might take the form of initiation, or at least, invitation by me and that I might be the first subscriber.

All I ask for is some protection against the sort of thing that nearly always happens when we have connections with the mainland. We give some concession to some very nice people, they bring along some less nice people, and the less nice people introduce some nasty ones who start ordering us about on our own Island and telling us where to get off."

(Harman 1946c)

The DBW&PS minutes of the meeting of 6th April record:

"...the most important business of the day came under consideration. This concerned further developments towards the possible achievement of Lundy Island as a base for a station devoted to the intensive study of bird migration in co-operation with the West Wales Field Society...

Mr L A Harvey who initiated the proposal at the previous meeting gave a report of his preliminary negotiations with Mr Martin C Harman, the owner of Lundy. On the whole these were reassuring.

...the scheme was to be commended, and many expressed their willingness to take an active part in the project. Accordingly a Lundy Field Committee to consist of the officers of our Society with Mr L A Harvey as convenor further to explore the possibilities of the scheme."

(DBW&PS 1946a)

After the meeting Harvey wrote to Harman:
> "I am delighted to be able to report that the Devon Bird Watching and Preservation Society agreed on Saturday to the formation of a Lundy Field Committee on the terms of your generous offer. They have asked me to act as Convenor, and I am going to set about collecting together a group of likely workers and members as soon as I have polished off one or two jobs which I must finish. I shall be very glad to have your views on the form of the Committee if you have a spare moment, and I hope very much that you will agree to my proposing you as the first President."
>
> (Harvey 1946c)

Harman replied to this "welcome letter" and warned of transport problems as the Admiralty had withdrawn its detachment on April 6th. He concluded:
> "I will keep in touch with you if necessary by telephone.
>
> With every good wish to you and to the embryo Lundy Field Committee."
>
> (Harman 1946d)

It seems likely that Harman and Harvey did speak, as by the end of May, Harvey refers, without explanation, to a Lundy Field *Society*. This probably reflects Harman's desire for an independent organisation of similar standing to the DBW&PS whose own minutes at their next meeting simply record "that the Lundy Field Society has been successfully launched."

(DBW&PS 1946b)

Harvey reported to Harman:
> "I called an informal meeting together yesterday [29 May 1946] at which we drew up the enclosed constitution for a Lundy Field Society, and inaugurated the society. We agreed unanimously to ask you to be President and in view of your last letter of April 9th, I am sure that you will accept this office. I may say that we shall, as soon as we call our next meeting, appoint among the other officers, a chairman who will take on all the work on conducting committee and other meetings, we shall not therefore call on you to do any more than you wish to do"
>
> (Harvey 1946d)

Harvey also indicated that he had never been to Lundy and that a reconnaissance party would be needed to identify the site for the trap.

Harman approved "a good job of work" which "interpreted my wishes in the constitution" and sent the promised £50 (Harman 1946e). Harvey also sent a copy of the minutes (presumably at the suggestion of Harman) to Felix Gade, then at the Hartland Quay Hotel, who responded positively and asked to join the LFS.

The early years

Correspondence continued between Harman, Harvey and Gade about the proposed visit that the LFS hoped to make on the 28th of June. Gade was asked to advise on the site for the trap. A position on the dam in Millcombe had been suggested but Gade recommended a site on the side of Hangman's Hill. Harman also offered accommodation: "pending the restarting of the normal life of the Island, you will be welcome to use the hotel and the furniture" but he warned, "You will find everything in an unbelievable dreadful mess" (Harman 1946f). For the future he suggested "The Old Lighthouse with its noble house adjoining would be ideal but for the distance from the trap" (ibid). This was another example of Harman's generosity for, after its occupation by the Navy, the Old Light was one of the best repaired buildings on the island.

Harman had been having difficulty obtaining reliable transport but the LFS had fewer problems than he predicted. Accordingly, on the 28th the first LFS party of 5 went to the island.

"[We left] Bideford at 6 am and arrived at the landing beach by nine after a wet crossing in the face of a stiffish westerly breeze. Capt. Pile's boat was the first to call at Lundy for a month, and we carried mail and stores in addition to our party and half a dozen visitors. We were met on the shore by Mr Heaysman, Mr Harman's agent, who gave us directions to the various places we wished to see and carte blanche to examine whatever we needed there."

(LFS 1946a)

On the island the party split into two, one going to the North End and the other looking at the trap site, and hotel...

"very generously offered with all its contents by Mr Harman as a temporary home until the end of the year. Having been warned, we were not surprised to find it somewhat forlorn, with many ceilings and walls badly damaged by rain through the unrepaired roof."

(LFS 1946a)

Hangman's Hill was rejected as a site for the trap but a promising site was located "between Hotel and House".

"Then over to the Old Light - our permanent quarters. It is good – plenty of room and "built like a battleship". No leaks here and all in good order after occupation by the Navy.

Lastly a visit to the Marisco Tavern to sample the beer we had ourselves brought over and down to the shore for the return. Just before three we weighed anchor and left the island, shining grey and green in the sunlight, with its lonely inhabitants waving us from the shingle. A quick passage with following wind and tide brought us to Bideford Quay by 5.30, our minds full of what has to be done, and how to do it."

(LFS 1946a)

The summer was spent organising the construction of the trap, not an easy task when many war-time restrictions on materials were still in force, and a second expedition was planned to leave on Friday 20 September. In the event they were delayed until the following Monday when they had a bad four-hour crossing. On the island they split, the three women cleaning up the hotel and the three men surveying the trap site and starting to dig holes for the posts. By Wednesday the posts had been erected and a small pond dug, fed by a convenient stream. Conditions were unpleasant as "the weather this day was foul ... no sign of sun since leaving Ilfracombe" (LFS 1946b). The condition of the Old Light had also deteriorated since June with a broken window and loose slates allowing the rain in. On the following day the sun came out and the skeleton of the trap was finished by lunch time, after which the whole party wandered up the west side and had tea with the keepers at the North Light. They returned to Ilfracombe on Friday and the work on the trap had to wait until October when another week's work saw the netting added and it could be described as virtually complete.

Sadly, much of this work was in vain as, at the first AGM on January 24, 1947, the trap was reported to have been "severely" damaged by the autumn gales. The meeting, however, was a success with membership reported at about 100 and a healthy bank balance. The meeting decided to appoint the first warden, Rowland Barker, who was later offered £100 per year and 10/- (50p) per visitor per week. He was the first of a number of wardens employed by the LFS to run the observatory and hostel accommodation in the Old Light.

The trap was destroyed twice during the first half of 1947 without having been used and, by June, other locations were being considered. It was decided to relocate the trap to "St John's Valley below the mission hut" (LFS 1947) with a second trap to be built in the quarries.

Harvey was also concerned with an issue that continues to this day and asked Harman whether he would permit some rat eradication using an experimental method. Harman agreed but warned "in my first year [ie 1926] I employed experts who at a cost of £350 nearly but not quite, cleared out all the rats" (Harman 1947a). The idea came to nothing as Harvey discovered that the supposed new method of rat control was only a rumour. Harman also suggested ideas to the LFS and suggested that a long-term project should be undertaken to repoint Marisco Castle. The AGM of the following year agreed to this after obtaining expert advice on whether this was appropriate for an ancient monument. This broadening of the LFS's interests is also reflected in the first Annual Report which, as well as birds, contained preliminary reports on terrestrial and freshwater habitats and marine ecology.

The traps continued to be a problem in 1948 and, in November, it was decided to build two new traps, one in the south quarry and one in the garden of the

Old Light. The Garden Trap was constructed in 1949 and a photograph of it appears in the third Annual Report. The year also saw the unveiling of the memorial to John Harman, VC, at which members of the LFS assisted with the 800 guests; the first suggestion that the LFS might assist with the Rhododendron problem; and the first suggestion that the LFS might undertake archaeological investigations "although such jobs ... must be done very carefully" (Harman 1949).

The Quarry Trap was built in 1950 but did not prove to be a success. It was replaced by the Terrace Trap in 1951 and a Quarter Wall trap followed sometime during the wardenship of Peter Davies (1951-4). The finances of the LFS were also causing great concern, particularly in 1952 when the University College at Exeter withdrew its grant, which had previously been of £200-300 per year.

Troubled times

Martin Coles Harman died suddenly at the end of 1954 and Leslie Harvey paid warm tribute to Harman's "advice, encouragement and help", reflecting that "The debt which the Society owes to M. C. Harman is beyond telling" (Harvey 1954). He was succeeded as President of the LFS by his son Albion and the Society decided to honour his father by founding and equipping a laboratory on the island named after him.

The later 1950s were a period of continual financial worries for the Society, brought about by reduced income and by the need for substantial repairs to the Old Light. Scientific work continued, however, with an archaeological survey begun in 1955 and the first mist-netting of birds in 1958. The gales of 1959 destroyed the Garden Trap and badly damaged the Terrace Trap, whilst the roof of the Old Light continued to cause concern.

These problems continued into the 1960s with, at one stage, Albion Harman concerned at the low number of visitors to the hostel and being reported as "agreeable to the Society continuing providing it can be made to work more efficiently" (LFS 1961). There were severe delays in the appearance of Annual Reports, caused in part by the lack of reports from the warden who was asked to resign. He was not replaced over the summer of 1961. The financial position of the Society worsened until 1967 when the treasurer reported a balance of £4/11/10 (£4.59). Some Annual Reports had had to be combined to save money, the last two years' had yet to be produced and the Old Light was reported to need at least £300 worth of repairs. Albion Harman had suggested that the LFS move out of the Old Light in 1965 and he repeated the suggestion with the offer of Tibbetts in 1967.

Drastic measures were called for. A prize draw produced £214 and an archaeological course run on the island made a profit of £100. These covered the backlog of Annual Reports. The committee decided not to fund a warden in 1968 and to relinquish the Old Light, requesting storage space for LFS property until better times would allow the re-establishment of a base on the island. These suggestions were endorsed at the AGM of March 1968.

Albion Harman, who had been ill for some time, died in June 1968 after 14 years as owner of Lundy and president of the LFS. Leslie Harvey recalled his interest and concern for the Society's welfare during these difficult years, despite his own financial problems in running the island (Harvey 1968). The LFS later placed a plaque on a seat in Millcombe and planted trees in the surrounding valley in his memory.

Agreement was reached with the Harman family that the Old Light hostel would be run by the island and a room above the bar would be made available for storage. John Harman became president of the LFS.

The Landmark Trust years

The following year, 1969, was a year of fundamental changes for both the Society and the Island. Professor Leslie Harvey, whose initial idea had resulted in the foundation of the LFS and who had served it as Secretary (1946-60) and Chairman (1960-69), retired from Exeter University and the chair of the LFS to live on the Isles of Scilly. Harvey's role in the foundation of the society, in obtaining grants from the University, and being involved in the running of the LFS for over twenty years had been pivotal in its development.

Three weeks after Harvey's retirement at the AGM, Lundy was put up for sale by the Harman family. The National Trust expressed interest in the island but had insufficient funds. An appeal was started to which the LFS made an immediate donation of £248, and hoped to raise £1000, but the fund-raising activities were overtaken by the donation of £150,000 to the National Trust by Jack Hayward (now Sir Jack). This, together with the agreement of the Landmark Trust to take a full repairing lease of the island for 60 years, enabled the National Trust to buy the island.

Discussions with John Smith (now Sir John), the chairman of the Landmark Trust, were fruitful with the Landmark Trust agreeing to the LFS choosing a warden, who would be funded by the Landmark Trust and run the Old Light as a hostel. The money donated by the LFS was to be used to assist with the repairs to the buildings.

The new era also brought the suggestion that the LFS should change its name to simply "The Lundy Society" but this was rejected by the members at the AGM in 1970. At the same time John Smith became the President in succession to John Harman who, together with Jack Hayward, became Vice Presidents. The Society also became registered as a charity which allowed it freedom from taxation but necessitated some constitutional changes.

In 1971 the LFS ran its first day excursion to the island offering guided walks for particular interest groups and this made a profit of £699. It was agreed that this money should be used to fund grants for

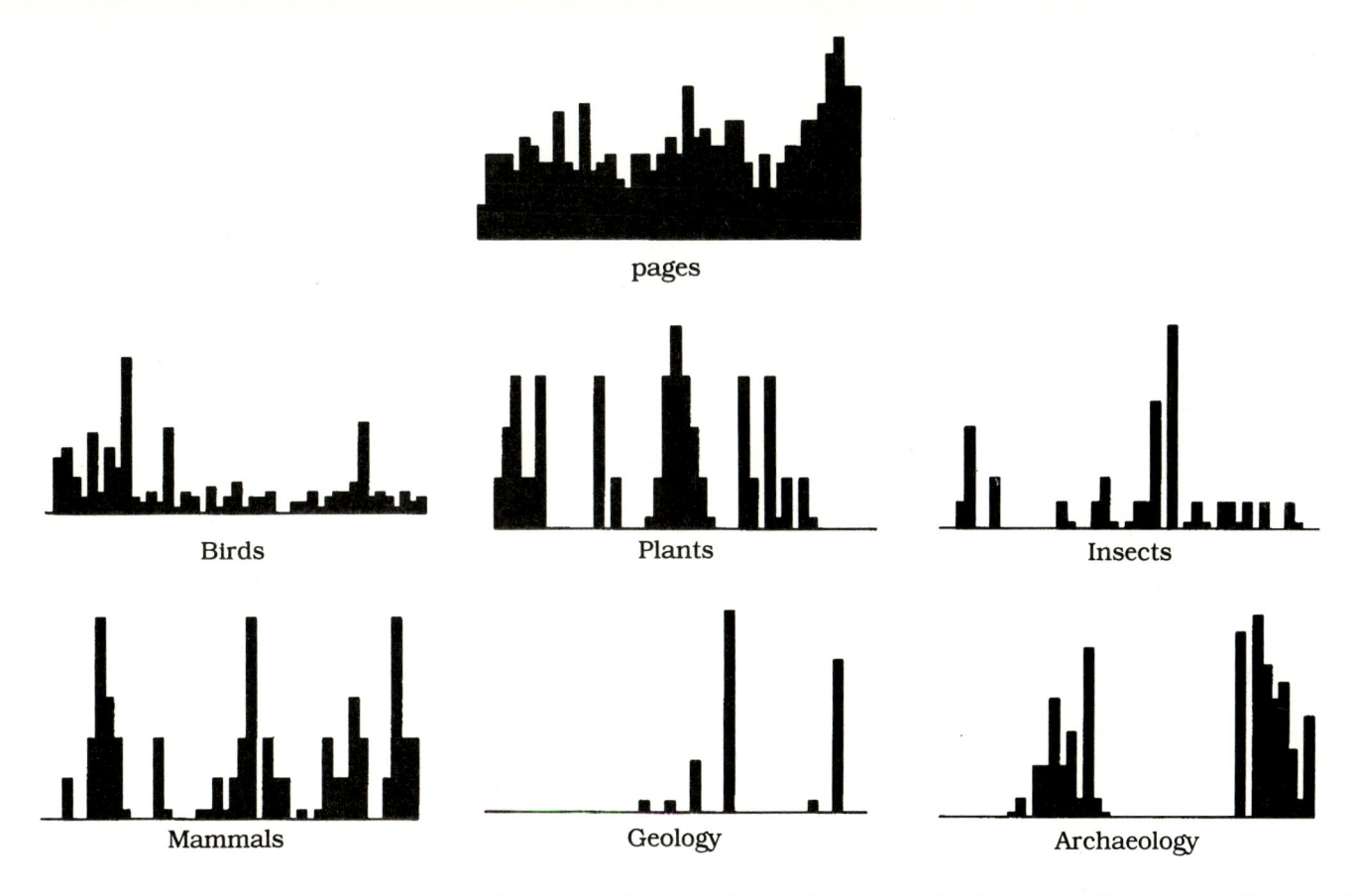

Fig. 2 Graphs showing total number of pages, and pages devoted to selected subjects, in the Annual Report of the Lundy Field Society. The graphs run from 1947 (left-hand side) to 1990 (right-hand side). All the figures are based on the index (Webster 1991) and are illustrative only as some papers may cover more than one subject and each has been rounded up to the next whole page.

fieldwork. Nick Dymond was appointed warden and Keith Hiscock produced plans for a marine nature reserve around Lundy.

The next year the excursion made £828. Despite this there was still concern that the Society's finances were not on a firm footing and stable, regular income was needed from the membership fees. The Terrace Trap was rebuilt and, the following spring, a Quarter Wall Trap was constructed before the warden left following his marriage. He was not replaced as it had been decided that the islanders should be subject to income tax and this had led to a sudden financial strain on the Landmark Trust.

The excursion continued to produce the bulk of the Society's income throughout the 1970s and early 1980s and much of the expenditure went to running courses on the island. This period saw a concentration on marine research organised around the promotion of Lundy as a marine nature reserve. This culminated in 1986 when the voluntary scheme was replaced by England's first (and so far only) Statutory Marine Nature Reserve (see Irving and Gilliland, this vol). The designation also led to the appointment of a warden by the Nature Conservancy Council and the Landmark Trust with some help from the LFS.

A sadder report during 1986 was that of the death of Leslie Harvey whose idea had led to the founding of the LFS exactly forty years before. He had run the society from then until his retirement in 1969 and without his energy, enthusiasm and commitment it is likely that the LFS would have foundered during those early years.

Bad weather on an excursion early in 1986 reduced the profits and there was also increased competition from other trips and the regular sailings of the MV Oldenburg which came into service that year. Profits recovered the following year but in 1988 the paddle steamer Waverley could not be filled and the trip only just covered its costs. Following this the excursion transferred to the smaller Oldenburg and profits returned but were not to last. Recently the excursion has broken even and is no longer used to provide funding for the society's work. Despite this, better financial control and realistic membership fees have allowed the LFS to expand research as can be seen from the increased size of the Annual Report during the 1990s (Fig. 2).

The changing role of the LFS

The origins of the LFS lay in the desire to establish a bird observatory on Lundy and Martin Coles Harman's insistence that this should be run independently of the mainland. These early years saw the employment by the LFS of a warden to run the bird observatory and a hostel for visiting members. However, increasing wealth and new leisure opportunities during the 1960s led to a contraction of interest in bird watching and similar pursuits. The costs of the warden and repairs to the hostel building were increasing at the same time as the income from the hostel was going down. The

LFS responded by enlarging its interests in fields such as archaeology and underwater research which were expanding.

It is clear that, from the start, the LFS was intended to have wider interests than ornithology. This may, in part, reflect the interests of Leslie Harvey whose own work on Lundy covered the ecology of the seashore. Work was concentrated during the early years on wildlife and the first foray outside this area was the proposal by Martin Coles Harman that the LFS should undertake some building conservation by repointing the walls of the castle. The first report of archaeological work was made in 1956, that on wrecks in 1967, and geology in 1968. The most recent addition to the fields of study has been animal psychology, which after a single paper in 1974 has been prominent in the past few years (Randle, this vol). There has also been an increase in the study of underwater archaeology (Robertson & Heath, this vol).

Throughout the range of subjects there have been noticeable peaks and troughs in interest as the graphs show (Fig. 2). Birds, as might be expected, form a constant theme throughout the years with a systematic list of species published in each Annual Report (These have not been included in the page counts). Peaks are visible, for example in the late 1980s when the warden, Neil Wilcox, published several surveys. The high figures during the early years are, in part, due to the length and number of rarity descriptions at that time.

Plants show peaks covering a few years, reflecting a continual interest with bursts of activity on particular topics. Insects and mammals show a similar pattern whilst geology has seen sparse but important contributions.

Archaeology shows a very different pattern with two peaks corresponding to the activities of Keith Gardner in the 1960s and, more recently, by work led by John Schofield and the National Trust. A new branch of archaeology has contributed to the totals since 1990, underwater archaeology, and it will be interesting to see if the growing popularity of sport diving leads to a long-term interest in this.

Today, bodies such as the National Trust, English Nature and English Heritage have taken over the formal protection of the island and surrounding sea. The LFS acts to promote research and conservation rather than organise them. This is carried out by means of grants, to the warden and others; a supply of volunteers to assist the warden; and by the members who provide a pool of expertise on all aspects of Lundy. The Annual Report which the LFS has produced since its first year provides an essential resource for documenting change and reporting new results. The Society continues to act in favour of Lundy's wildlife and antiquities, making representations where changes would affect these.

Fifty years' work by the Lundy Field Society have seen the island and its sea recognised for their national and international importance. The LFS has weathered many storms but has remained true to its objectives and this has led to Lundy becoming one of the most studied places on earth.

Acknowledgements

The first part of this paper (Origins) is based, largely, on a draft prepared by Tony Langham shortly before his death. The remainder has had to be compiled from the LFS archives without the benefit of his encyclopaedic knowledge of the island. I am very grateful to Myrtle Ternstrom for sorting out the LFS material from among Tony's papers and for her extremely valuable comments on an earlier version. John Woodland very kindly gave access to the DBW&PS minutes.

from a photograph by E.C. Pyatt

References

DBW&PS, 1945. *Devon Bird Watching and Preservation Society minutes of 45th meeting* 8/12/1945.
DBW&PS, 1946a. *Devon Bird Watching and Preservation Society minutes of 46th meeting* 6/4/1946.
DBW&PS, 1946b. *Devon Bird Watching and Preservation Society minutes of 47th meeting* 10/7/1946.
Harman, M C, 1943a. Hoopoe on Lundy. *British Birds* 37, 38.
Harman, M C, 1943b. First breeding of the Fulmar in the South West. *British Birds* 37, 97.
Harman, M C, 1946a. *Letter to L A Harvey*, 1/1/1946 in LFS archive.
Harman, M C, 1946b. *Letter to L A Harvey*, 27/3/1946 in LFS archive.
Harman, M C, 1946c. *Letter to L A Harvey*, 30/3/1946 in LFS archive.
Harman, M C, 1946d. *Letter to L A Harvey*, 1/4/1946 in LFS archive.
Harman, M C, 1946e. *Letter to L A Harvey*, 1/6/1946 in LFS archive.
Harman, M C, 1946f. *Letter to L A Harvey*, 15/5/1946 in LFS archive.
Harman, M C, 1947. *Letter to L A Harvey*, 22/4/1947 in LFS archive.
Harman, M C, 1948. *Letter to L A Harvey*, 19/1/1948 in LFS archive.
Harman, M C, 1949. "Owner's Letter". *Annual Report of the Lundy Field Society* 3, 42.
Harvey, L A, 1946a. *Letter to M C Harman*, 3/1/1946, copy in LFS archive.
Harvey, L A, 1946b. *Letter to M C Harman*, 29/3/1946, copy in LFS archive.
Harvey, L A, 1946c. *Letter to M C Harman*, 8/4/1946, copy in LFS archive.
Harvey, L A, 1946d. *Letter to M C Harman*, 30/5/1946, copy in LFS archive.
Harvey, L A, 1954. "Martin Coles Harman" *Annual Report of the Lundy Field Society* 8, 4-5.
Harvey, L A, 1968. "Albion Harman" *Annual Report of the Lundy Field Society* 19, 2.
LFS, 1946a. Lundy Field Society. "1st visit Friday June 28th 1946" *LFS Log Book*, LFS archive.
LFS, 1946b. Lundy Field Society. "Log of second trip (working party)" *LFS Log Book*, LFS archive.
LFS, 1947. Lundy Field Society. *Minutes of committee meeting* 30/6/1947.
LFS, 1961. Lundy Field Society. *Minutes of committee meeting* 11/2/1961.
Webster, C J, 1991. *Annual Report. Index and Contents* 1947-1990. Lundy Field Society

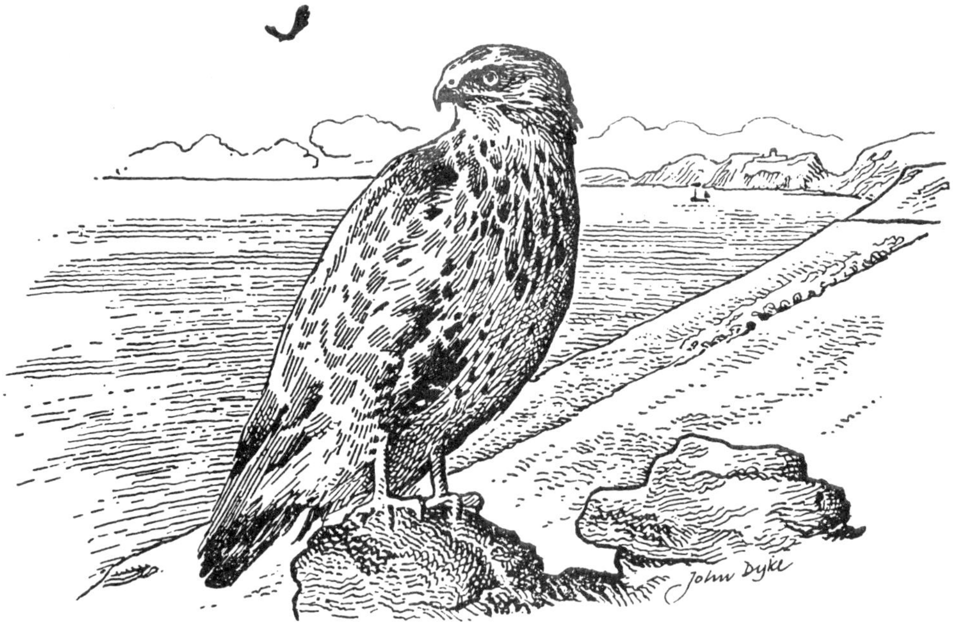
John Dyke

Lundy's Lost Name

Charles Thomas

Within the broader field of toponymy, the scientific study and analysis of place-names, the names of islands always present special problems. Around the coast of mainland Britain there are hundreds of islands large and small, some constituting proper archipelagoes like Orkney, Shetland and Scilly, but a great many hardly known beyond the nearest parish. All, of course, possess names. Many have, or have had, more than one name, and not necessarily at successive times. The names of a few extremely isolated islands come to us only from post-medieval records; that of Rockall, which is 191 miles west from St Kilda, first appears as 'Rocol' in Willem Janson's map of 1606. At the other end of the scale we have those large islands continuously inhabited since prehistory, where a single name has long been fixed. It is beyond serious dispute that the Isle of Wight is the *Vectis* of Pliny's "Natural History" and Ptolemy's "Geography", and the *Vecta* of Bede around AD 700; and it is highly probable that Ptolemy's *Malaios* or *Maleos* (in Greek) and Adamnán's *Malea* in the late 7th century is the island of Mull.

So what of Lundy? On the testimony of archaeology – but not history – Lundy was inhabited within the last few centuries BC and the first few AD by (at most) a couple of peasant families farming part of the plateau; remains of field-systems point to some kind of settled agriculture and there is no reason to deny them livestock. Unless these folk were exotic beyond all probability, they spoke British, the Celtic language ancestral to Welsh and Cornish, and people living (sparsely) in the nearest part of what is now north Devon would have spoken the same. It is inconceivable that the latter would not have had (at any given time during this period) a fixed indicative name for so large a feature, visible out to sea for most of the year and from a long stretch of the coastline; just as it is inconceivable that British-speakers in the southern parts of counties Pembroke and Carmarthen, where Lundy can also be seen if slightly less often, lacked an appropriate name. But this by no means implies that it must have been the *same* name. As for the handful of Lundy inhabitants, we can suppose that in the early centuries AD they might well have had the odd small boat; inadequate for crossings to the mainland except in the best of conditions, but perfectly suitable for offshore fishing. We can picture two such folk, out long-lining in dodgy weather, with a mist coming down, and one saying to the other, "Let's get back to the island" (in British *sindan inissan*, accus sing fem). In the same fashion how often do we say, "I'm just popping into town" or, "Let's drive over to Fred's place", without using a place-name at all? We might also picture, on Lundy in AD 250, the excitement – the wary reception

– of a larger, strange boat arriving, to buy (or steal) a sheep, and the visitors asking, "What's this place called, then?" To which the answer might be, "Well, we just call it The Island", or then "But some people over there call it X" and, "There were some people here a while back, they came from [Wales], and *they* called it Y".

The defectiveness of the island-name record, insular toponymy, is linked to all these factors: a muddle between *internal* names (those used – especially on small islands – by, probably discontinuous, inhabitants), and *external* names (those used by groups at one or more mainland viewpoints, let alone quite separate labels applied by seafarers from afar); and the fragility of the written record in respect of small or remote island properties with little value, and limited appeal as residences. Add to this a well-documented Western British propensity for name *replacement*, and the search becomes even harder. The many islands, ranging from the medium-sized to the tiny, within the Severn Sea exemplify this in abundant detail. Caldey, which is about the same size as Lundy, is easily reached by a short boat-trip from Tenby and is visited annually by thousands. It actually has two names; Caldey (or Caldy – both are used) is recorded as *Caldea* in the early 12th century, *Kaldey* and *Caldey* in 1291 (Norse *kald, ey* 'cold island'), but an alternative Welsh name is Ynys Byr ('kaldey yw ynys pyr', 15th cent., 'Caldey is Ynys Byr'). A supposed saint Piro was abbot of a small monastery here around 500, according to the early 7th-century Life of St Samson, and it is perfectly possible that in archaic Old Welsh (6th-7th cents.) the island was locally known as 'Enis Pir[o]'. It is equally clear that before Piro's day, when this part of coastal Wales was fully inhabited, the island must have had some other name altogether.

The generic, non-locative nature of internal names can also be demonstrated from the small archipelago of Scilly. The full story of Scilly's place-names is of extreme complexity but the oldest stratum is British. There was apparently a general place-name used in west Cornwall, bearing in mind that Scilly is often visible from high ground in several parishes of the Land's End peninsula; it last appears (in Cornish) at the end of the 17th century as Sillan, Zillan, and as with *Vectis* and 'Wight' it represents some continuation of the *Silinna – Sillina – Sylina* forms of Classical authors ('Scilly' and the French *Sorlingues* are from English and Scandinavian forms). However until the Middle Ages, when rising sea-levels and erosion began to produce the separate islands we see today, much of Scilly was one large block, not much smaller than modern Guernsey, centred on the present St Mary's. A few years ago, I showed that this had an internal name – ie. what the several hundreds of inhabitants called it – which just survives as a modern label for the odd road and house, Ennor. This is Old Cornish *en-Noer* (12th cent., *Enor*; 13th, *Inoer*; 14th, *Enoer, Enor*), meaning 'The Land', and there is no reason to exclude the strong chance that it was as old as the Roman period and began as British *sindos diiaros*, same meaning. And here again we have a very fine example of multiple naming in the present Old Town, St Mary's, a pleasant deep inlet and beach flanked by the 12th-century parish Church of the Blessed Virgin and an originally-small fishing village. The internal medieval name for this locality was Porthenor, 'landing place of En(n)or'; Scandinavian visitors about 1150 called it Maríuhöfn, 'Mary's Haven' from the new church; because the village was in a natural dip, Norman-French churchmen re-named it in the 13th century as La Val, 'the Down-there place'; and when a new main settlement grew up at present Hugh Town in Tudor times, the village (before c.1600, probably an Dre 'the town' to its inhabitants, *Enor* to others in Scilly) became 'Old Town' and Porthenor became 'Old Town Bay'. In saying that, happily, sufficient dated records have survived to permit this muddle to be sorted out. I would add that the Old Town story almost certainly typifies a great many other, less well recorded, cases along similar lines.

The present name 'Lundy', as we all know, surfaces in the 14th-century texts of the mid-12th century *Orkneyingasaga*; it may have been quite widely used after c.1100 (1199, *Lundeia*, Charter Rolls) and it represents Old Norse *lundi* 'puffin' and *-ey* 'island'. We must assume puffin in the sense of the bright little bird *Fratercula arctica* and not *Puffinus puffinus*, the Manx Shearwater, though in medieval sources 'puffin, pophin' etc., sometimes means the latter. Lundy goes with all the other Severn Sea island names ending in -ey, -y, and -holm (hølmr, 'islet', generally small) as evidence to the dominating currency or names used by people whose constant sea-traffic required precise identifications, and in their own Scandinavian tongue. The history of the Pacific Ocean in recent centuries, dotted as it is with Midway, Christmas, Easter, Society, Norfolk, Marshall, Fanning, Lord Howe, Three Kings, Henderson, Washington (etc.) islands – all of them ousting perfectly good internal and external names of Polynesian or Melanesian character – somewhat precludes us from criticising the Norse seafarers.

These Norse names are by and large simple and descriptive; they are what might be expected from people whose perceptions were from passing ships. To Lundy and Caldey we could add those in Pembroke, Skomer and Skokholm (which Dr B G Charles has explained as *skálm-ey*, 'Cleft Island' and *stokkr-hólmr* 'island in the sound'); and this has been carried over into English with names like Flat Holm and Steep Holm. Appearance of such, originally alien, labels during the 10th to 12th centuries, does not mean that others ceased to use older names; merely that records of the latter have not always survived. Because Caldey happens to lie offshore from that part of Pembroke containing some of the royal seats (Narberth, probably Carew, possibly Tenby Castle) and because it has been, since the 500s, more or less continuously home to successive religious establishments, the Welsh preference for (and retention of) Ynys Byr is quite explicable. In the Severn estuary-mouth, it happened to be the religious associations of Steep Holm and Flat Holm that led to historical records of their non-Germanic names (non-Germanic, because both had Old English names as well as Norse ones: *Steopan-reolice* and *Bradan-reolice*. 'Steep' and 'Broad'(= 'Flat') plus *re(o)lice* 'Christian burial-ground(?)', like Old Irish *reilig* 'cemetery, cemetery with chapel', Late Latin *reliquiae*). Production in the late 11th to 13th centuries of (Latin) Lives of several major Welsh saints gives us however *Ronech* as the British (Old Welsh) name of Steep Holm, and *Echni* for Flat Holm.

Because of intervisibility with parts of Wales, we might expect some record, even an oblique one, of a Welsh name for Lundy. In fact we have two, though both are oblique indeed. The remarkable collection of early Welsh tales lumped together in modern times as 'The Mabinogion' represents selective transmission of oral recitations with heroic, royal and mythological themes committed to literary form in the Middle Welsh period. They are exceptionally difficult to understand and to analyse, but the material is plainly pre-Norman and some of the stories may have originated in the court circles of *Demetia* (Dyfed, or the former south-western counties of Pembroke and Carmarthen). Linked to them are what survives of a body of ancient poetry; and in the Book of Taliesin there is a poem *Preiddeu Annwn* which, as Professor Roger Loomis showed, must mean 'The Spoils (or Plunder) of the Other-World', and whose language, despite the medieval recension, Sir Ifor Williams would compare to composition of c.900.

The poem's contents need not concern us, except that the Welsh concept of the otherworld preferably embraced, not the subterranean regions or the sky but mysterious islands; and it begins with mention of *karchar gweir ygkaer sidi* 'the prison of Gweir, in the Fairy Castle'. Of this, Sir John Rhys had commented, "It is not improbable that the legend about Gweir located his prison on Lundy, as the Welsh name of that island *appears to have been* Ynys Wair, 'Gwair's Isle'". The italics are mine, because there is an implication we cannot now check, that in the last century Rhys had encountered this name, somewhere in Dyfed, still known as a name for Lundy. In her vast study of another collection of Welsh sources, the *Trioedd Ynys Prydein* or 'Triads', Dr Rachel Bromwich drew attention, first to a triad naming 'Three Exalted Prisoners of the Island of Britain' of which the third is Gweir, son of Geirioedd, again; and second, from what is admittedly a late text (The Names of the Islands of Britain), a reference to Britain's 'Three Adjacent Islands', and twenty-seven subordinate ones. Only the former, *teir prif rac ynys* ('three prime (chief) fore-islands' – cf. the same usage in Cornish, where *Raginnis* is the real name of the little St Clements Isle, the 'adjacent-isle' just off Mousehole) are named. The first two are Môn and Manaw, Anglesey and the Isle of Man. The third should of course be the Isle of Wight, the Roman-period *Vectis* or *Vecta*, whose name in Old Welsh was *inis Gueith* (Nennius), and later Ynys Weith. In fact the triad has 'Ynys Weir'. One disagrees reluctantly with Dr Bromwich's authority in her own field, but it strikes me as inherently more likely that this — for some reason we cannot recover, connected with the composition of the tract — is the name of Lundy, and not an alternative label for Wight at all.

If Ynys Wair (or Weir) is a name for Lundy originating in pre-Norman times and still dimly recalled in Sir John Rhys's lifetime (1840-1915; his *Celtic Folk-Lore: Welsh and Manx* appeared in 1901), I think it probable that it arose in that region of south-west Wales where Lundy can be seen on the horizon, and was indeed confined to that region. There is a rather similar case in Scilly, where the scatter of high rocks and islets called 'the Eastern Isles' can be just seen from, and is closest to, Land's End. All the components now have their own names but until rising sea-level separated them they formed a tract whose British (Old Cornish) name we might reconstruct as *Guenhyly* (possibly 'briny waste; unenclosed salt-sprayed area'; the name partly survives in (Great and Little) Ganilly, two of the islets). Some of these once-hillocks exhibit large and prominent megalithic cairns with passage tombs, visible from a boat. The role of distantly-seen islands all over the Celtic-speaking world as 'Isles of the Blessed' or 'of the Dead', quite apart from acting as Prisons, needs little comment. The present 'Great Arthur', which has about ten such cairns, was *Arthurs Ile* in 1570 (a Godolphin lease). How far back this ascription may be pushed we cannot tell, possibly not before the Arthurian 'revival' of Geoffrey of Monmouth's mid-12th century writings; but we can suppose that, among west Cornish stories, one of them regarded this tomb-studded ridge in the nearest and just visible, *Guenhyly*, part of *Sillan* as a local claimant to the site of 'Avalon' and Arthur's resting-place.

The second potential Welsh name for Lundy is peculiar, perhaps unique, in that it must be an invention and not a genuine 'organic' place-name at all. I have previously given a re-assessment of the results of the work in 1969 at the Beacon Hill cemetery, Lundy's main Early Christian site, and suggested that the burial-ground's focus — probably in the latter half of the 6th century — was the elaborate special grave in a rectangular setting of granite slabs, filled with a mound or cairn, where the primary cist-burial had been exposed and emptied in a secondary (7th-century?) phase (Thomas 1992). Rather fuller discussion appeared in my book *And Shall These Mute Stones Speak? Post-Roman Inscriptions in Western Britain* (Cardiff, 1994, especially chaps.8 to 10), where the person so entombed is identified as Brachan or 'Brychan', the eponymous ruler of the early Welsh Brycheiniog (roughly, the northern part of the county of Brecon or Brecknock). Assuming that, towards the end of his life, Brachan retreated to what was then a small Christian community, a monastery, on Lundy — implied by the oldest inscribed stones and by the archaeology of Beacon Hill — I argued (and would still argue) that his remains were exhumed and enshrined at the nearest mainland British monastery, now represented by the church and surrounds at Stoke (St Nectan), Hartland; and furthermore that the 'Saint Nectan' of subsequent (10th-12th cents.) writings and a medieval cult is none other than Brachan under his name assumed as a monk.

The earliest source for the history of Brycheiniog is an internal writing, a compendium now called *De Situ Brecheniauc* 'About the region Of Brycheiniog', surviving (in Latin) in a sole and late, c.1200, manuscript (British Library Cotton Vespasian A, xiv). In yet another book, too intricate in content to be summarised here, I want to show that *DSB* contains a genuine, shorter historical tract probably written in the later 7th century, to which other items were added; the whole then being paraphrased (in the 10th century) in a second compendium, *Cognacio Brychan*, which we know only from a transcript made after 1500. Those added items include a statement about the graves of four men from the royal house of Brycheiniog; Brachan's father Anlach, who was an aristocrat of Irish descent from Pembroke, Brachan himself, his first son *Canauc* ('Cynog') who became the patron saint of Brecon, and his second son Rein, who succeeded him as king. The little list must post-date the deaths and burials of Cynog and Rein, both of whom cannot have lived later than 565-575, and I am inclined to see it as not necessarily much later than 600. The graves of Anlach, Cynog and Rein were all at known Early Christian locations in Brycheiniog (now Llansbyddyd, Merthyr Cynog and Llandefaelogfach). Brachan's was not. It was not even within his kingdom, and the admission of so unusual a fact alone implies that this must have been common knowledge at the time of writing, and therefore presumably true.

The original Latin text of *DSB* can, apart from the several-times updated spellings of proper names, be reconstructed with a good deal of confidence. The entry for Brachan was: *sepulchrum Brachan est in insula que vocatur Enis Brachan que est iuxta Manniam*, 'The grave of Brachan is in the island which is called 'Island of Brachan', which is next to *Mannia*.' The last word, which occurs in another item in the compendium, is the result of two miscopyings by later hands who no longer recognised what it was meant to be. The context makes it plain that it almost certainly began as *Damnoniam* or even *Damnaniam*, and we can see how continuous script, *iuxtadamnaniam*, might carelessly yield *iuxtamanniam*. It is a post-Roman version of the general, Roman-period, term for the southwest peninsula; Gildas in the 6th century wrote it as *Damnonia*. We have an 'adjacent island', and the Latin *iuxta Damnaniam*, if it had ever been turned into written Old Welsh, might have appeared as *rac Divnein(t)*.

The whole of the county of Brecon, and early Brycheiniog as a small kingdom centred on the upper Usk Valleys, is land-locked. If Brachan, who may have lived from c.490 to 550, planned to end his days in Christian retreat on Lundy, his most likely route would have taken him down the Usk to its mouth at Newport, where (under the present St Wooloo's Cathedral) there may have been a royal seat overlooking the mouth of the Usk, a seat of the Prince Gwynllyw who in medieval sources is said to have married Brachan's daughter Guladis. In a direct line, and because of the Glamorgan bulge it is a curve, Lundy is 86 miles from Newport and certainly not visible from the Usk mouth. Alternatively, from Brycheiniog, one can travel down the river Neath to its outflow, which is about 46 miles from Lundy (and, skirting the Mumbles, a direct line). Lundy *is* sometimes visible from the high ground, the southern spurs of Fforest Fawr or the Brecon Beacons. Possibly in the 6th century AD it had a name, though there is no reason to think that (as in Dyfed) the name was necessarily Ynys Wair.

The most, by way of information, that may have trickled back to Brycheiniog was that their elderly king, having reached the coast, went by boat to an island known to lie offshore from Damnonia, as Devon-and-Cornwall; where, at this period, any small monastic house is likely to have been an offshoot of one of the many major late 5th-century establishments in south-east Wales. By definition, as with Piro and Ynys Byr, it cannot have been called 'Enis Brachan' until Brachan had been buried there. Nor can one see, with any persuasion, why those few persons on the Glamorgan coast who had any reason ever to use the name of so small and distant a feature should adopt a fresh name involving the dead ruler of another, inland, kingdom. We have to see Enis Brachan as a pious invention, a literary figure, supplied by a writer who knew that the island existed but had absolutely no idea of its actual contemporary name, or names.

Turning, at last, to what the British-speaking inhabitants of north-west Devon and north Cornwall, the viewers-from-land *en masse* as opposed to a tiny minority of indigenous mariners, may have called Lundy, there is not much left to say. It is curious that none of the Classical geographers seems to have named Lundy. Ptolemy's 2nd century Geography gives certain island names around Britain and Ireland, though none of the few unlocated names can be identified as Lundy. Cornish *enys* 'island' (it has other meanings, like 'isolated place, land beside waters') is found in Innis Pruen (Mullion Island), the *-innis* of St Clements Isle, Mousehole, and only a few among the hundred-odd isles and rocks of Scilly. The last mentioned includes Innisidgen – 'Ox Isle', Innisvrank – 'Frenchman's Isle', Illiswilgic or Inniswilsack – 'Grassy Isle', and Innisvouls – meaning uncertain, which are all pretty small and uninhabitable. Around the coasts of Devon and Cornwall are larger islands, like St George's Isle off Looe, whose pre-English names have simply not survived. It is therefore no better than a guess to suggest that, from the relevant stretches of Devon and Cornwall in pre-Norman times, Lundy's name may have involved *enis* 'island'; on its own, or with an adjective (like the Irish 'High Island'; Ardoileán, Co.Galway), or a personal name (like 'Ynys Wair'). It may on the other hand have been of the same type as *Ronech* for Steep Holm and *Echni* for Flat Holm; both of very uncertain meaning (Echni may be a personal name). I offer one last suggestion. The place-names of North Devon have not been exhaustively studied (what area in Britain has been?) and one can never be sure that extremely localised names will not be found in unpublished early documents of private origin, like grants and leases. The vast parish of Hartland does have a very few surviving names of British, not Old and Middle English, origin; Trellick, in 1249 *Trevelak*, is an instance. As far as I know, the place-name 'Hartland Quay' is entirely modern. Some few years ago, for West Cornwall, Peter Pool's careful examination of the obscure Penheleg Manuscript of 1580 (the rights of the Arundells of Lanherne, as lords of Penwith hundred) brought to light correct readings of scores of place-names whose significance had never been observed. They included the hitherto-unknown *Gonhellye under Meen*, and *Porth Gone Hollye*, both for the 'porth' or landing-place at the southern end of Whitesand Bay, Sennen, which faces Scilly. Subsequently I was able to show that the forgotten 'Porth Goonhilly' (or similar) was so-called because it was the beach for 'Goonhilly', the Eastern Isles of Scilly as the nearest landfall across; as if Millbay at Plymouth was now re-named 'Roscoff Dock'. It is at least possible that, even as late as the foundation of Hartland Abbey, the difficult but convenient landing-place at Hartland Quay retained the element *porth* (if so, as Port-) and this may even have been followed by the name of Lundy in its pre-Norse guise. Hartland parish has 18,000 acres. Down to the lowest level of field, cliff and rock names, it must have possessed thousands of place-names, only a fraction of which have been collected and published. Most such place-names will remain in obscure, and private, manuscript settings. Here is a real challenge to another generation of Lundy enthusiasts.

References

Bromwich, R, 1961. *Trioedd Ynys Prydein. The Welsh Triads*. Cardiff: University of Wales Press.
Charles, B G, 1992. *The Place-Names of Pembrokeshire* (2 vols). National Library of Wales, Aberystwyth.
Gover, J B, Mawer, A, & Stenton, F M, 1931. *The Place-Names of Devon* (2 vols). Cambridge: English Place-Name Society vols viii & ix.
Howells, R, 1984. *Caldey*. Llandysul: Gomer Press.
Loomis, R S, 1956. *Wales and the Arthurian Legend*. Cardiff: University of Wales Press.
Padel, O J, 1985. *Cornish Place-Name Elements*. Nottingham: English Place-Name Society, vol lvi/lvii.
Pool, P A S, 1959. The Penheleg Manuscript. *Journal of the Royal Institution of Cornwall* n.s. iii, 163-228
Rendell, S & J, 1993. *Steep Holm. The story of a small island*. Stroud: Alan Sutton.
Rivet, A L F, & Smith, C, 1979. *The Place-Names of Roman Britain*. London: Batsford.
Thomas, C, 1985. *Exploration of a Drowned Landscape. Archaeology and History of the Isles of Scilly*. London: Batsford.
Thomas, C, 1992. Beacon Hill re-visited: a reassessment of the 1969 excavations. *Annual Report of the Lundy Field Society* 42, 43-54.
Thomas, C, 1994. *And Shall These Mute Stones Speak? Post-Roman inscriptions in Western Britain*. Cardiff: University of Wales Press.

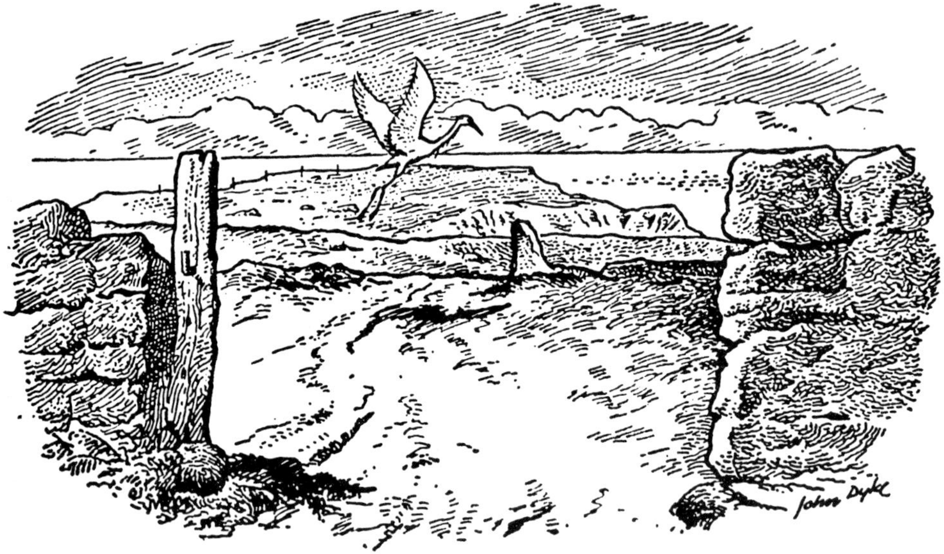
John Dyke

Rebels and Recluses: Lundy's history in context

Clive Harfield

Lundy's geographic isolation dictates a recurrent theme through history: it has been a redoubt for the rebel and the recluse, the reactionary and the refugee. As a consequence it has historical significance but a significance confined more to the footnotes of history than its main text. For all the island's rebellious associations, both political and economic, it has never enjoyed anything greater than regional importance, more often than not being the source of a little local irritation.

Had the port and market at Bristol assumed greater economic importance than London early on, the story might have been different. But London enjoyed closer proximity to continental Europe, and the invading Romans, Saxons and Normans necessarily established beach-heads in the south-east, before seeking to control the rest of the British mainland. Not until the trade routes to the New World were established was the economic and geographical focus of the kingdom re-balanced. By then London's political pre-eminence was unassailable. Lundy, therefore, stood on the threshold to the back-door during the formative centuries of English history and it is within this framework that Lundy's history must be explored.

The history of Lundy has been the subject of much recent attention, notable of which is the work of the late Tony Langham (1994; Langham and Langham 1984), and Myrtle Ternstrom (1994). Both have produced detailed histories of the island, and it is not the intention of this chapter to replace them in any sense. Where this chapter does differ is that it has been written, as it were, from the outside in: viewing Lundy from the wider perspective of its contemporary political landscape, as opposed to exploring islanders' attitudes towards the outside world.

An historical framework

Lundy's history, in the sense of documented evidence of past events, begins in 1140 when episodes from the *Orkneyinga Saga* describe the squabbles of settlers largely oblivious to, and unaffected by, contemporary events in mid-twelfth century Anglo-Norman England. In the spring and summer of that year, Hold – a chief from Wales – used the island as a base from which to plunder the Scandinavian settlements on the Isle of Man in retaliation for earlier raids on the Welsh coast. The Vikings of Man, under the leadership of Svein Asleifarson, besieged Hold on Lundy but to no avail, returning to the Isle of Man in the autumn. The following year Holdboldi, who had taken part in the raids on Wales with Svein, revolted against him and sought refuge on Lundy, being welcomed there by Hold

(Palsson & Edwards 1981, 146-7).

The western coastal regions to the north of the south-west peninsula were, at this time, mostly untroubled by authoritarian government. The sons of Harold Godwinson chose Devon as the area in which to launch an uprising against William I in 1068 and 1069, but the former Saxon king had been no more popular in this region than his Norman conqueror, and the sons failed to find support for their cause (Golding 1994, 38-9). On the northern shores of the Bristol Channel, King William had avoided the argumentative Welsh princes by establishing the Palatinate earldoms (Loyn 1982, 179) to keep the ungovernable at bay. And by the mid-twelfth century when Hold used Lundy, the Angevin empire of Henry II was emerging from the ashes of civil war which characterised Stephen's reign, and the politics of England were focused towards western France, from Normandy to Gascony. Taking advantage of this void, which persisted when the Francocentric Henry II was succeeded initially by the crusading Richard I, then the politically inept John and eventually the nine year-old Henry III, the Marisco family seized Lundy probably for no other purpose but to ensure privacy from royal government and baronial intrigue (the rightful possessors of the island were the Knights Templar: Lees 1935, 141).

It has been suggested tentatively that a direct blood link existed between the thirteenth century Mariscos and William the Conqueror (Langham 1994, 14). However, the lack of sources renders the Marisco genealogy before the twelfth century impossible to trace with any certainty (Powicke 1941, 290), and the idea that the Mariscos wished to use the island as a base from which to mount a claim to the throne in 1238 (Langham 1994, 18) is speculation. It is a fact that the island was used by certain individuals of the family to avoid being brought to justice for the murder of a minor royal official. Professor Powicke's meticulous recounting of this incident (Powicke 1941) is probably as erudite and explicit an explanation as it is possible to achieve given that there were living contemporaneously more than one branch of the family, and a number of individuals named William de Marisco. Indeed the ministers enforcing the justice of Henry III seized the lands of the wrong William de Marisco on one occasion (*ibid*, 299), and if contemporaries could be so easily confused, it is understandable that later historians find it difficult.

The actions of the Mariscos were typical of the age. The barons under Stephen and Matilda had the opportunity to assume virtual political independence and supported whichever of the two claimants suited them at any time in the conflict (Poole 1955, chapter 5). Richard I was never at home long enough to establish direct control over his tenants-in-chief. John succumbed to baronial power at Runnymede in 1215, acceding to the Magna Carta which, far from being the bill of rights it is so often claimed to be, established in codified form baronial privilege to exploit the lower social orders free from undue royal interference (*ibid*, chapter 14). The baronial label itself described a seigneurial rank within which were to be found a wide variety of tenurial and economic circumstances in a fluid social order (Mortimer 1994, 79 & 87).

Lundy's setting, physically removed from mainland influence, was the ideal place for a secondary branch of a minor baronial family to establish some small token of seigneurial independence. The limits of Marisco influence can be measured by their absence from, or at best their infrequent occurrence in the indices of major history books (McKisack 1959; Poole 1955; Powicke 1962). The Lundy Mariscos did however cause a significant nuisance in the Bristol Channel through piracy (Powicke 1941, 297-300). It was for this crime and his treachery that William de Marisco was executed in a fashion devised specifically for him (hanging, drawing and quartering: Langham 1994, 17, fn 21; Lewis 1987, 234-9). (See Fig.1.)

The family's notoriety was achieved through a single murder which is known about only because, by chance and unusually, the records of the judicial inquiry have survived (Maitland 1895). After the capture of the Mariscos (Powicke 1941, 300-301) Henry III took steps to secure his control of the island by placing his own men in charge of it. Arguably the king attached considerable importance to the island (Langham 1994, 19), though it is difficult to see why. Although in effect Lundy was a natural fortress, it was far from any centre of political significance; nor was it held by a major baronial family. Above all, the economic resources of the island were insufficient to sustain a full knight's fee (Langham 1984, 49), never mind a concerted rebellion. The interest shown by Henry III in disposing of the island once it had been forfeit to the crown was no more than would have been shown to any other escheated estates.

Rebellion continued into the fourteenth century with civil war in the reign of Edward II. In 1326, fleeing from the rebel army, the king travelled from Bristol to Chepstow apparently intending to take refuge on Lundy and from there counter-attack. Storms prevented him sailing to the island and he was captured at Neath Abbey (McKisack 1959, 24, 86). If his only refuge in his own kingdom was a tiny island some twelve miles off the coast then the king's cause was probably lost already.

The south-west peninsula was as much a problem to Edward VI (1547-53) as it had been to the Conqueror nearly five hundred years earlier. The Cornish had rebelled against taxes under Edward's grandfather Henry VII in 1497, and in 1548 another rising swelled in Cornwall and spread to Devon, this time against the imposition of a vernacular prayer book intended to replace the Latin mass at a time when the Cornish spoke their own language; they could recognise the Latin liturgy but comprehended not a word of English (Beer 1982, chapter 3). The independent nature of those living in the south-west had never properly been challenged. Royal rule was tolerated up to a point but local government was entirely in the hands of individual squires, none of whom had especially close affiliations to the politics of the royal court. Although the Tudor administration created the basis of modern government, their influence was weak in the south-west, and probably weaker still on Lundy. This was still true a century later: with the country in the grips of a civil war yet again, Lundy was once more home to a lost cause.

Possession of the island had now passed to Sir Bevil Grenvile, a member of the gentry classes who enjoyed much independence in the south-west. Grenvile also held land on the mainland and in 1641 had written, "make it known to all my neighbours and tenants.... that I shall take it ill if they grind not at my mill" (Davies 1937, 266). The seigneurial right of a lord to force his tenants to use the manorial mills and pay for the privilege rather than use their own mills or hand-querns, like all banalites, enabled feudal lords to exploit the economic surplus produced by their peasants (Bennet and Elton 1975; Harfield 1990, chapter 3). That it should still be enforced in the seventeenth century speaks volumes about social and economic relationships in the south-west peninsula at this time.

Grenvile mortgaged Lundy to raise money for the royalist cause (Langham 1994, 38). On his death the island passed to another royalist, Thomas Bushell. The fact that Lundy was one of the very last royalist outposts to be surrendered to Parliament indicates not that it had withstood military force to the end, nor that it was an important stronghold, but simply that it had no military or political significance and was thus not a target for Cromwell. The surrender of the island was achieved through negotiation after Bushell had sought permission from the imprisoned king.

This was the last occasion an occupier of the island was willing openly to defy the government of the day with force of arms. It was not, however, the last time an occupier would dissent from government. For William Hudson Heaven among the attractions of his new purchase in 1834 were the rights and privileges which it was claimed pertained to the island. Such claims were a throw-back to the days of baronial independence and civil war and do not appear to have been founded upon royal charter[1]. Whatever the perceived rights and privileges, Heaven was keen to preserve them. He was mindful too, to preserve a foothold in democracy and so retained possession of certain mainland estates in order to maintain his electoral

---

1   It has been suggested that Lundy's unique tenurial circumstances were referred to in correspondence between Elizabeth I and Bishop Tunstall in 1559 (Langham 1994,199) but this correspondence demonstrates merely that Lundy had traditionally been omitted from royal treaties; probably originally an error, this was perpetuated since Elizabeth I did not see fit to correct it. As such this is evidence of royal indifference, not of special tenurial privileges or rights of independence (*Calendar of State Papers, Foreign Series*, Elizabeth I: 12th and 16th May 1559).

THE DEATH OF WILLIAM DE MARISCO

Fig 1 The Death of William De Marisco
From the Darawings of Matthew Paris edited by M R James
(Walpole Society 1926)

franchise. But as far as Lundy was concerned, his word was law. In 1871 he challenged the right of a mainland law court to hear a trial for manslaughter, following a death on the island. Having succeeded in his challenge, and therefore in making his point, he formally requested that the trial take place on the mainland (Langham 1987, 10). In the same year the authorities demonstrated some ambivalence towards the island when Devon magistrates objected to employing constables on the island in view of uncertainty as to whether or not the island fell within Devonshire's administration (Langham 1994, 200)[2].

By 1929 the magistrates at Bideford were satisfied that they did indeed have judicial responsibilities for the island, and convicted the then owner, Martin Coles Harman (Fig.2), of issuing his own coinage contrary to the Coinage Act 1870. Arguing that he was the owner and therefore governor of a self-regulating Dominion outside territorial waters which paid no taxes and received no central government services, Harman appealed against conviction on the grounds that the Bideford magistrates had no jurisdiction over him. The Lord Chief Justice found against him and an important test case had been established (Langham 1994, 203).

Harman also wished to make a point about Lundy's independence regarding the armed services. From 1929 onwards he charged landing dues to any uniformed military personnel who visited the island and at the outbreak of war in 1939 he publicly denied the right of the Government to requisition material or supplies from the island. Notwithstanding his claim to independence, he was prepared to offer full co-operation in a time of national emergency (*ibid*, 203-4).

The political independence claimed for Lundy in the last 150 years is merely symbolic, all the more so because the island, besides being *de facto* militarily dependent, was also completely economically dependent upon the mainland. The nineteenth and early twentieth centuries were thus periods of defiance and dissent rather than open rebellion. The island's tenurial circumstances in relation to the rest of the kingdom were clearly anomalous, but it was not until 1973 that the Government took the significant step of imposing taxes upon Lundy's residents. The Boundary Commission the following year incorporated the island into the county of Devon.

To summarise, two themes emerge from this overview: rebellion, both in the form of piracy and smuggling, and reclusion, and these display a chronological dimension which merits further consideration.

---

[2] The magistrates were prepared to consider police provision if the island's occupiers were prepared to meet the cost (Myrtle Ternstrom, pers comm).

ISLAND STUDIES

Themes and variations

Piracy
The lifestyle of many of the settlers along the west coasts of Britain and its islands was not far removed from that which many would recognise as piracy. The need for subsistence piracy was simple: Lundy has only limited agricultural potential for the law-abiding. Those wishing to isolate themselves from contact with the mainland, including trading at markets, have virtually no means of surviving for long periods of time on what the island alone can sustain.

By the Tudor period sufficient information becomes available to place piracy in the Bristol Channel into perspective. The anonymous author of *The Libel of English Policy* called upon the Crown to clear English waters of pirates (Warner 1926, 31). The coastal waters of the Bristol and St George's Channels appear to have been particularly prone to piracy (Williams 1979, 244), although shipping in the English Channel was also at risk (Black 1959, 126).

There were some twenty ports in England in the reign of Henry VII, to which can be added any number of creeks and small harbours (Mackie 1952, 219). Bristol developed trade with Ireland, Iceland and the Iberian peninsula and as early as 1461, William Cannings of Bristol controlled a fleet of ten merchant vessels which made him a powerful trading merchant. Henry VII actively encouraged English traders by

Fig. 2   Martin Coles Harman

forbidding the use of foreign vessels to conduct trade abroad if English ships were available, and by supporting Merchant Adventurers in the competition for trade with the Hanseatic League and the Venetian traders (*ibid*, 220).

In 1496, John Cabot began exploring the potential for trade with the New World from Bristol, and ten years later Bristol traders formed themselves into The Company Adventurers into the New Found Lands. Increased trade meant more prey for the pirates. The rewards were not great, but this was compensated for by the regularity of the captures (Mathew 1924, 338; McGrath 1950, 70-72, argues that losses to local pirates were minimal compared to losses to Turkish pirates in the Bristol Channel).

Lundy was not the only base for pirates in the Bristol Channel as the rugged coastlines of the south-west peninsula provided numerous hiding places and landing areas. Local landowners actively participated in piracy providing both custom and protection for the pirates (Williams 1979, 244). Collaboration between the pirates, the gentry and local officials ensured that pirate bases from Ireland to Dorset were safe from sudden attack (Mathew 1924, 337). Piracy had developed from a subsistence strategy to a commercial concern (*ibid*, 334).

Piracy complicated the then delicate relations between England and Spain. For example, in 1534 Don Pedro de la Borda, Vizino de las San Sebastion and Pero Minez de Malles, all Spanish sea merchants, were put ashore on Lundy having had their ships seized by English pirates (Langham 1994, 28). Thirty years later the failure to address successfully the problem of piracy, despite the best efforts of the Privy Council, aroused suspicions in Spain that English piracy against Spanish shipping was unofficially condoned by the Crown. Indeed the activities of Sir Francis Drake in the waters off Central America supported such a supposition (Black 1959, 126, 248). On the other hand there were valid suspicions in the English court that Irish pirates exploiting English shipping were acting on the orders of Spain, thus linking piracy with treason (Mathew 1924, 344-5).

Effective action against the pirates was hindered by the independent inclinations of the local south-west aristocracy and gentry, and by the fact that the rewards for fighting piracy were out-stripped by the rewards of engaging in it. Crime paid. The Deputy Vice Admiral of Bristol was accused of taking bribes from pirates, the Vice Admiral of Wales was prosecuted for piracy (Mathew 1924, 337, 341), and in 1549 Lord Seymour, the High Admiral of England, was executed for piracy and consorting with pirates including with those on Lundy with whom he sought refuge (Langham 1994, 28). It is hardly surprising when those in charge of suppressing piracy were themselves engaged in it, that lesser, local gentry also became involved.

Lundy's position was vulnerable. It could only be a temporary base for pirates. It did not provide them with a market for their plunder. It was not the home of a local minor aristocrat willing to sponsor pirate raids. If action against mainland pirates was ineffective because of the role duality in law-breakers enforcing the law, no such problems existed on Lundy where there were no persons with law-enforcing responsibilities. Under these circumstances Lundy witnessed official action against pirates. In 1587 the authorities at Barnstaple launched a raid on pirates staying on Lundy (Langham 1994, 31). It seems to have been successful as no pirates were reported there when Sir Richard Grenville visited the island a year later. Lundy was the only place in the south-west where the authorities could be seen to be taking effective action against pirates, and where corrupt public officials could act without adversely affecting their own private interests.

Success against the Lundy pirates was only temporary. The eviction of those in 1587 merely afforded others the opportunity to base themselves on the island in later years. In 1620 the mayor of Bristol reported to the Privy Council that £8,000 had been lost in one year due to piracy, and that consequently Bristol merchants could not pay their full contribution towards the cost of suppressing it (Stephens 1974, 158; McGrath 1970, 69 & 73). This suggests not only a recipe for disaster for the merchants, but also ultimately for the pirates who were seriously damaging the trade on which they preyed.

War with France and Spain, and the pirates based at Lundy, were specifically blamed for the decrease in trade at Bristol at this time (Stephens 1974, 159). In 1625 Turkish pirates seized the island (Langham 1994, 36), and the following year as many as fifty ships were reported lost in the Bristol Channel to pirates or shipwrecks (Stephens 1974, 159; McGrath 1950, 78). In 1628 a French fleet raiding the Severn also attacked the island (Langham 1994, 36; Stephens 1974, 159), and in 1631 a pirate called John Nutt proclaimed himself admiral of Lundy (Ternstrom 1994, 7). Such a catalogue could be presented for the rest of the seventeenth century, but in this period also there emerged a second form of economic rebellion which was eventually to supersede piracy.

Smuggling

Smuggling was recorded on Lundy in 1723 by customs officials who had been posted in the area since 1698 (Langham 1994, 46). Throughout the eighteenth century and the first quarter of the nineteenth century smuggling was a major problem for the authorities. The nature of surviving government records suggests that the problem was far more serious along the coasts of Essex, Kent, Sussex, Hampshire, and Dorset than it was in the West Country, although clearly absence of evidence is not necessarily evidence of absence (Atton and Holland 1908, 1910; Harper 1966, chapter 9; Smith 1989, 65). Once again it was the proximity of England's south-east coast to continental Europe which focused economic activity. Apart from the country houses of the squirarchy, London provided the main market for smuggled goods. The economist Adam Smith remarked upon the hypocrisy of those who denounced smuggling when so many enjoyed its fruits (Harper 1966, 112). The Bristol Channel not only lacked a large customer-base; it also suffered perilous waters and a coastline far less suited to mass smuggling than the Kent and Sussex coasts (Smith 1989, 66).

Information about smuggling in the West Country comes largely from two smugglers who wrote autobiographies (Carter 1900, writing about a Cornish smuggling family; Rattenbury 1837, writing about smuggling in Devon). Compared with the trade along the south-east coast, smuggling in the south-west peninsula was economically insignificant to the extent that Smith has described it as "small fry" (1989, 65). When the number of dragoons employed to combat smugglers was doubled in 1733, it was to Essex, Kent and Sussex that the reinforcements were sent (Atton and Holland 1908, 231). The north Devon coast had to make do with four unarmed customs officers (Smith 1989, 116-7).

The government could not mount any effective action against smugglers such was the demand for smuggled goods. Accounts presented to the House of Commons in 1825 show that smuggled goods worth £282,541 in excise duty had been seized during the previous three years, but at an enforcement cost of £2,070,528 (Harper 1966, 160-2). Trade restrictions, too complicated even for customs officers to understand (Atton and Holland 1908, 211), were relaxed in the second quarter of the nineteenth century (Atton and Holland 1910, 135). All the islands in the Bristol Channel were bases for smugglers (Smith 1989, 66). Those principally involved came from Ireland, and from the large number of pilots who worked the Channel waters (ibid, 62-3, 77, 79). The advantage Lundy had over the other islands was two-fold. Pilotage was compulsory from Lundy and therefore the opportunities to engage in smuggling under the cloak of legitimacy were many. Secondly, Lundy fell outside the jurisdiction of the Smuggling Acts (ibid, 79, 124). Customs officials were aware of the smuggling based at Lundy but could take no direct action against the island.

This legislative loop-hole was exploited by a Bideford merchant, Thomas Benson, who smuggled tobacco and also transported convicts to the island (ibid, 123-5; Langham 1994, 47). His contract with the government was to transport convicts to Virginia, but Benson's attitude to Lundy was like that of many of its owners. Having acquired the island in 1748 it had become his personal fief, separate from the kingdom of England. In transporting convicts to the island to work for him, Benson felt he had fulfilled his part of the bargain to remove the convicts from the kingdom. His smuggling base and private colony was strongly defended against Customs officials by gun platforms (ibid, 52).

Benson's removal from the island, following a fraudulent insurance claim on a ship he himself caused to be sunk (*ibid*, 50), left it free for others to use as a smuggling base. In 1782 Customs Officers seized 128 ankers (9 gallon kegs) of brandy. Three years later a smuggler called Knight, who operated on a scale similar to Benson, occupied Lundy having been driven from Barry Island (*ibid*, 57; Smith 1989, 126). As late as 1856, a tenant farmer on Lundy was convicted of the crime, but by this period the relaxation of trading legislation meant smuggling had become less lucrative. Lundy then entered a third phase of its history when those hiding from authority were replaced by those choosing merely to withdraw from wider society.

Reclusion

With the compensation he received following the emancipation of his Jamaican slaves, William Hudson Heaven (Fig.3) bought Lundy in 1836 for the price of £9,870 (Langham 1987, 10)[3]. His intention was to use it as a summer residence although financial necessity eventually forced his permanent removal to the island (Ternstrom pers comm). Lundy had entered the Victorian age, described memorably by scholar of Victorian studies, Gertrude Himmelfarb, as a mirror

---

3   Langham (1994, 62) indicates the sale took place in 1834 but Ternstrom, who has access to the Heaven papers, can find no authority to support this (Ternstrom pers comm).

Fig. 3   William Hudson Heaven, 1869

image culture in which, "the underworld of pornography co-existed comfortably with the outer world of prudity" (1968, 277). The golden age of the English country house inspired by Palladian mansions visited on the Grand Tour was almost over (Royle 1987, 227), but for a Victorian gentleman aspiring to the squirarchy (if not actually the aristocracy) a country seat was a pre-requisite. Heaven immediately commissioned the building of his own Villa on the island, the house now called Millcombe (fig.4).

Educated at Harrow, Oxford and on the Grand Tour (Langham 1987, 10) and himself the son of a gentleman, Heaven married well and was listed in Burke's Landed Gentry. He was typical of his age. The price he paid for the island appears at first sight to place him in the greater rather than the lesser gentry bracket (Thompson 1963, 112), at a time when 29% of all the land in Devon was held by the gentry classes (coincidentally the national average for land in each county held by the gentry, *ibid*, 113-5).

Marriage alliances and the magistracy were the principal aims of the Victorian gentry classes (*ibid*, 128; Altick 1973, 26), and in acquiring his own island Heaven had gone one better than many of his class. He was not only in effect his own magistrate, but also his own law-maker, choosing at times to accept the jurisdiction of the mainland courts when his tenant farmer was prosecuted for smuggling, but (as demonstrated above) also challenging the rights of a mainland coroner to inquire into a death on the island.

Heaven found the island too expensive to maintain simply as a country seat (Langham 1987, 10), even though with Lundy at just over 1000 acres, he ranked as only one of the smaller landowners (estate size not necessarily determining social status: Thompson 1963, 109, 115). Attempts to sell the island in 1840, 1856, 1906 and 1912 all failed. Between 1856 and 1906 Heaven, succeeded on his death in 1883 by his son the Reverend Hudson Heaven, attempted to supplement his income by leasing the rights of quarrying on the island (Langham 1994, chapter 20) with a number of ventures only the first of which ever enjoyed brief success.

The Reverend Hudson Heaven's life on Lundy to some extent reflects the careers of his ecclesiastical contemporaries on the mainland (Altick 1973, 26; Thompson 1963, 208). He concerned himself with rebuilding the church in stone taken from abandoned buildings on the island, and with a night school and a Sunday School for the island families, leading the way to Spiritual redemption through education in much the same way as the Reverend John Coker Egerton was doing at the same time in the Weald, and the Reverend John Wycliffe Gedge tried to emulate in Buriton, Hampshire (Wells 1992; Harfield 1994, 203-6). Permanent residence on the island, a consequence of financial necessity, isolated the Heaven family from the mainstream of Victorian shire society and the 'Provincial Season', a gentry version of the aristocratic 'Season' in London (Royle 1987, 227-231). Between

Fig 4   View of Millcombe taken between 1885 and 1897

1870 and 1905 the family kept a diary of their time on Lundy, some short extracts from which have been published. One entry in particular seems to sum the island up: "everybody did nothing in particular and the rest looked on" (Langham 1987, 15).

In 1918 the island was sold to Augustus Langham Christie whose stated ambition was that of the landed recluse because he "could not bear to see from his house any land that he did not own" (Blunt 1968, 51). In 1926 Martin Coles Harman, "an enthusiastic naturalist and individualist" bought the island (Langham 1994, 67)[4]. His defiance against the mainland authorities by issuing both coinage and stamps for the island demonstrates perhaps recalcitrance as much as reclusion. His passion for Lundy was manifest in his founding of the Lundy Field Society, the fiftieth anniversary of which marks his enduring legacy, and is celebrated with this volume.

Harman's vision for Lundy was as a place of resort for like-minded persons. It was a vision which has persisted through the generosity of both Jack Hayward (Fig.5), who provided the finance which enabled the National Trust to purchase the island, and of the Landmark Trust, whose leasing and subsequent investment in the island has helped to sustain it since 1969. Whether visitors today come simply to observe the flora and fauna, or whether they choose to excavate into the island, hang off its cliffs or dive round its rocks, Lundy now offers a temporary refuge from the day-to-day mundane world of the mainland. The growth of the leisure industry has provided the opportunity of economic viability as greater spending power among the majority allows others to share the peace and tranquillity sought by the island's owners from Heaven to Harman. The irregularity of leisure patterns in the late eighteenth and nineteenth centuries has been replaced by the twentieth century concept of structured holidays (Royle 1987, 260), arranged in week-long parcels which the Landmark Trust markets to such good effect.

Conclusions

It is worth considering finally the uses to which the various authorities have considered putting the island. The fact that the Government did not take formal responsibility for the island until 1973, suggests that, in these terms, no real use for the island was envisaged before then, yet suggestions had previously been made which imply that this was not necessarily the case. For example, the authorities from time to time considered Lundy as a repository for those unwanted in society. In 1765 Merchants at Bristol suggested using the island as a fever colony (*Exeter Flying Post* March 29th 1765). Twenty-one years later the government speculated about the island's future

---

[4] The conveyances for the sales of 1918 and 1926 are preserved in the Lundy Museum Archive. There appears to be no authority for the date of 1928 suggested by Langham (1994, 67).

Fig. 5   Sir Jack Hayward's visit to Lundy, 1969

as a penal colony (*The Times* October 25th 1786). Thomas Benson MP had, after all, already demonstrated the potential in this idea in the sort of parliamentary scandal which so exercises the Press of today. Nothing came of it on this occasion, but the Earl of Malmesbury noted in his diary for October 22nd 1852 that the idea was once again seriously considered in government (Langham 1994, 63). Finally, in 1915, a suggestion that the island be used to house prisoners of war was rejected because of the logistical problems in feeding and accommodating a large number of persons on the island (*ibid*, 67).

Closer government attention to Lundy might have been expected had the island been of any particular military significance. In fact there has been little to gain by housing a garrison there. Henry III built the castle on the island after he had seized Lundy from the Marisco family (after whom the castle is misleadingly named). His intention apparently was to prevent the island's use by pirates (Ternstrom 1994, 1). Given the later history of Lundy, this plan appears to have been a well-intentioned failure.

The island was noted as a good anchorage in the Armada Pilots Survey of the English Coastline, October 1597. The traitorous Captain Eliot sought permission from the King of Spain to seize Lundy and garrison there 100 Spanish and 40 English soldiers. How useful the island would have been in the event of an invasion is uncertain, but only four years later the idea was still current because Robert Basset set up a base on the island in order to assist an anticipated French invasion (Langham 1994, 31-3). Significantly Queen Elizabeth ignored Basset's presence on the island and did not regard him as any particular threat. He fled Lundy for France in 1603, the hoped-for invasion never having taken place.

The French threat during the reign of Queen Anne caused the government to survey the defences on Lundy in 1787. A note was made of the guns in position around its coast. But when the French did invade south Wales in 1797, they appear to have paid the island no notice other than to shelter in its undefended lee (*ibid*, 58; Smith 1989, 48). In 1881 Vice Admiral Phillimore, reviewing the nation's defences, advised that three large guns with a range of two and a half miles be placed on Lundy in order to assist in the defence of the Bristol Channel. Technology overtook this idea almost immediately, and the defence of the Bristol Channel was left to the crews of the new and versatile torpedo boats. The guns were never sent to Lundy (Langham 1994, 65).

When the Second World War broke out, ironically the island and its lighthouses guided the Luftwaffe on bombing raids to Bristol. The Admiralty leased the Old Light from Martin Harman for £400 a year, and stationed a sixty-year old Lieutenant and six ratings on Lundy to staff a watching post. Their presence, although only the most minor of naval shore stations, ensured that the islanders received regular supplies of food during the war. Despite the fact that the

Women's Land Army sent one volunteer across to help with the farm, the Devon War Agricultural Committee did not regard Lundy as a viable farming project. No further help was sent to the island (Gade and Harman 1995). The islanders themselves contributed to the war effort by staffing boats which were used to patrol the waters between Lundy and the Devon shore, and by forming a four-man Home Guard unit on the island which captured Luftwaffe air crew from the two planes which crashed there.

The chronology of events in Lundy's past have been well catalogued elsewhere (Langham and Langham 1984, Langham 1987, Langham 1994, and Ternstrom (formerly Langham) 1994). The themes into which these events fall are defined both by the circumstances of the island itself, and those of the ages through which it has been occupied. Never at the centre of national events, its peripheral position has enabled lesser individuals to earn a place in the pages of local history.

It is difficult to think of any square mile of the United Kingdom which has been so-much studied by amateur and professional alike, across such a broad spectrum of academic and scientific disciplines. Its days of petty politics and piracy over, Lundy is now enjoying a new significance founded upon the natural beauty of its isolation and the bounty of its nature.

Acknowledgments

I am grateful to Myrtle Ternstrom for commenting on a later draft of this chapter and for providing information from documentary sources in her possession. John Schofield and Chris Webster assisted in locating source material and commented on earlier drafts.

References

Altick, R, 1973. *Victorian People and Ideas*. London: Dent.
Atton, H, & Holland, H, 1908. *The King's Customs: an account of maritime revenue and contraband traffic in England, Scotland and Ireland from the earliest times to the year 1800 (Volume 1)*. London: Murray.
Atton, H, & Holland, H, 1910. *The King's Customs: an account of maritime revenue, contraband traffic, the introduction of free trade, and the abolition of the Navigation and Corn Laws from 1801-1855 (Volume 2)*. London: Murray.
Beer, B, 1982. *Rebellion and Riot: popular disorder in England during the reign of Edward VI*. Kent State University Press.
Bennet, R, & Elton, J, 1975. *Some Feudal Mills*. Wakefield: EP Publishing Ltd.
Black, J, 1959. *The Reign of Elizabeth 1558-1603 (2nd edn)*. Oxford: Clarendon.
Blunt, W, 1986. *John Christie of Glyndebourne*. London: Geoffrey Bles.
Carter, H, 1900. *Autobiography of a Cornish Smuggler*. London: Gibbings.
Davies, G, 1937. *The Early Stuarts 1603-1660*. Oxford: Clarendon.
Gade, M, & Harman, M, 1995. *Lundy's War: memories of 1939-45*. Appledore: Gade & Harman.
Giles, J, 1852-4. *Matthew Paris's English History* (3 volumes). London.
Golding, B, 1994. *Conquest and Colonisation: the Normans in Britain 1066-1100*. Basingstoke: Macmillan.
Harfield, C, 1990. *Feudal Economics*. Unpublished MPhil thesis: University of Southampton.
Harfield, C, 1994. A Rector's Legacy. *Proceedings of the Hampshire Field Club & Archaeological Society* 50, 193-207.
Harper, C, 1966. *The Smugglers*. Newcastle: Graham.
Himmelfarb, G, 1968. *Victorian Minds*. London: Weidenfeld & Nicholson.
James, M R (ed), 1926. *The Drawings of Matthew Paris*. Walpole Society.
Langham, A, 1994. *The Island of Lundy*. Stroud: Alan Sutton.
Langham, A & M, 1984. *Lundy* (2nd edn). Newton Abbot: David & Charles.
Langham, M, 1987. *A Lundy Album* (2nd edn). Reigate.
Lees, B, 1935. *Records of the Templars in England in the Twelfth Century: the inquest of 1185 with illustrative charters and documents*. London: British Academy.
Lewis, S, 1987. *The Art of Matthew Paris in the Chronica Majoiria*. Aldershot: Scholar Press.

Loyn, H, 1982. *The Norman Conquest*. London: Hutchinson.
Luard, H, (ed) 1872-83. *Matthew Paris: Chronica Majoiria*. London.
Mackie, J, 1952. *The Earlier Tudors 1485-1558*. Oxford: Clarendon.
Maitland, W, 1895. The murder of Henry Clement, 1235. *English Historical Review* 10, 294-7.
Mathew, D, 1924. The Cornish and Welsh pirates in the reign of Elizabeth. *English Historical Review* 34, 337-48.
McGrath, P, 1950. The Merchant Venturers and Bristol shipping in the early seventeenth century. *Mariner's Mirror* 36, 69-80
McKisack, M, 1959. *The Fourteenth Century 1307-1399*. Oxford: Clarendon.
Mortimer, R, 1994. *Angevin England 1154-1258*. Oxford: Blackwell.
Palsson, H & Edwards, P, 1981. *Orkneyinga Saga*. London: Penguin.
Poole, A, 1955. *From Domesday Book to Magna Carta 1087-1216*. Oxford: Clarendon.
Powicke, M, 1941. The murder of Henry Clement and the pirates of Lundy Island. *History* 25, 285-310.
Powicke, M, 1962. *The Thirteenth Century 1216-1307* (2nd edn). Oxford: Clarendon.
Rattenbury, J, 1837. *Memoirs of a Smuggler*. Sidmouth.
Royle, E, 1987. *Modern Britain: a social history 1750-1985*. London: Arnold.
Smith, G, 1989. *Smuggling in the Bristol Channel 1700-1850*. Newbury: Countryside Books.
Stephens, W, 1974. Trade Trends at Bristol 1600-1700. *Transactions of the Bristol & Gloucester Archaeological Society* 93, 156-61.
Ternstrom, M, 1994. *The Castle on the Island of Lundy: 750 years 1244-1994*. Ternstrom: Cheltenham.
Thompson, F, 1963. *English Landed Society in the Nineteenth Century*. London: RKP.
Warner, G, (ed) 1926. *The Lybelle of Eynglyshe Polycye*. Oxford University Press.
Wells, R, (ed) 1992. *Victorian Village: the diaries of the Reverend John Coker Egerton of Burwash 1857-1888*. Stroud: Alan Sutton.
Williams, P, 1979. *The Tudor Regime*. Oxford: Clarendon.

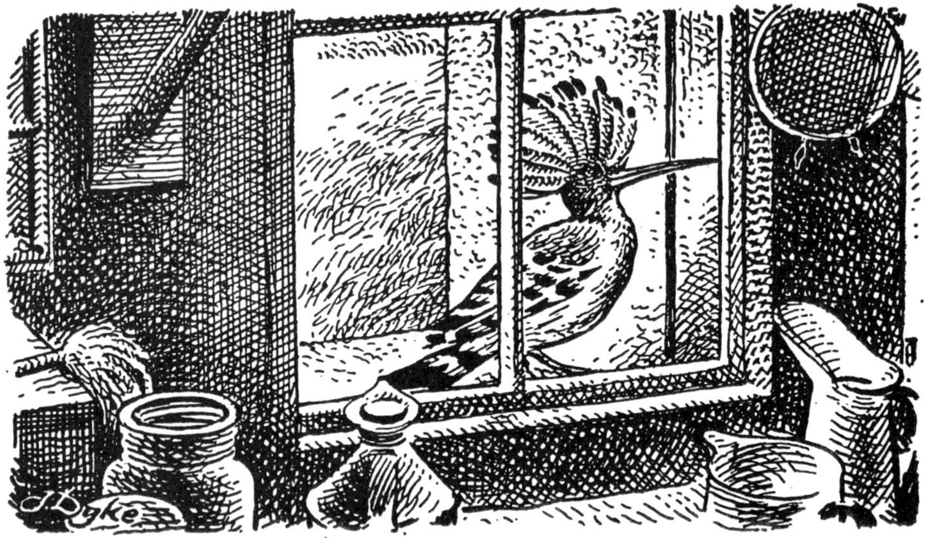

The Geology of Lundy

Sandy Smith and Clive Roberts

Introduction

Lundy, although a small island, has attracted and intrigued geologists since the nineteenth century, as it is formed from rocks that are of a very different type and age to the nearby rocks of Devon and South Wales. It is formed mainly of granite (a coarse-grained igneous rock, composed of the minerals feldspar and quartz, often with biotite and amphibole) intruded into metamorphosed sedimentary rocks. Both of these rocks are themselves intruded by dykes, sheet-like intrusions of igneous rock that have a vertical or near-vertical orientation.

The metamorphic rocks occur in the south-east peninsula of the island, around the Landing Beach (Plate 1). They are correlated with the Upper Devonian Morte Slates or Pilton Shales of North Devon which form Morte Point south-west of Ilfracombe. The Lundy granite appears similar to the granites of Devon and Cornwall, which were emplaced in Carboniferous times, 362-290 Ma (million years ago) and was originally thought to be the same age. However, radiometric dating of the Lundy granite showed that it was much younger (59-52 Ma), belonging to the Tertiary period. This makes it part of the British Tertiary Volcanic Province (BTVP) which is composed of intrusive complexes and their associated dykes, mainly located in Scotland and Northern Ireland (Fig. 1). Lundy is therefore of special interest in that it is the southern-most complex of the BTVP. It also differs from the Scottish part of the BTVP as it is emplaced into rocks of Hercynian age (345-245 Ma), which are younger and compositionally different to those in the North.

The Lundy granite

The Lundy granite is easily visible in the quarries on the east side of the island and in the tops of the cliffs. The granite has been studied by a number of researchers, in particular Dollar (1941), Edmonds et al (1979) and Thorpe et al (1990) and this summary is based on their accounts.

The Lundy intrusion is mainly a coarse-grained granite, containing large white alkali feldspar crystals about 20-30 mm in size surrounded by a groundmass of alkali feldspar, quartz, plagioclase, biotite and muscovite of about 1-2 mm grain size (Plate 2). The main granite can also appear as a very coarse-grained pegmatite, composed mainly of alkali feldspar and tourmaline. The granite crystallised from a relatively water- and fluorine-rich magma. As it did so, the less volatile components crystallised first changing the composition of the remaining magma as it cooled. This fractionation concentrated the volatiles into the late stage magma, forming the pegmatites, and also thin sheets and veins of fine-grained aplite and microgranite which intruded the main mass.

The accessory minerals of the granite are similar to those found with the Devon and Cornwall granites, including anatase, arsenopyrite, apatite, beryl, cassiterite, a columbite-tantalite series mineral, cordierite, epidote, fluorite, garnet, magnetite, molybdenite, monazite, pyrrhotite, rutile, sphene, topaz, tourmaline, uraninite, xenotime, wolframite, zircon and zoisite.

The Lundy granite has been dated by methods that use ratios between naturally occurring radioactive isotopes in the rock; potassium-argon, argon-argon and rubidium-strontium. The results give the age of the granite between 52 and 59 Ma, of Palaeocene-Eocene age within the Tertiary period. This confirms the granite as part of the BTVP, despite being physically closer to the older Devon and Cornwall granites.

Strontium and neodymium isotope data show that the Lundy granite originated from fractional crystallisation of a mixture of material, partly derived from a basic (alkaline) intrusion and partly from melting of the lower crust that also formed the source of the Devon and Cornwall granites. This explains the similarity of the Lundy granite to the granites of Devon and Cornwall. The basic intrusion would have been generated by partial melting of the mantle caused by stretching at the same time as, but distant from, where the North Atlantic was opening. Lundy is associated with positive gravity and magnetic anomalies, which are consistent with the presence of an underlying gabbro intrusion (composed of the minerals feldspar and pyroxene) below Lundy and with a larger volume than the granite. After mixing of the basic and crustal magma, and fractional crystallisation, the magma rose and then cooled in the upper crust, where it assimilated some of the country rock, indicated by xenoliths (inclusions) of the metasediments in the granite near the contact of the rocks.

Lundy dykes – remnants of a volcano?

The Lundy granite and the metasediments to the south are intruded by a swarm of dykes (Plate 3). These dykes have been studied by Dollar (1941, 1968), Mussett *et al* (1976), Edmonds *et al* (1979), Thorpe and Tindle (1992) and Roberts and Smith (1994) amongst others.

The dykes were emplaced into joint fractures within the granite and metasediments. They are slightly younger than the granite, with radiometric ages of 45-56 Ma. They range in thickness up to 2.3 m, and erode readily, forming prominent gullies within the sea cliffs.

Most of the dykes are dark-grey dolerites (a medium-grained igneous rock composed of feldspar and pyroxene), but with about 10 per cent of the dykes intermediate or acid in composition: trachytes or rhyolites. Field relationships indicate that the dolerites and trachytes/rhyolites were emplaced contemporaneously, with both dyke-types cutting the other in different places. They both often show evidence of hydrothermal alteration and may contain gas cavities, indicating emplacement at a high level near the Earth's surface. Some of these gas cavities have been infilled by secondary minerals such as chlorite, calcite, analcite, natrolite and thomsonite.

The main trend of dykes in the BTVP is northwest-southeast (Fig. 1), due to the northeast-southwest regional extensional stress field at the time of emplacement, associated with the opening of the North Atlantic Ocean. Some of the dyke trends in the BTVP are locally also related to central intrusive complexes, and do not follow the main dyke trend. As the plateau of Lundy is covered with superficial sediment, dykes can only be mapped directly in the sea cliffs around the island, which does not allow their trend to be ascertained. Instead, the presence of dykes has been inferred from magnetic measurements, as dolerite dykes (but not the trachytes or rhyolites) have a much higher magnetic susceptibility (degree of magnetisation) than the granite or metasediments, so these dykes produce magnetic anomalies. These have been mapped around Lundy (Fig. 1) and on the island (Fig. 2).

The trend of dykes around Lundy is similar to the BTVP northwest-southeast trend, but the dykes mapped on Lundy also show a radial trend, mainly northwest-southeast towards the south end of the island, but east-west at the centre and northeast-southwest towards the north end. Extrapolation suggests a focus and source for the dykes 2 to 3 km to the west of Lundy.

This is consistent with the origin of the dykes as interpreted from their mineralogy and chemistry. Basaltic magma (the same composition as in gabbro) was formed from partial melting of the mantle (the layer beneath the crust), with minor crustal contamination. Fractional crystallisation of the basaltic magma produced trachytic and rhyolitic magma. Most of the rhyolite dykes have a peralkaline composition (rich in sodium and potassium), but rarer subalkaline rhyolites were also formed from the basaltic magma through a separate fractional crystallisation path. There is only minor evidence of any interaction of the dyke magmas with the granite into which they were intruded, and the intrusion must have occurred rapidly, at a high level in the crust.

The origin of the dykes is connected to the granite through the initial basaltic magma chamber. Following emplacement of the granite, the basaltic magma chamber remained active and during further fractional crystallisation yielded dolerites, trachytes and rhyolite magmas emplaced as dykes into the cooler, jointed granite. The chemical characteristics and silica distribution within the dolerite/trachyte/rhyolite association reflect fractional crystallisation of compositionally varied basaltic magma and the rapid transition from basalt to rhyolite over a relatively small crystallisation interval. This process was accompanied by rapid emplacement of the dyke magmas into joints within the cool Lundy granite, accompanied by minor crustal-

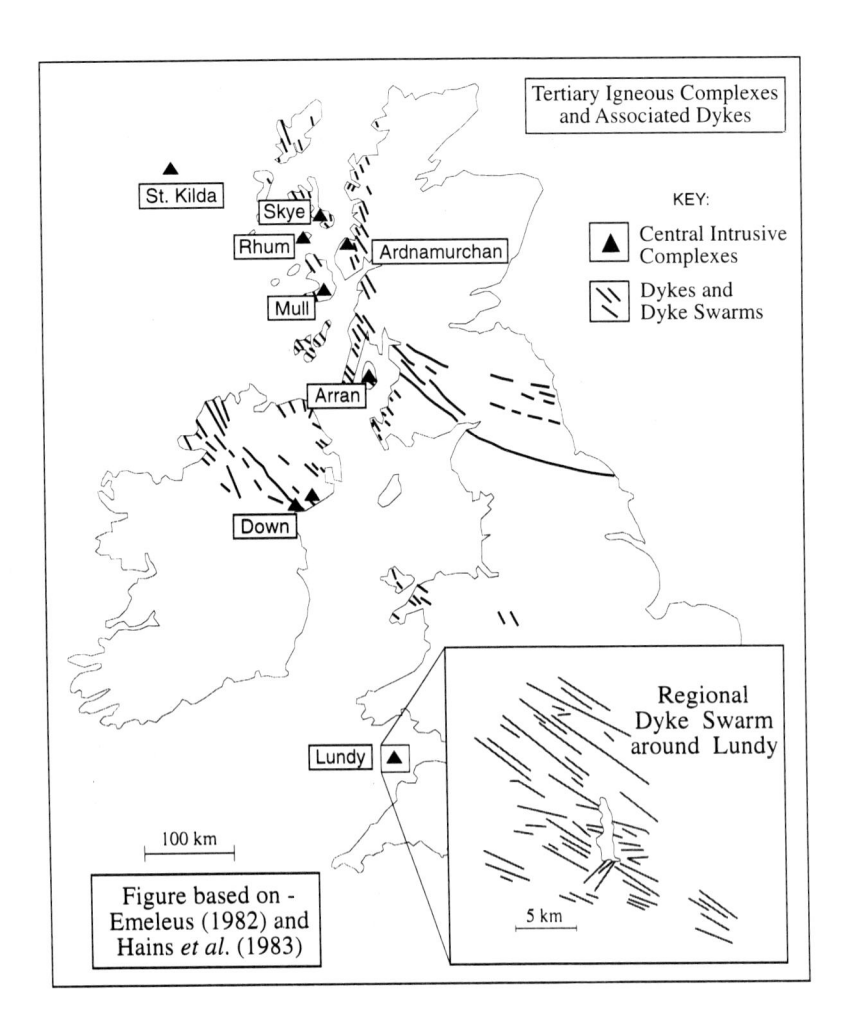

Fig. 1

granite interaction. The focus of the dyke swarm to the west of Lundy and the positive gravity anomaly to the west suggest this was the site of the basaltic magma chamber.

This rapid emplacement of the basalt, trachyte and rhyolite magmas at a high level in the crust makes it possible that the magma erupted at the surface, forming a volcano above Lundy. This would be consistent with the extrusive volcanic rocks at other BTVP centres. By similarity with volcanoes in similar settings, the Lundy volcano would have been 10-20 km in diameter, and composed of rhyolite and trachyte pyroclastic (fragmental) flows and airfalls associated with rhyolite domes and basaltic cones and flows. This Lundy volcano would have been one of the most spectacular geological events in this area.

Geomorphology

The subsequent geological history of Lundy is one of erosion, eventually leaving the harder granite protruding and now surrounded by the sea. The island is a relatively flat plateau, sloping from a height of 140 m in the south to 90 m in the north, surrounded by steeply-inclined sidelands, at the base of which are near-vertical cliffs. The geomorphological history of Lundy is confused and in many ways, unresolved. The top of the island clearly displays planation surfaces and relatively flat platforms, but whether these are of a marine, glacial or even subaerial origin is debatable. Mitchell (1968) reported gravels in the north-east of the island and assigned them to the effects of a retreating ice sheet, which also "carved" Gannets' Combe. He also noted the occurrence of roche moutonées and glacial erratics as further evidence of an ice sheet. However, many of the rounded erratics over the northend are composed of locally derived Lundy Granite, which (*senso stricto*) should not be termed erratic material. Glacial erratics normally consist of rock types such as Scottish granites and Welsh slates, that have been transported great distances, for example to North Devon, by slow moving ice sheets, of a type seen in present day Antarctica and Northern Canada.

It is likely, however, that ice sheets did reach the North Devon coastline (and presumably Lundy as well) in either the Middle Pleistocene Wolstonian stage (128,000 - 195,000 years ago) as proposed by Kidson (1977) or the Anglian stage (251,000 - 297,000 years ago) as postulated by Bowen *et al* (1986). Recent research indicates that age relationships around these periods are complicated, but at least this gives a crude indication as to the age of glaciation.

The glaciations and warmer interglacials (including the present one) were accompanied by sea level changes as water frozen on the land was not returned to the sea. This is complicated by the rising of the land. Absolute sea level around the coast of south-west England has been much lower than the present day level for much of the last 1 million years (Heyworth and Kidson 1982). Possible marine features now seen above sea level are therefore good indicators of how Lundy (and indeed most of south-west England) has moved vertically over time. This has mostly been the result of powerful Earth movements and it is interesting to note that the Lundy granite crystallised from a molten magma at a possible depth up to 10 km below ground level. Although erosion has removed an unknown thickness of overlying sediments above Lundy, these recent land movements are small compared to those in the Tertiary period after Lundy was formed.

Cullingford (1982) summarised the consensus of opinion on the existence of marine platforms and raised beaches in Devon and listed them at about 210, 180, 130, 100, 85, 45, 15, 7, 4 and 0 m OD. The two highest could not be expected on Lundy but to what extent the last eight can be seen is unclear. Queen Mab's Grotto at Brazen Ward correlates with the 15 m platform and wave-cut features can be detected at both 4 and 7 m in the same region. Langham (1985) correlates bluffs around the Cheeses and Jenny's Cove to the 85 m horizon and the flattened island surface to 130 m level. A more detailed investigation of geomorphological features over the island may unravel more of the complicated recent sequence of events. Weathering and erosion have certainly destroyed much of the evidence.

The orientation of the streams that drain the island depends on the features of the underlying rocks. Some of the streams develop along the line of the softer

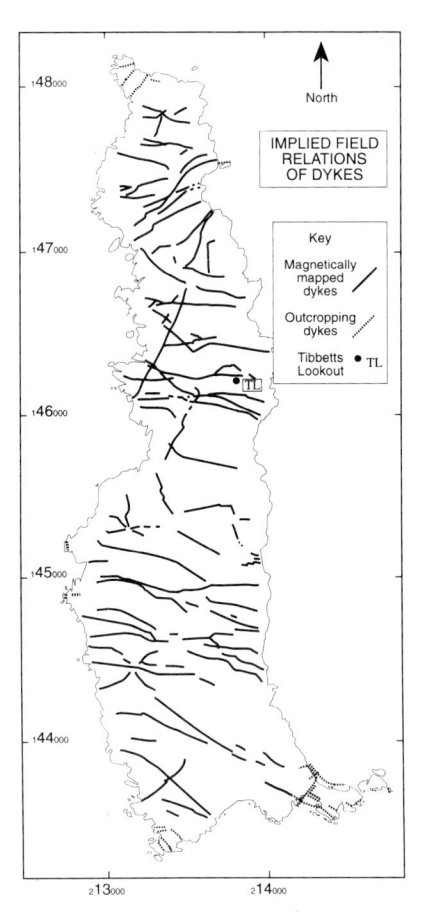

Fig. 2

ISLAND STUDIES

dykes (most of the Gannets' Combe streams follow, or partly follow, dykes) and, in the south-east, streams are influenced by linear features in the metasediments.

Quarrying The Lundy granite is an excellent and easily available building stone, and was used for the lighthouses, castle and other buildings on the island. The Old Light is an excellent example of granite masonry, formed of carefully curved blocks. The quarries on the east side of the island were used not only to supply stone for use on Lundy, but also elsewhere by the Lundy Granite Company, registered in 1863; blocks were lowered down the cliff face to Quarry Beach, then transported to the mainland by ship. Most of the stone was used in Devon. Unfortunately for Lundy this export of stone became uneconomic by 1868.

References

Bowen, D Q, Rose, J, McCabe, AM and Sutherland, DG, 1986. Correlation of Quaternary glaciations in England, Ireland, Scotland and Wales. *Quaternary Science Review 5*, 299-340.

Cullingford, RA, 1982. "The Quaternary". In E Durrance and DJ Laming (eds), *The Geology of Devon*, 249-290.

Dollar, A T J, 1941. The Lundy complex: its petrology and tectonics. *Quarterly Journal of the Geological Society Of London*, 97, 39–77.

Dollar, A T J, 1968. Tertiary dyke swarms of Lundy. *Proceedings of the Geological Society In London*. 1649, 119-120.

Edmonds, E A, Williams, BJ and Taylor, RT, 1979. *Geology of Bideford and Lundy Island*. Memoir of the Geological Society of Great Britain.

Emeleus, C H, 1982. "The central complexes". In DS Sutherland, *Igneous rocks of the British Isles*, 369-414.

Hains, B A, Edmonds, E A, Briden, J C and Tappin, T R (compilers) 1983. *Lundy, Solid Geological Map, Sheet 51N-06W*, (1:250 000). Institute of Geological Sciences.

Heyworth, A and Kidson, C, 1982. Sea-level changes in south-west England and Wales. *Proceedings of the Geological Association*, 93(1), 91-111.

Kidson, C, 1977. "The coast of south west England". In C Kidson and MJ Tooley (eds), *The Quaternary history of the Irish Sea*, 257– 298.

Langham, A F, 1982. *Geology of Lundy*. Lundy Field Society leaflet.

Mitchell, G F, 1968. Glacial gravel on Lundy Island. *Annual Report of the Lundy Field Society*, 19, 39-40.

Mussett, A E, Dagley, P and Eckford, M, 1976. The British Tertiary Igneous Province: palaeomagnetism and ages of dykes, Lundy Island, Bristol Channel *Geophysical Journal of the Royal Astronomical Society*, 46, 595-603.

Roberts, C L and Smith, S G, 1994. A new magnetic survey of Lundy Island, Bristol Channel. *Proceedings of the Ussher Society* 8, 293-297.

Thorpe, R S and Tindle, AG, 1992. Petrology and petrogenesis of a Tertiary bimodal dolerite-peralkaline/ subalkaline trachyte/rhyolite dyke association from Lundy, Bristol Channel, UK. *Geological Journal* 27, 101-117.

Thorpe, R S, Tindle, A G and Gledhill, A, 1990. The petrology and origin of the Tertiary Lundy granite (Bristol Channel, UK). *Journal of Petrology* 31(6), 1379-1406.

The Archaeology of Lundy

Caroline Thackray

In terms of the history of human settlement, Lundy is quite remarkable. Its very remoteness has resulted in an archaeological survival rarely to be found in such rich concentration on the neighbouring mainland. Mesolithic flints, Bronze Age and Iron Age settlement and field systems, medieval enclosures and farmsteads survive as earthwork remains on the plateau (Plate 4), while the Early Christian burial ground at Beacon Hill containing its mysterious inscribed memorial stones, lies in the shadow of Daniel Alexander's granite lighthouse. Above the landing beach stands Marisco Castle, its stark outline dominating the skyline. The thirteenth-century keep was extensively repaired and garrisoned for the king by Governor Bushell from 1645 until 1648, when he was finally forced to relinquish the island to Parliamentarian forces. The gun platform and breastwork at Brazen Ward, on the east coast, is the best survival of a number of coastal defences, possibly built to counter the threat from Spain during Queen Elizabeth's reign, but almost certainly re-used during the Civil War and perhaps in later wars against France. Of more recent interest are the industrial remains of the workings of the Lundy Granite Company, a short-lived enterprise which was established on the island from 1863, but foundered into bankruptcy and was dissolved by 1868; the archaeological survival is remarkably good, but (ironically for something so recent), the supporting documentary evidence is almost non-existent, the books having been lost when the company was liquidated.

The Antiquaries

Antiquarian interest in Lundy has pointed to the indications of former settlement and land-use in terms of a number of ruined buildings and the degraded and abandoned remains of what were once extensive field systems. Westcote, writing in 1620, observes:

"...that it hath been tilled in former times the furrows testify yet plainly..."
(quoted in Oliver and Pitman-Jones 1845, 343-6)

While Grose (1776) describes:
"...many ruins of old walls...which were fences to inclosures, and plainly prove a great part of the island to have been cultivated..."

Chanter (1877) alludes to signs of past cultivation and to the settlements which accompanied them:
"There are traces of no less than seven or eight groups of cottages or villages in various parts of the Island, some of which have traditional names attached to them, but no records remain as to when they were abandoned and fell into ruin"

The most notable early archaeological finds must be those of the "kistvaen" or "ancient stone burial-place", whose discovery in 1851 is described by Gosse (Loyd 1925), and the "Giants Graves", which were uncovered by Mr Heaven's workmen in 1856 whilst digging for the foundation of a wall at the north of the cattle sheds (Chanter 1877 and Loyd 1925). Much study and speculation has been given to these burials – to the outlandish stature of the skeletons, to the intriguing glass beads (variously attributed to Early Iron Age, Roman or Viking period by the British Museum in 1925, and to ninth-century Danish origin by Bristol Museum in 1960) and the fragments of gilt-bronze and sherds of red pottery said to have been found with them. The words of William Hudson Heaven in a letter to John G Heaven (May 7, 1856, quoted in Langham 1986):

> "...I shall not be surprised if in clearing away the turf and mould under it, which it is intended to do, in order that the walls may afford more protection to the rick barton, which they are to enclose, more bones will be found..."

were to find a fitting response in the subsequent twentieth-century archaeological exploration of Bulls Paradise by Bristowe in 1928, by Dollar and Lethbridge in 1933, and by members of the Lundy Field Society under the direction of Keith Gardner in 1962. All of these excavations were to find more skeletal remains, grave slabs, and midden material, ranging in date from approximately the thirteenth to the seventeenth centuries, and lying close by what Gardner has suggested may be the foundations of a former chapel site (Gardner 1962).

A further chance discovery with profound archaeological implications was made on the island in 1905 during the digging of a grave for Miss Amelia Heaven. This was the uncovering of an inscribed memorial stone (TIGERNUS), since dated to the late sixth century (Thomas 1994, 288). It was excavated from within the ruined chapel inside the old burial ground on Beacon Hill (Loyd 1925).

The Lundy Field Society

It is somehow historically satisfying that exactly one hundred years after the discovery of the Giants Graves, the first archaeological paper should be published by the LFS. Keith Gardner's "Prehistoric Settlement – Gannets Combe, Lundy" appeared in the 10th Annual Report in 1956 and it was to be the first of many. Early work by Gardner concentrated on a review and analysis of existing archaeological evidence, which was to form a basis for future research. This first article made comparisons between the Lundy settlement remains and similar sites on Dartmoor, attributed by Ralegh Radford to the Middle Bronze Age. The following year he reviewed Dollar's findings of flint scatters in 1932, and the 1957 collection of over 1,000 flint pieces from Brick Field, pointing to the existence here of a Mesolithic settlement (Gardner 1957). A further preliminary discussion was presented by Gardner (1959a), concerning "Dark Age Remains on Lundy".

Using evidence derived from Chanter (1877) and Loyd (1925), Gardner re-examined the Giants Graves and the Early Christian "Tigernus" stone, raising questions for the archaeologist and historian about post Roman occupation of Lundy and the origins of the Early Christian burial ground and chapel site.

This and similar questions arising from these early papers led Gardner, under the aegis of the Lundy Field Society, to embark on a series of research investigations over the next decade which were to extend Lundy's archaeological record, and in the nature of much research, to both enlighten and mystify.

Brief reference has already been made to the discovery of further burials and a likely chapel site in Bulls Paradise, but Gardner's 1962 excavations there also established this as the likely site of the twelfth- century de Marisco stronghold, pre-dating the royal castle of AD1243. During the ensuing years, survey and excavation work concentrated on a number of different sites. A rectangular earthwork in Widow's Tenement was examined and planned, yielding flints and both Early Iron Age and thirteenth-century pottery. These together with its form suggested a long-house-type dwelling, which may have developed from a former prehistoric site (Gardner 1964). Excavations of hut circles in Middle Park, and within the North End settlement system, produced Iron Age and Late Bronze Age pottery respectively (Gardner 1963-4, 1965-6, 1968). Surveys were carried out of the field systems in Middle Park, Ackland's Moor, and west and south-east of the Old Light (Gardner 1965-6 and 1968). Plans were also produced for a number of batteries at North End, including Brazen Ward (from which trial excavations had produced sixteenth-century pottery) and for John O'Groats house (Gardner 1968). A platform structure above Jenny's Cove was examined, and the discovery of thirteenth-century pottery, combined with its form and structure and documentary reference, led to the proposal that this was the site of a mangonel platform – part of Lundy's medieval defence (Gardner 1965– 6).

Of prime importance among Gardner's archaeological achievements on Lundy was his collaboration with Charles Thomas and Peter Fowler, supported by both students and Lundy Field Society members, in the excavation and analysis of the burial site at Beacon Hill in 1969 (Plate 5). This had been prompted by the discovery within the burial ground of three more inscribed stones: one in 1961 by Gardner and Langham (POTITI) and two others by Douglas Hague in 1962 (RESTEUTAE and OPTIMI). Thomas now attributes dates of late fifth to early sixth centuries AD to these latter, whilst a mid to late sixth-century origin is thought more appropriate for TIGERNUS and POTITI (Thomas 1994).

The excavation attempted to discover why these stones were placed here and to see if they could be related to graves of this early date within the graveyard. In summary (Thomas, Fowler and Gardner 1969) the main finding was a central feature marked by large slabs, which showed a complex process of use and reuse. They also showed that the likely date for the foundations of the small chapel was the twelfth or thirteenth century. The excavations revealed that the central feature was built over, and partly from, the remains of an earlier circular house. This adjoined the traces of a lynchet (a low bank caused by ploughing) running underneath the centre of the burial ground, which formed part of a system of earlier fieldbanks and hut circles, south and west of Beacon Hill, surveyed by Peter Fowler at the same time as the 1969 excavation.

A recent re-analysis of the excavation evidence by Professor Charles Thomas (1990), has resulted in some intriguing observations, expanded on more recently (Thomas 1994) when Lundy is identified as "Enys Brachan", and the empty central grave on Beacon Hill as that of the Welsh king Brychan, himself.

The culmination of Gardner's archaeological research was the publication of his Archaeological Field Guide in 1972. This provided an inventory of sites for the island and is accompanied by a commentary describing these and their state of research and suggesting an interpretation and likely chronology.

The recording and explanatory work by Gardner had two-fold importance. In the first instance it provided a sound basis for further research, revealing for the first time the remarkable breadth and range of archaeological survival on Lundy. It also alerted the profession to the need to maintain and conserve this special survival, and accordingly in 1970, a number of sites on the island were scheduled, giving them legal protection and special status in terms of their management.

The National Trust Survey

The acquisition of Lundy by the National Trust in 1968, and its lease to the Landmark Trust with consequent restoration and building, led to a different focus on the island's archaeology, with an increased concern for the management and conservation of sites – an emphasis which has continued into the 1990s. Work has been undertaken by both Trusts as part of the management process, and has also been extended by the Field Society, close cooperation being sought by all parties.

Excavation and survey by the Central Excavation Unit of English Heritage (Dunmore 1982) in 1978 preceded the Landmark Trust's renovation of three derelict cottages within the castle keep. Similar work was undertaken on the parade ground by the National Trust (Thackray, D 1985) prior to consolidation of the curtain wall and Benson's "Old House" in 1984-5, but the main thrust of National Trust archaeological work on Lundy in recent years has been field survey.

Concern that lack of knowledge was leading to damage to important sites led to a National Trust archaeological report for the island (Thackray, C 1989), which inventoried existing sites, stated their location and condition, and gave recommendations for their management. It was accompanied by an account of Lundy's land-use history. The objective of the ensuing project was to compile over a 4-year period a topographic survey of the island which would identify and document in detail all visible traces of past land-use, ranging from evidence of prehistoric and medieval occupation to the industrial remains and other survivals of the more recent past. Existing records were incorporated where appropriate, but the majority of the survey was the product of new measurement by electronic theodolite survey, and large-scale, detailed drawings. All sites were described and photographed. Further contour information, aerial photographic and other existing mapped detail will ultimately be combined with the 1:1000 metrical survey to produce a final plan of the island as a whole. By examining the archaeological landscape in this way, it is hoped to achieve two things: an improved understanding of Lundy's historic evolution; and the creation of an up-to-date and consistent record for management and conservation.

This historic landscape survey was undertaken by National Trust staff, and volunteers (among them LFS members) over four years, in 2-week periods during late April/May from 1990-1994. The raw material of the survey is currently (1996) being written up; annotated plots of the island's archaeology have been produced, and details of every site (amounting to almost 2,000) are being entered onto the Trust's computerised database. Interpretation is ongoing, but the suspicions mooted by Gardner in the 1960s that almost the entire island plateau shows evidence of previous farming and settlement, are being borne out, with field systems clearly continuing to the south of Halfway and Quarter Walls, and into and below the village. It is only through seeing these patterns emerging in plan that informed analysis and interpretation of these remains and their relationships to each other may be deduced. An especially high degree of detail has been employed for recording Beacon Hill Cemetery, with both a contour survey and a feature survey of its interior. Detailed drawings of central features (the excavated graves and thirteenth-century chapel remains) together with written descriptions and photographs were completed. The Quarries were also treated in great detail, and it is hoped that the resulting plan will give a better understanding of the operations there.

Part of the work of the survey was to record the architectural detail of those ruined buildings which have survived in more substantial form, and some fine plans, elevations, and suggested reconstructions have been drawn for Belle Vue Cottages and the Quarry Hospital, the Battery Cottages and associated buildings (Fig. 1); similar detailed recording has been given to the recording of John O'Groats House, Widow's Tenement long-house and enclosure, Bull's Paradise, and some of the more complete earlier ruins.

As with the results of Gardner's work in the 1960s, it is intended that this research will give rise to publication, both at an academic level, and to provide the interested visitor to the island with an updated archaeological field guide and other information. It will also,

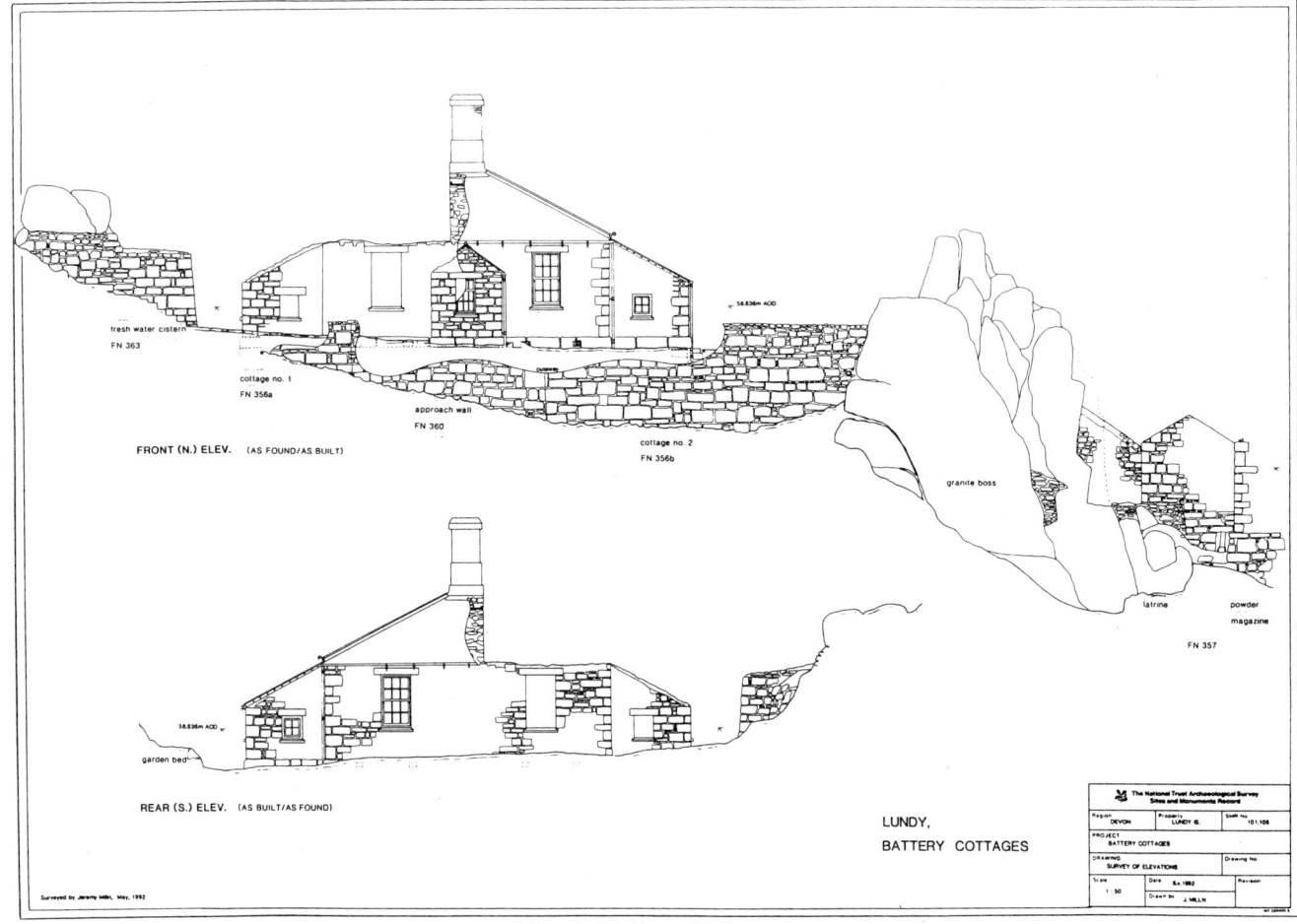

Fig. 1 Battery Cottages

through its reinforced statement of the overall archaeological importance of the island, lead to a revision of existing Scheduled Monuments and a likely increase in their number under English Heritage's Monuments Protection Programme.

Running concurrently with the NT survey has been the research undertaken in recent years by John Schofield and Chris Webster with the support of the Lundy Field Society. This has focused on the areas where earthworks have, for the most part, been ploughed away: the fields to the south of Quarter Wall. Techniques employed have been geophysical prospection and test-pit excavation. Existing collections of flint artefacts have been examined (Schofield 1991) and comparisons made with other flint finds and those arising from test-pits, particularly in Brickfield, Tillage Field and St Helen's (Schofield 1988). Artefact concentrations in Airfield and Lighthouse Field have also been examined (Schofield & Webster 1989, 1990), the evidence reinforcing the impression that this area was fairly intensively used in both the Mesolithic and Post-Medieval periods. A geophysical survey of Bull's Paradise (Webster 1991) both supports Gardner's previous evidence and also indicates new features. It will be interesting to compare the geophysical findings with the NT survey plan of the area.

Now that the National Trust survey is substantially complete, the resulting Sites and Monuments record for Lundy and the research undertaken by Schofield and Webster may be studied together, along with the extant documentary record and current historical research being undertaken by Caroline Thackray and Myrtle Ternstrom. In addition, it is hoped that the opportunity will arise for a programme of environmental analysis, including a reassessment of pollen analysis results from Gardner's 1960s investigations. Further geophysical research may also be considered.

A further important observation of the 1989 National Trust report had been the existence of a large archive arising from past archaeological work on Lundy, chance finds, or personal observations which was scattered and largely anonymous. The recommendation that an attempt should be made to embrace this problem has led to the collaboration of Myrtle Ternstrom (for the Field Society) and Caroline Thackray (for the National Trust), and work is already well-advanced in locating, cataloguing and indexing this dispersed archive.

Finally, articles in the two most recent Field Society reports (Heath 1993, Robertson 1994, and Heyes 1994) have given an indication of a new direction in archaeological research to be closely followed in the future – that of underwater exploration. There already exist two wreck sites off the island (*Iona II* & Gull Rock) which are afforded statutory protection under The Protection of Wrecks Act of 1973, and there is a growing awareness of the importance of underwater archaeology – both as a possible aid to understanding the people who occupied the island and because of Lundy's position in the path of national and international trade.

Inevitably, in such a brief review, much will have been omitted from the catalogue of archaeological progress made during the fifty years of the Field Society's existence, but it is hoped that the serious enquirer will be able to use the bibliography below, and the Index to the LFS Annual Report, to pursue a deeper interest. Space has not allowed a discussion of the challenging and lively articles on the archaeo-astronomy of Lundy, by Bob Farrah (1991), or his thoughts on the symbolic orientation of St Helen's Church (Farrah 1992, 1994). Nor has direct reference been made to the invaluable historic research of Tony and Myrtle Langham (now Ternstrom), and many other LFS members, whose curiosity and love for Lundy have set them poring through documents and extending our knowledge and understanding of the island's history by publishing their results. For all this is archaeology, too, and the interplay of research into material remains and related documents is vitally important wherever it can be called into effect.

And what of the future?... The archaeological record for Lundy is looking good. A very great deal has been done to establish its position as ranking high in management considerations for the island, holding its rightful place beside the nature conservation considerations of an SSSI, and the special concerns of a Marine Nature Reserve; the need to maintain satisfactory levels of stocking and grazing of a working farm, and its special provision as a refuge for those who seek and delight in remote island seclusion, however temporarily. The balance is delicate, and maintaining it requires cooperation and understanding. It is not just the archaeology of Lundy which is special, any more than its ecology or its ornithology. Balance is all, and our challenge for the next fifty years must be to hold on to this concept – advancing our scientific knowledge and understanding of the island, whilst not allowing its special magic to slip away in the process.

References

Chanter, J R, 1877. *Lundy Island*.

Claris, P D, 1989. Historic landscape survey of Lundy: an introduction. *Annual Report of the Lundy Field Society* 40, 48-49.

Claris, P D and Thackray, D W R, 1990. Historic landscape survey of Lundy: first interim report. *Annual Report of the Lundy Field Society*, 41, 26-33.

Dunmore, S, 1982. The castle in the Isle of Lundy. *Proceedings of the Devon Archaeological Society*, 40, 153-162

Farrah, R W E, 1991. The megalithic astronomy of Lundy: evidence for the remains of a solar calendar. *Annual Report of the Lundy Field Society* 42, 55- 65.

Farrah, R W E, 1992. The symbolic orientation of St Helena's Church, Lundy. *Annual Report of the Lundy Field Society* 43, 78-91

Farrah, R W E, 1994. Further thoughts on the symbolic orientation of St Helena's Church. *Annual Report of the Lundy Field Society* 45, 43-57.

Gardner, K S, 1956. Prehistoric settlement at Gannets Combe. *Annual Report of the Lundy Field Society* 10, 56-57.

Gardner, K S, 1957. Report on flint implements found in the Brick Field, Lundy, 1957. *Annual Report of the Lundy Field Society* 11, 32-34.

Gardner, K S, 1959a. Dark Age remains on Lundy. *Annual Report of the Lundy Field Society* 13, 53-62.

Gardner, K S, 1959b. Archaeological note. *Annual Report of the Lundy Field Society*, 13, 63-64. [On items in Bristol Museum.]

Gardner, K S, 1961. Preliminary report on archaeological excavations in The Bulls Paradise, Lundy. *Annual Report of the Lundy Field Society* 14, 22-26.

Gardner, K S, 1962. Archaeological investigations on Lundy, 1962. *Annual Report of the Lundy Field Society* 15, 22-23.

Gardner, K S, 1963-4. Archaeological investigations, Lundy, 1964. *Annual Report of the Lundy Field Society* 16, 29-32.

Gardner, K S, 1965-6. Archaeological investigations, Lundy 1966/7 *Annual Report of the Lundy Field Society* 17, 30-33.

Gardner, K S, 1967. Lundy – a mesolithic peninsula? *Annual Report of the Lundy Field Society* 18, 24-28.

Gardner, K S, 1968. Lundy archaeological investigations, 1967. *Annual Report of the Lundy Field Society* 19, 41-44.
Gardner, K S, 1969. Pollen analysis – a brief note. *Annual Report of the Lundy Field Society* 20, 18-19.
Gardner, K S, 1972 *The Archaeology of Lundy: A Field Guide*. Landmark Trust.
Grose, F, 1776. *The Antiquities of England and Wales*, IV.
Langham, M, 1986. The Heaven Family of Lundy, 1836-1916. *Report and Transactions of the Devonshire Association for the Advancement of Science* 118, 93-121.
Loyd, L R W, 1925. *Lundy, its history and natural history*.
Oliver, G and Pitman-Jones, 1845. *A View of Devonshire*.
Schofield, A J, 1988. Archaeological fieldwork 1988: the results of test-pit excavations and geophysical prospection south of Quarter Wall. *Annual Report of the Lundy Field Society* 39, 31-45.
Schofield, A J, 1991. The Langham Collection and associated finds: a large assemblage of chipped stone artefacts from Lundy. *Annual Report of the Lundy Field Society* 42, 70-84.
Schofield, A J and Webster, C J, 1989. Archaeological fieldwork 1989: further test pit excavations south of Quarter Wall. *Annual Report of the Lundy Field Society*, 40, 34-47.
Schofield, AJ and Webster, C J, 1990. Archaeological fieldwork 1990: further investigation of artefact concentrations south of Quarter Wall. *Annual Report of the Lundy Field Society*, 41, 34-52.
Thackray, C, 1989. Lundy – *National Trust Archaeological Survey Report*. Vols 1 & 2 (unpublished).
Thackray, D W R, 1985. *Lundy Island: Marisco Castle Parade Ground Excavations*, 1984-5 (Preliminary Report).
Thomas, C, Fowler, P and Gardner, K S., 1969. Beacon Hill – Early Christian Cemetery. *Annual Report of the Lundy Field Society*, 20, 14-17.
Thomas, C, 1990. Beacon Hill re-visited: a reassessment of the 1969 excavations. *Annual Report of the Lundy Field Society*, 42, 43-54.
Thomas, C, 1994. *And shall these mute stones speak? Post-Roman inscriptions in Western Britain*. Cardiff: University of Wales Press.
Webster, C J, 1991. A geophysical survey of the archaeology of Bulls Paradise. *Annual Report of the Lundy Field Society*, 42, 66-69.
Webster, C J, 1992. Geophysical surveys of artefact concentrations south of Quarter Wall. *Annual Report of the Lundy Field Society*, 43, 68-77.

Marine Archaeology and Lundy

Philip Robertson and John Heath

Introduction

Beneath the waves off Lundy remain some fascinating relics of the island's rich maritime past. Out of sight for most of Lundy's visitors, these archaeological sites should not be out of mind. It is with the study of these wrecks, as well as other material evidence of mankind's historical relationship with the sea that marine archaeology is principally concerned. As a subject, marine archaeology developed after the invention of the aqualung in the 1940s and was pioneered in particular by archaeologists in the Mediterranean in the 1960s who learned to apply land techniques under water on excavations of Bronze Age shipwrecks off the coastline of Turkey. Since the 1960s marine archaeology in Europe has brought to light vital information of our maritime past from famous wrecks such as Henry VIII's *Mary Rose*, the magnificent *Wasa* in Stockholm (Sweden), the Viking ships at Roskilde (Denmark), the cargo vessels of the Classical Mediterranean, and the ships of the Spanish Armada. While shipwrecks are perhaps the most obvious line of enquiry for the marine archaeologist, landscapes submerged by rising sea levels since the last ice age, fish-traps, and ancient harbours are just a few other examples of what interests this discipline.

An historical view

As far as research into the marine archaeology of Lundy is concerned, the overall aim has been to learn about the island's role within the maritime setting of north Devon and the Bristol Channel; to learn about the design and function of some of the ships wrecked on its coasts; and to record for the future a resource of great value to Lundy and to the UK.

The first objective for any study of the marine archaeological resource must be to assess the potential of the area. Given evidence for Lundy's occupation since the Mesolithic (9000-5000 BC) when a land bridge may well have linked Lundy with the mainland, there is potential for locating evidence of human settlement of those land surfaces which have since gradually inundated. Rising sea levels following the last ice-age probably cut Lundy off from the mainland around 7000 BC and from this period on, settlers on the island relied on boats for access to and from their home. No material evidence this old has been found under water off Lundy but if anything has survived, then the more favourable burial environment and soft sediments found off the east coast of the island should be the first priority for any search. As a general rule the archaeological potential of the west coast is limited by its exposed coastline, particularly inshore where the destructive effects of wave surge are greatest. Archaeological deposits may only have survived relatively intact where they have come to rest in deeper water offshore or in localised areas where accumulated sediment in offshore gully systems offers a stable resting place.

The Bristol Channel was in common use as a sea road by the 11th century and its importance grew after the 16th century with the opening up of English colonies in the New World and with the growth of trade in coal from the ports of South Wales to national and international destinations (Davis 1962). Lundy's maritime history is inextricably linked with the economic fortunes of Barnstaple, Bideford and Bristol, and to a lesser extent of Clovelly, Hartland and Ilfracombe. However, apart from localised trade in quarried granite, the island played only a small part in the wider maritime picture; its renown originates more from its position as an awkward obstacle to shipping traffic in the Bristol Channel. Given the lack of navigational technology available to ships until the 20th century, Lundy, situated in mid-channel with its dangerous rocks and tidal races, constituted a serious hazard to shipping. A number of developments, starting with Trinity House's recognition of the need for a lighthouse on the island at the end of the 18th century (Langham 1994), indicated the seriousness of this threat. The completion of the beautifully-built but inadequate Old Light in 1820, was followed by the development of a fog battery on the west coast, and eventually the construction of two further lighthouses at the island's north and south ends.

Nevertheless, many vessels continued to founder around the island's shores. The history of Lundy's wrecks has been fairly well researched and several good accounts have been published (see Heath 1991; Larn, R & B 1995; Bouquet 1967, 1969; Langham 1994; and Gibson 1993). The earliest record of a wreck on the island is that of the collier *Marie*, lost on 19th September 1757. Gibson (1993) states that since this date "over 200 shipwrecks have been recorded around the island" and we may presume that many wrecks occurred before this date. Occasionally, the location on the island where a shipwreck occurred would thereafter bear the ship's name. Thus Jenny's Cove on the west side is named after the three-masted schooner *Jenny* which sank there in February 1797. Returning from Africa to Bristol with a cargo of ivory (elephant tusks) and gold dust, she struck rocks and swiftly broke up, with the loss of all crew bar one. Apparently much of the ivory was salvaged but the leather bags containing the gold dust were soon washed away (Langham 1994).

Unfortunately, references to wreckings were usually given in fairly vague terms (ie. 'inside Lundy'), and this makes attempts to identify a newly located shipwreck from bibliographic sources difficult. Those which have been surveyed by marine archaeologists to date are indicated in Fig. 1.

Of the 200 or more recorded losses, divers have located at least 13 (English Nature 1994) and perhaps as many as 20 wrecks. The discrepancy in figures between the potential resource and the number of located sites (say 10-15%) can be put down to several

ISLAND STUDIES

factors. Many of the ships which were wrecked, particularly those lost on the island's exposed north, south, and west shores probably broke up quickly with little coherent structure remaining today. Even on the more sheltered east coast, the MV *Kaaksburg* has now broken up completely since she was wrecked as recently as 1981.

With wreckings a common occurrence, a salvage industry evolved. Tugs were often called in, and unless serious damage had been incurred, sunken or beached boats were often raised to the surface, repaired and pressed back into service. The sad tale of the wooden barge *Rover* recalls one particularly disastrous salvage attempt. Following the loss of the 2188 ton SS *Salado* at the Mousehole and Trap on the east side of the island in March 1897, salvage barges were called in. The *Rover* however, sank in August the following year during a north-easterly force 7 whilst moored to the *Salado* before she had broken up.

Marine archaeological survey work

The task of locating and identifying individual sites under water presents its own problems. Lack of funding and the logistical difficulties of operating on an exposed island, combined with the environmental and physical constraints of cold water, tidal currents and limited available time under water, are all complicating factors. As a starting point, archaeologists have relied heavily on second hand knowledge gained from local diving clubs and individuals who dive frequently

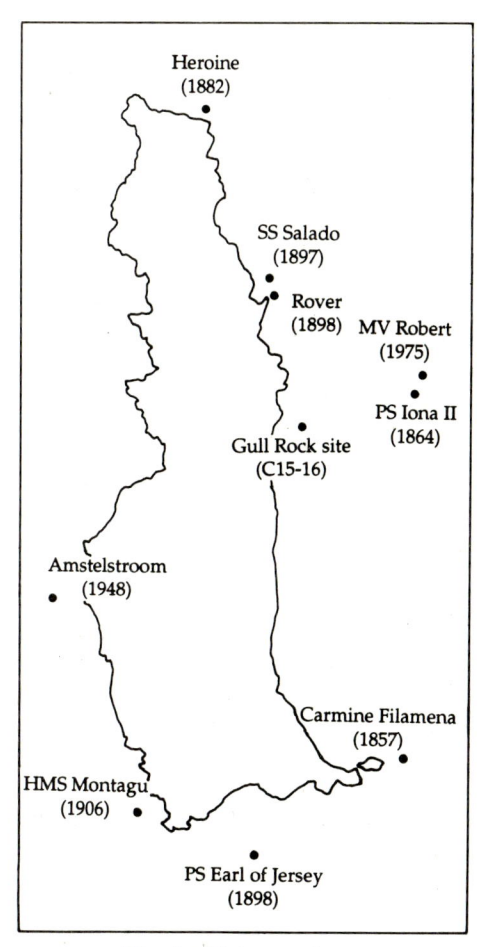

Fig. 1 Shipwrecks

around the island and have been responsible for locating most of the sites known to date. Yet, these individuals are often reluctant to publicise their information for fear of souvenir hunting by other groups on a 'virgin wreck'. However, their secrecy complicates the task of compiling an accurate estimate of the extent and importance of the resource, and of managing it accordingly. Finally, some of the island's wrecks may have come to rest in deep water below 30 metres, and beyond the range of recommended air diving limits. Archaeology must look to attempts in the future to deploy remote sensing equipment to locate these.

While archaeologists have long been conducting fieldwork on the island itself, survey work under water has only been undertaken fairly recently very much in the wake of pioneering biological studies on the island's marine life, but enough work has been done to gain a good overall impression of the significance of the island's underwater heritage. The earliest discovery of importance was made by John Shaw, one of Lundy's diving pioneers. Diving in the vicinity of Gull Rock in 1968, he located some stone cannon balls and iron cannon. Unfortunately the remains were well camouflaged and the site was not found again until 1983. Since then a series of surveys have shed light on what may be Lundy's most important underwater site.

John Shaw himself carried out a pre-disturbance survey in 1983 and 1984 and raised four 6" stone cannon balls for identification. Following a visit in 1989 by the Archaeological Diving Unit based at St. Andrews University in Scotland, it was decided that the remains were of national importance and the Gull Rock Site was therefore designated under the Protection of Wrecks Act, 1973. This conclusion was based on the probable 15th-16th century date of the armament found on the site combined with the existence nearby of soft, mobile, sand sediments providing favourable burial conditions for any organic remains which would have become buried during the wrecking process if indeed a wreck occurred. The limited coverage of visible remains, and the absence of any visible ship structure suggest that the guns and cannon balls might alternatively have been jettisoned from a ship without necessarily any wreck occurring.

A second pre-disturbance survey was carried out under licence by John Heath and members of the Appledore Sub-Aqua Club in 1993 to record the site and its environment more accurately and to compile a photographic record of artefacts. The team established a detailed site plan of the visible features of the site, namely eight 5" limestone cannon balls, two wrought iron cannons, and one breech gun (Fig. 2) along with some material of a more recent date which possibly originates from other wrecks nearby.

Lundy's other officially protected wreck is the Clyde-built paddle steamer PS *Iona II*. Built in 1863 at Govan as a fast ferry for use around the Clyde coast, with an overall length of 245 feet, a beam of 25 feet, draught of 9 feet, paddle wheels 20 feet in diameter, and a twin cylinder oscillating engine of revolutionary design, this ship was capable of a top speed of 24 knots. Shortly after her construction, the ship was bought by Charles Hopkins Boster of Richmond, Virginia allegedly to break the Federal blockade of Confederate supply routes during the American Civil War. Although initially well decked out, the PS *Iona II* was stripped for her first trans-Atlantic voyage in 1864 and was loaded with enough coal for the long voyage from Glasgow to Nassau, a voyage for which the ship was not well suited. Her narrow clipper-like hull design with shallow draught and flat bottom would have made her very unstable in the steep seas of the north Atlantic. In the event, under the command of a Captain Chapman, the PS *Iona II* sank off Lundy but her 39 man crew were saved, and taken to Ilfracombe (Farr 1967). Eye witness accounts of the day told of salvage operations in progress using a diving bell. Nevertheless, the wreck of the PS *Iona II* was still fairly intact when she was relocated during a search for the nearby wreck of the MV *Robert* in 1976. Divers salvaged material from the wreck, some of which has been deposited in Greenock Museum.

Iona II was designated in 1989 under the Protection of Wrecks Act 1973 because of the revolutionary design and function of the vessel and the intact condition of her engineering. The gradual deterioration of her hull and paddle wheel assemblies, caused mostly by corrosion of her iron fittings in seawater but exacerbated possibly by the trawling of fishing gear over her hull, prompted the need for a baseline survey to be undertaken. The first work was undertaken in 1990 by Potters Bar Sub-Aqua Club under the guidance of Nick and Carol Rule (Rule 1991). With the aid of secondary video footage, stills photography, and the original ship plans, Carol Rule compiled a detailed isometric sketch of the ship as she lies on the sea-bed (Fig. 3). As the diagram shows, the PS *Iona II* remains fairly intact, consisting of hull ribs and plating at the bow and stern of the ship protruding from a sandy gravel sea-bed, with remains of the coal cargo, intact boilers, twin cylinder oscillating engine and paddle wheel drive shaft clearly visible.

No survey measurements were taken to compile the isometric sketch so in 1995, and 1996, Philip Robertson led two field school expeditions of members of the Nautical Archaeology Society with the aim of compiling baseline measurement data, using tape-measures, and photographic recording. The resulting data is currently being used to enhance the isometric sketch so that it can be re-drawn to scale and this final record will be useful as a baseline with which to assess deterioration of the wreck as seen during future visits to the site, as well as for interpretation as part of the activities of the Marine Nature Reserve.

Under the Protection of Wrecks Act 1973, diving on the Gull Rock Site and PS *Iona II* is limited to holders of a survey licence issued upon application to the Department of National Heritage. Although those diving on a designated site without a licence are committing a criminal offence and can be prosecuted,

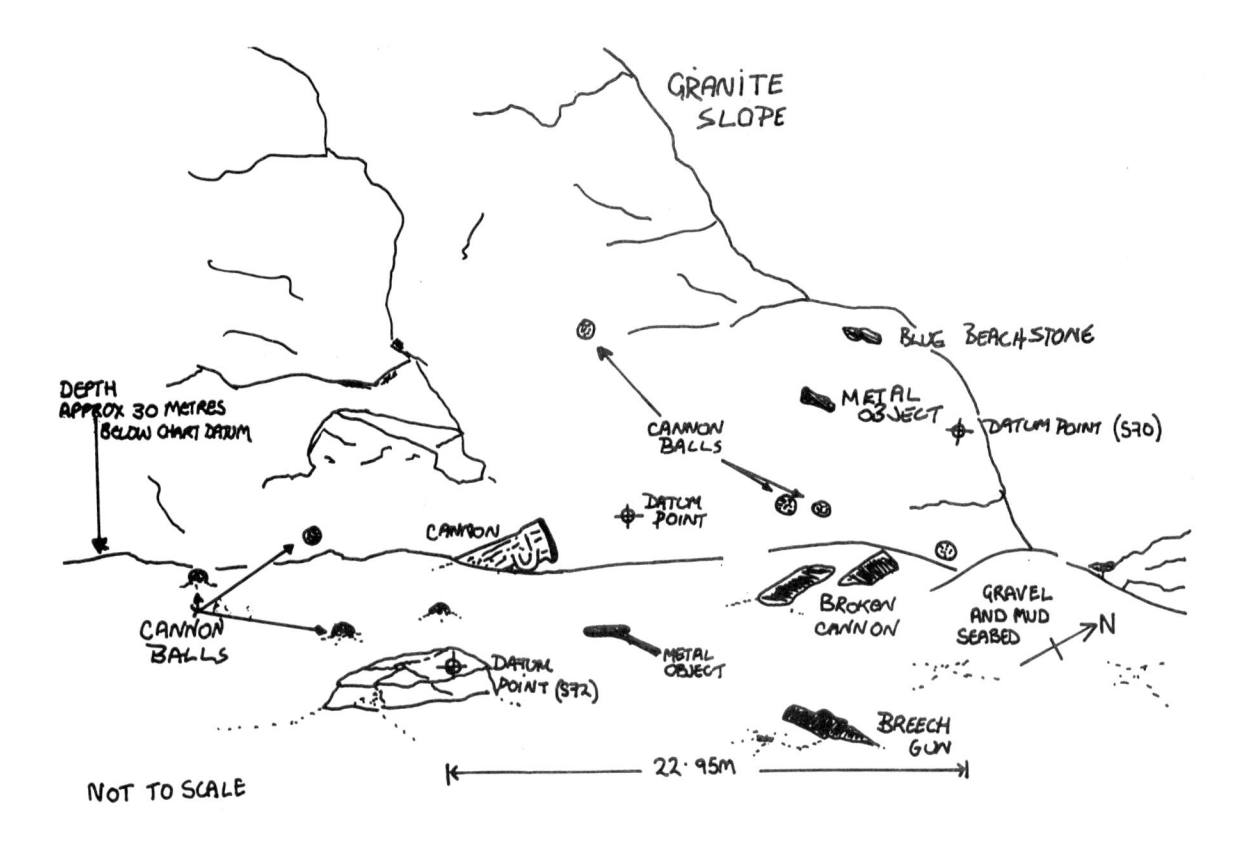

Fig. 2 Sketch of the Gull Rock Site showing layout of datum points, artefactual remains and environmental information (John Heath)

unlicensed local charter boats and diving clubs frequently dive PS *Iona II*. On the other hand, they are apparently causing little damage to the wreck and most respect the importance of leaving the site untouched. This situation is clearly unsatisfactory. With the introduction of a trial 'open day' on the wreck in 1996 enabling controlled access to visiting divers, it appears that the stance of the regulatory body for the Protection of Wrecks Act 1973 – the Advisory Committee on Historic Wrecks, may be warming to the idea of visitor schemes. It must be hoped that Lundy may move to a position whereby the Warden will be allowed to facilitate legal access to the wreck to visitors on the grounds that they are provided with educational material about the wreck and about the importance of conserving Lundy's shipwrecks for the future.

While the two wrecks discussed above are Lundy's most important wrecks and have received most attention from archaeologists, an overall assessment of the importance of the island's other wrecks was undertaken in 1994. Using tick-in-the-box recording forms being jointly promoted by the Nautical Archaeology Society (NAS) and the Royal Commission on the Historical Monuments for England (RCHME), a team of divers led by Philip Robertson completed basic assessments of most of the known wrecks. All the sites surveyed were of post-medieval or of modern date, and most are of iron construction. Their condition varies from intact (MV *Robert*) to semi intact (PS *Earl of Jersey*), broken up (SS *Carmine Filomena*, HMS *Montagu*) and scattered (SS *Salado*, *Amstelstroom*, *Heroine*). The famous Duncan class battleship HMS *Montagu*, wrecked at Shutter Point in 1906, would have been of significant importance but commercial salvage and the quick disintegration of her hull have diminished this. None of the others are of national archaeological importance but they are of local interest because studying them helps build up a picture of trade and maritime activity in the Bristol Channel. For instance, several of the ships wrecked around Lundy were engaged in the coastal and international trade in coal from the ports of SW Wales which was so important to the economy of the Bristol Channel area. One such example was SS *Carmine Filomena*, a steam driven Italian cargo vessel of 5,287 ton displacement carrying a cargo of coal to Genoa from Cardiff. The steam-powered SS *Salado* lost in fog in 1897, and the single screw coaster MV *Robert* capsized off Lundy in 1975, were also involved in the coal trade.

On the MV *Robert*, the intact hull, deck railings, windlass wheels and air vents have all become adorned with marine life, providing an artificial haven for plumose anemones *Metridium senile*, conger eels *Conger conger*, lobsters *Homarus gammarus*, and shoals of bib *Trisopterus luscus* and frequent wrasse (Labridae). Many of Lundy's other wrecks are also of great value to nature conservation (see also Hiscock, this volume). Of particular note, biological surveys have identified communities of the phoronid worm *Phoronis hippocrepia* on the limestone cannonballs of

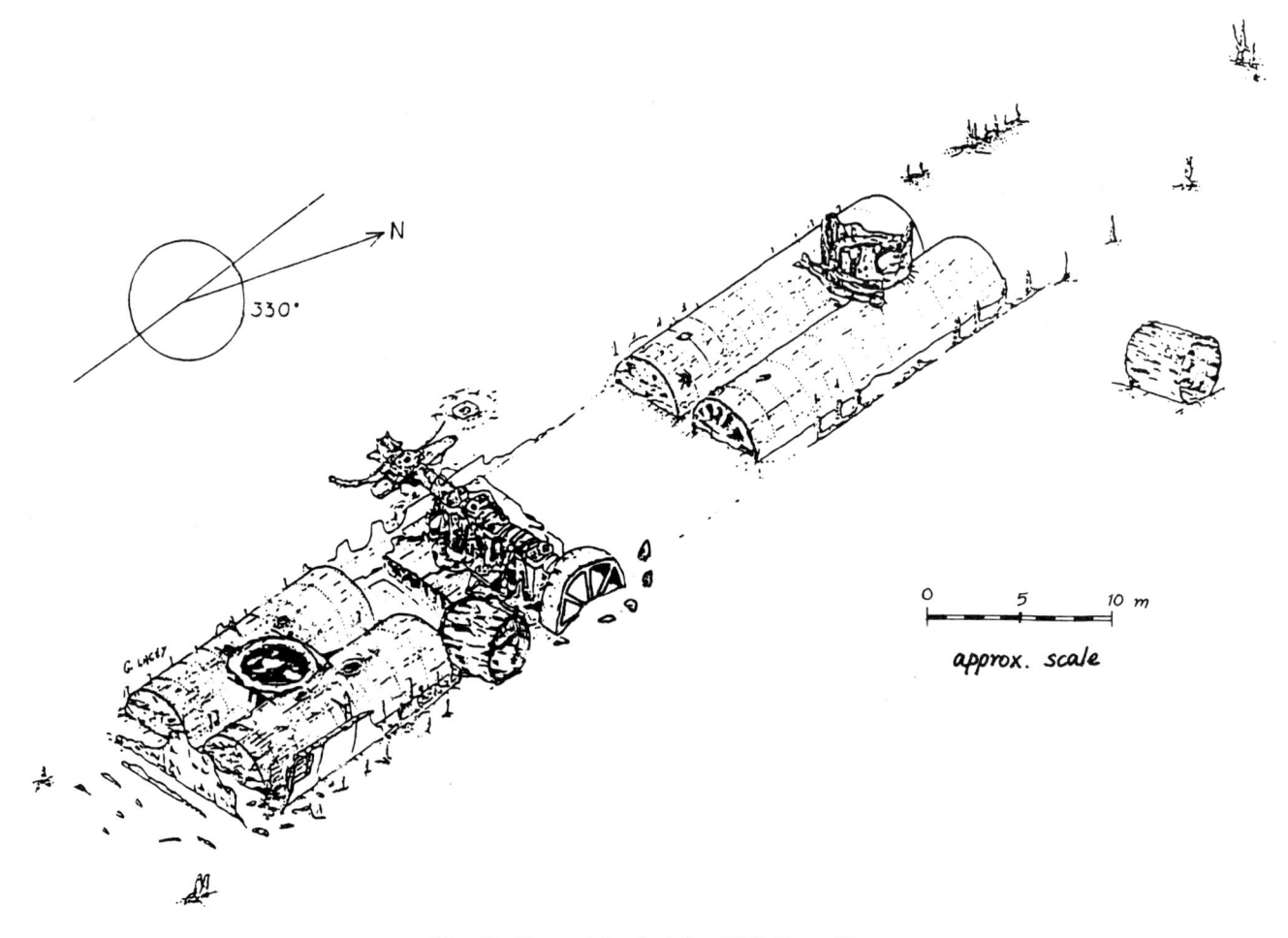

Fig. 3　Isometric sketch of PS Iona II

the Protected Wreck at Gull Rock, consistent with limestone bedrock in other parts of the country, but not occurring elsewhere under water around Lundy (Irving *et al.* 1995). It seems that by the artificial introduction of a limestone source into the area, a unique localised habitat has been created.

In conclusion

Alongside Lundy's renowned clear waters and rich marine habitats, it is the scenic qualities of the wreck of MV *Robert*, and the history surrounding the sinkings of the PS *Iona II*, and HMS *Montagu*, that attracts so many sport divers to Lundy. The island's wrecks also provide a rich artificial habitat for marine life increasing the diversity of the vital marine ecosystem of England's only Marine Nature Reserve. Marine archaeologists have a role to play in recording sites and in promoting the importance of conserving Lundy's shipwrecks in the face of intentional human interference: the stripping of historic wrecks for commercial gain, and the casual souvenir hunting that threaten the future of many of the UK's most interesting wrecks. The problem is that archaeological sites are non-renewable; once a wreck has gone, it has gone forever.

As diving around Lundy becomes more popular with the growth of the sport in the rest of the UK, more wrecks will be located and the true archaeological potential of the waters of Lundy will become clearer. Several useful steps can be taken to further knowledge in the short term. A programme of remote sensing research off the island's east coast using techniques such as side-scan sonar and magnetometry combined with visual confirmation by remote operated vehicles (R.O.V.) would help to identify shipwrecks which have yet to be found by divers. Diving fieldwork should concentrate on monitoring the Gull Rock Site and PS *Iona II* protected sites to assess change to each. In the case of the PS *Iona II*, it would be possible to undertake corrosion potential studies on selected parts of the wreck to identify whether anything can be done *in situ* to conserve the ship. There would be no advantage in lifting or excavating any of the wrecks within Lundy's waters but research from Australia and elsewhere in the UK suggests that large iron wrecks like PS *Iona II* can be partially conserved on the sea-bed, for instance using sacrificial anode protection. The best museum for Lundy's underwater heritage is the sea-bed itself, where divers may continue to visit these memorials to the island's maritime history, and marine life can continue to thrive in an environment that is all the more diverse for the presence of these enriching artificial habitats. Let us promote the waters off Lundy as a flagship for the sustainable management of our underwater heritage, to be a shining example for the rest of the UK and Europe.

Acknowledgement

The authors would like to thank Steve Waring, of the Royal Commission on the Historical Monuments of England, for his contribution towards this paper.

References

Bouquet, M 1967, Lundy Shipwrecks. *Annual Report of the Lundy Field Society* 18, 19-23.
Bouquet, M 1969, More Lundy Shipwrecks. *Annual Report of the Lundy Field Society* 20, 22.
Davis, R 1962, *The Rise of the English Shipping Industry in the Seventeenth and Eighteenth Centuries.* Newton Abbott.
English Nature 1994, Managing Lundy's Wildlife: a management plan for the Marine Nature Reserve and Site of Special Scientific Interest. Okehampton: English Nature.
Farr, G 1967, *West Country Paddle Steamers.* London.
Gibson, C 1993, Lundy Shipwrecks Map. Lundy.
Heath, J 1991, 'Diving around Lundy'. *Lundy Field Society Newsletter* 21, 4-5.
Irving, R A, Holt, R & Moss, D 1995, Selected reports from the Marine Conservation Society's diving working party to Lundy, 3-10 June 1995. *Annual Report of the Lundy Field Society* 46, 54-65
Langham, A F 1994, *The Island of Lundy.* Stroud: Alan Sutton.
Larn, R and B 1995, *Shipwreck Index of the British Isles.* Lloyd's Register of Shipping.
Rule, N 1991, 'Potters Bar Sub-Aqua Club 1990 Survey of IONA II' *Nautical Archaeology Society* Newsletter 1, 8-9.

Further Reading

Duffy, M 1992, *The New Maritime History of Devon 1.* Conway Maritime Press, London.
Duffy, M 1994, *The New Maritime History of Devon 2.* Conway Maritime Press, London.
Robertson, P. 1994. Marine archaeology and Lundy Marine Nature Reserve – an assessment. *Annual Report of the Lundy Field Society* 45, 57-76.
Throckmorton, P. (ed.). 1987. *History from the Sea.* London.

The Buildings of Lundy

Julia Abel Smith

A stay in a Landmark is meant to offer not just a holiday but an experience, of a mildly elevating kind, a fresh window on life, to be looked through, or not, as you please.

Introduction

For a small and remote island, Lundy has a fine and unusual collection of buildings. In 1969 when the Landmark Trust took over the management of the island, it was clear that for the foreseeable future the island should depend mainly on holiday revenue for its survival. Its buildings, which for Landmark had been one of the island's selling points, were immediately recognised as a valuable resource: places where holiday-makers might enjoy a holiday in a beautiful and unspoilt place.

The Landmark Trust is a charity which was set up in 1965 to rescue buildings in distress and bring them back to useful life. Each restoration is undertaken with great care and much thought is given to the way the building was used in the past. For those who stay in our buildings, there is an album of historical notes, plans and photographs, showing how the place was when we found it and what we have done to it. Thus, research on each of our buildings is an integral part of our work. We believe that by knowing about the building in which you are staying you can gain more from your holiday. In the words of our Handbook:

In 1989 when we came to write the Lundy history albums, it became clear that there had been very little research done on the buildings themselves. There was a great deal to be found on bird or marine life and archaeology but nothing specific on the built environment. The only properly researched building was the Castle. In 1928 Martin Harman had commissioned Charles Winmill of the Society for the Protection of Ancient Buildings to do a report on its condition, but due to the high cost of the proposed works, the report was ignored.

Three of the buildings; the Castle, Old House and the Old Light were listed Grade II and had cursory entries in the Statutory List. Beyond this, research on the buildings meant talking to people who used to live on the island, those who had built up collections of memorabilia, and of course our builders.

We came to rely on the publications of Tony Langham and Myrtle Ternstrom about the island generally, and Tony Langham's extensive collection of photographs of Lundy past and present, generously placed at our disposal, was invaluable. We also had Felix Gade's *My Life on Lundy* covering the years when he was agent, from 1926 until his retirement in 1971.

This was a useful source of information on what day to day life was like in those sometimes difficult years. *The Illustrated Lundy News* which ran from 1970-1975 was also helpful.

The scale of our project on Lundy was different from those on the mainland. Here we were faced with the problems of restoring more than twenty buildings of differing styles, materials and age. One factor however, unites them all: the weather. Lundy has very little natural shelter and at times is cruelly exposed to the wind and the wet. For a building to last on the island, it must be built in a more robust manner than those on the mainland and builders and restorers must be ever-mindful of Lundy's special conditions in their selection of materials and techniques. The original builders had mainly used Lundy granite: it was on site and it was durable. Like those before them, the Landmark workforce had to import every other material such as timber and slate – an operation which immediately raised costs.

With the notable exceptions of the Castle and the Old House (just), most island buildings date from the nineteenth century when Lundy enjoyed the fruits of Victorian public and private spending. The buildings fall loosely into groups, those built at the instigation of the Heaven family and their tenants, those erected by Trinity House, and those of the Lundy Granite Company. In this century, the Harmans began to use some of the buildings to let for holidays. In its turn, the Landmark Trust has overseen the restoration and repair of every building (except Signal Cottages) and the new building of Government House and Square Cottage.

The Buildings

The Castle
The oldest building on Lundy is the Castle built in 1244 by Henry III to prevent Lundy's use as a base by rebels and fugitives. On a commanding site overlooking the harbour, it seems to have been Lundy's principal building until the end of the 18th century when the island entered a period of calm and the focus of affairs moved to the present village centre. With its cottage on the north side, the Castle now provides four holiday cottages. The history of the castle has been recently published (Ternstrom 1994) and will not be repeated here.

The Old House
The Landmark Trust has restored the Old House to something like its original appearance. It is very likely that this is the house referred to in 1787 in a description printed in the North Devon Magazine of 1824, as "lately built by Sir John Borlase Warren" the MP for Marlow and future Admiral, who owned Lundy from 1775 – 1781. Mary Ann Heaven's drawing of it dated August 1838 shows a single storey central section

flanked by two storey twin towers. It was here that the late Georgian owners and their agents or stewards lived.

When Mr Heaven bought Lundy he removed the tower roofs, built up the single storey and covered the whole with a shallow pitched roof. As the Heaven family lived at their new house in Millcombe, Sir John's house became the Farm House. Further details and plans of the development of the house are given by Langham (1994).

The Old Light
The Corporation of Trinity House is the General Lighthouse Authority for England, Wales and the Channel Islands. In the 19th century, it played an important part in the life of the island for it was responsible for the Old Light complex, the Battery, the cottage at Stoneycroft, and at the end of the century, the North and South Lights.

Lundy has always been a danger to shipping in the Bristol Channel. At the end of the 18th century, a group of Bristol merchants, mindful of possible business losses, decided to build a lighthouse on the island's highest point at Beacon Hill. This choice of site, 470 feet above sea level, was in fact an unsuitable one. Although foundations were laid, nothing happened until Trinity House acquired the site on a 999 year lease and asked Daniel Asher Alexander, their Surveyor, to design his exceptionally fine lighthouse of 1819.

It was built of Lundy granite – an entirely suitable material for the monumental style he chose. During its restoration, Landmark's builders discovered that the Old Light tower (96 feet high) has a cavity wall, and unusually, both skins are of granite. The cavity wall was a brick technique whereby the regular thickness of the two walls made it possible to separate the outer and inner skin with a uniform cavity. Such a technique was obviously easier when bricks, fashioned from identical moulds, were used. Alexander used this method for masonry on his Heligoland lighthouse tower in 1811 but Lundy was exceptional in having two granite skins. The challenge for his masons was to cut perfectly even blocks and in this they succeeded because the cavity is consistent, measuring 3" all the way up.

The lighthouse – the highest light in Britain – was first brought into use on 21st February, 1820. It had cost £36,000, a very considerable outlay on the part of Trinity House. The upper beam revolved by clockwork every 16 minutes and there was a flash every two minutes. The light could be seen from a point 18 foot above sea level from some 32 miles. There were commodious quarters for two keepers and their families at the side of the tower and later a house for the Principal Keeper was built in the south-east corner of the walled compound. This was demolished when the South Light was being built in 1897.

After the 1939-45 War when the Old Light was requisitioned by the Admiralty and housed a naval detachment, Mr Harman gave it rent-free to the Lundy Field Society. The Society used it for many years as their headquarters with a hostel in the care of a resident warden.

Also within the compound is the little building known as Old Light East which originally housed the compulsory pigs, advocated by Trinity House, and the latrines. After the closure of the lighthouse, it became a store and later a ringing room for the Lundy Field Society before it was turned into an extra bedroom.

The Battery

The choice of Beacon Hill by the Bristol merchants and later by Trinity House, for the lighthouse site was an unhappy one. It was always too high to be seen by ships in fog. The light was therefore supplemented by a fog battery halfway down the west side, a site chosen in 1863 and equipped with two 18 pounder guns. When it was foggy, one gun was fired every ten minutes. Two families lived in the tiny, and now roofless, cottages uphill from the little powder house. By 1897 it was clear that both the Battery and Lighthouse were not reliable safeguards and Lundy North and South Lights were built.

Stoneycroft

The pleasant little one storey cottage to the east of the Old Light is Stoneycroft. It appears in a drawing of Mary Ann Heaven of 1838 and may have been built about that time for Mr Grant, the Collector of Customs at Barnstaple, who was also a Trinity House Agent. In 1988 Landmark converted it into a holiday cottage for four people.

Millcombe House

In 1836 William Heaven – a gentleman from Somerset educated at Harrow and Oxford – bought Lundy for £9,870. At first it was a place to spend summer holidays but after Mrs Heaven died in 1851, Mr Heaven became the first owner to live there permanently. It was at this time that the island became much more civilised in a most Victorian way.

Mr Heaven's first job was to build himself a house suitable for him and his young and growing family. Arriving at Lundy, the view of Millcombe is obscured until right at the last minute. Then as the boat moves towards its anchorage, the valley where Millcombe has been sheltering, reveals this unexpectedly attractive classical house of cream stucco. It is an antidote to the ruggedness which surrounds it and as, Nikolaus Pevsner says in the *Buildings of England* series, the only place where Lundy can be seen in so gentle a mood.

Building Millcombe was not easy. The majority of the materials, apart from granite, and all the Heavens' furniture and effects had to be hauled up the beach path on carts by donkeys and oxen. Soon after this Mr Heaven set about building the present beach road which Trinity House would not help with and told him was impossible.

Mr Heaven's resident agent, William Malbon, supervised the works which clearly did not run smoothly, as before completion and account settling a survey and report was carried out detailing the shortcomings: shoddy joinery, plumbing and decoration as well as a poorly designed roof. Whatever the truth of such a damning document, Millcombe is a very pleasing and sociable house to stay in. It is compactly designed on the ground floor round a central hall and upstairs round a top-lit central staircase with well-proportioned rooms making the best of the views towards the Landing Bay.

The Rev. Hudson Heaven, son of William Heaven, died on the mainland in 1916 and, two years later, the island was sold to Mr Christie and then in 1925 to Martin Coles Harman. The Heavens had called their house The Villa but by then it was known as The House. The Harmans renamed it Millcombe after the mill at the bottom of the valley or combe which had stood near the little pond to the right of the gates.

In 1961 it had been necessary to replace the roof with a cheaper flat roof after dry rot eradication. When Landmark began its refurbishment, we replaced the copper-lined inward sloping roof. We also removed the front and back porches which had been added at a later date as well as making a north window in the kitchen, facing the site of a demolished latrine. The walls around the terrace were erected in 1989 to give those staying at Millcombe some privacy.

The Old School (Blue Bungalow)

Rev. Heaven, known by the family as "Phi" short for philosopher due to his bookishness, was headmaster at Taunton College until 1863 when he moved to Lundy. In 1886 he erected the School Bungalow primarily as a Sunday school. It is built of timber and corrugated iron and was originally one room inside. Internal partitions were added in 1918 when it became a dwelling and has been used to house staff, or let for holidays as it is now, ever since.

Bramble Villa

The original bungalow here was built by Rev. Heaven in 1893, partly as an overflow for Millcombe and partly to house Mr and Mrs Ward, the coachman/gardener and cook. It was built in a colonial style with an east-facing verandah. Rev Heaven used the sitting room as his study, no doubt something of a refuge for writing sermons.

By 1970 this building was derelict and Landmark decided to replace it with a similar building which was designed by our architect, Philip Jebb, and made by a firm called Timbaform in sections to be erected on the island.

The Church

William Heaven suffered a stroke in 1875 and his son, the Rev. Hudson Grosett Heaven, took over the running of the island. At first when congregations were small, Sunday services had been held in the hall or dining room at The Villa but something larger was soon required. In 1885 Mr Heaven built a modest church immediately to the north of the present Government House where its site may be still seen (photo in Langham 1994, 124). It was described by the Bishop of Exeter as a "corrugated irony". Undaunted, Rev. Heaven then achieved his long-held ambition and erected a much grander church consecrated by the Bishop in 1897.

The Lundy Granite Quarry Company's buildings
Often short of funds themselves, the Heavens sought other investors to bring prosperity to Lundy. The Lundy Granite Company was inaugurated in 1863 working the quarries on the east side. It flourished for five years but then closed down amid rumours of inefficiency and malpractice. The cottages built for the managers and the hospital are now picturesque ruins at the top of the cliffs but the Company also developed what is now the kernel of the island, the village itself.

When it was set up, the Lundy Granite Company took over a lease of most of the island including the Farm. To the north of the Farmhouse (Old House) they built a Store which is now the outer bar of the Marisco Tavern with a store-keeper's cottage, now the main Tavern. At the other end was a bakehouse with the baker's quarters above – in the present office.

Behind the south end of the Farmhouse they built a wing, later known as the Big House, which was still unfinished when the Company went out of business. It seems to have been used occasionally by the Heavens for Sunday services. In 1885 the farm was let to Mr Wright, gentleman farmer, who furnished the Big House for himself and laid out the tennis court in front of the Farm House which then became more of a farm cottage. In 1890 Mr Wright built the Linhay, premises of the present shop. (The Barn may well have been built in 1839 as it does not appear in the right place in Mary Ann Heaven's drawing of the village in 1838 and Mr Heaven's agent, Mr Malbon, mentions a new barn in 1839.)

After 1899 Mr Taylor – a tenant of the Heavens – made the Big House into a hotel and only in 1926 did Mr Harman run the Farm House and the hotel behind into one, making the Manor Farm Hotel. When the Landmark Trust took over Lundy, it realised that it would be impossibly expensive to restore the Hotel as it was, and for some years Millcombe was the island hotel.

The Admiralty Lookout (Tibbetts)
Lundy's most famous wreck, that of HMS *Montagu*, happened close to Shutter Rock in 1906. Three years later the Admiralty built this isolated signal and watch station which was in use until 1926 and originally had a lookout room on its roof which was removed in 1971 being beyond repair.

Recent years

The Harmans realised that Lundy made an excellent place for holidays. Admiralty Lookout, known for many years as Tibbetts, was the first building they made available for holidays and in 1960 Albion Harman and his two sisters opened Castle Cottage. In 1964 a battlemented and flat-roofed farm shed set against the wall dividing St. John's Valley and 'The Common' was made into the much-loved holiday cottages known as St. John's.

The aim of the Landmark Trust on Lundy has been to retain its special atmosphere. This has meant restoring and improving what was already there but, in addition, the Trust has erected three new buildings.

The Quarters

One of the main problems at the outset was accommodation for the work force. This was overcome by putting up in 1972 the prefabricated Quarters. They now serve a useful life housing staff and larger visiting parties.

Square Cottage

As it was too expensive to repair, the "Big House" wing of The Manor Farm Hotel was demolished and Square Cottage built in its place. Its pyramidal roof is deliberately reminiscent of those on the Borlase-Warren house.

Government House

Philip Jebb designed Government House which was built in 1981 mainly of dressed granite reused from the demolition of the Manor Farm Hotel. It was originally proposed that the island's agent should live there but now it provides one of the most comfortable places for visitors to stay on Lundy.

Conclusion

Lundy is not known for its buildings. It is famous for its bird and marine life, flora and fauna, and for the fact that it is an island. However, the buildings on Lundy are a bonus and in such a small place, the variety is remarkable. There is the castle with its origins in the middle ages, there is the highest lighthouse in Britain, a church of truly Victorian proportion and a classical small country house. On Lundy, every building is accessible and in the great majority, you can spend a very special holiday.

References

Langham, A F, 1994. *The Island of Lundy*. Stroud: Alan Sutton
Langham, M, 1995. *A Lundy Album*, privately published.
Ternstrom, M, 1994. *The Castle on the Island of Lundy*, privately published.

The Birds of Lundy

Tony Taylor

Introduction

51°10' N, 4°40' W:– Lundy's position is the key to its significance for birds. Three snapshots will give a glimpse of its ornithological value.

On a fine morning early in May, with a breath of wind from the south, a walk over the southern part of the island reveals several new arrivals: a bright male redstart and a couple of whitethroats, perhaps, and twenty willow warblers. The willow warblers are not just in their expected woodland habitat in Millcombe, where several are singing, but also on stone walls and flitting among tussocks of sedge out in the fields. Then, near the battlements at the head of St John's Valley, one flies across from the south and into the gorse. A minute later it has moved on but a second arrives, to be replaced in turn by a third. Then closer observation of the birds out on the field walls shows them working their way gradually north. It becomes clearer as the morning progresses that any repeat of the walk would still produce twenty willow warblers but a different twenty every time. Ringing shows the same story: fifty willow warblers have been caught in the day with never more than five at one time in the netting area.

Late June, again sunny, but with a westerly breeze. Seen from the long slope next to the Devil's Chimney, Jenny's Cove is alive with birds. Serpentine lines of guillemots and razorbills litter the sea surface. Other busier, noisier guillemots jostle on their cliff ledges, with continual confrontations between experienced breeders guarding chicks and immature birds prospecting in preparation for next year. More circle over the water, sometimes rising to inspect an area of cliff more closely or to land there. A loud call from a breeding guillemot heralds its mate's arrival a few seconds later with a fish for their chick (how on earth can the pair recognise each other individually, in flight at fifty metres, among so many?). Much smaller numbers of puffins and shags, together with herring, lesser black-backed and great black-backed gulls, fulmars and the screeching kittiwakes in Deep Zawn, complete the picture.

Now to a more precise snapshot: 27th October 1989. Again there is a breeze but this time it is cold and there are just occasional bouts of hazy sunshine as a strong westerly brings clouds streaming across the island. Migration is more immediately apparent than in May, with a succession of tightly-bunched flocks of starlings flying purposefully south along the island. Suddenly, a bird is seen leaving the clump of willows near Quarry Pond and flying into the rhododendrons below. Tantalising glimpses between the leaves reveal one of the small North American cuckoo species, but not enough to tell which. After a few minutes of excited but frustrating eye-strain, its watchers finally see it clearly as it emerges to feed among the dead bracken – a yellow-billed cuckoo obligingly showing all its diagnostic characteristics. Others are called to admire it, hurrying from the North Quarry where they have been watching Lundy's first olive-backed pipit, discovered three days earlier. Two rarities are within a couple of hundred metres of each other, one looking understandably tired after having survived a transatlantic crossing, the other remarkably active and healthy considering that it had just strayed four thousand kilometres west from the species' nearest breeding area in Russia.

Lundy receives large numbers of migrants because birds working their way north or south across the Bristol Channel will prefer to make the flight in two stages rather than one. They will leave the mainland coasts from several points in South Wales or North Devon and Cornwall, scattered along a broad front, but then be focused in on the island to produce high concentrations there. The same strategic positioning leads to Lundy's high quotas of rare, vagrant species from Europe and Asia.

The great majority of migrants swept from the eastern seaboard of North America in autumn gales undoubtedly die at sea. The next land that the few survivors see and struggle towards may be the Scilly Isles or southwest Ireland but there is plenty of sea-space in between and for birds in this corridor, Lundy will frequently be the first visible target.

For seabirds, Lundy provides a breeding site completely surrounded by rich feeding areas and safe from many potential predators.

The Society's ornithological work

The main objectives in the Lundy Field Society's work on birds have been to monitor the population sizes of the island's breeding species, particularly with a view to detecting any significant changes resulting from pollution, climatic and oceanographic changes, overfishing or other influences; to record the species and numbers of birds migrating via Lundy, the timing of these movements and any significant changes in numbers; to investigate, through ringing, the migration routes, longevity, causes of mortality and other aspects of the biology of Lundy's breeding and migrant birds; and to encourage field studies into all other aspects of Lundy's birds such as their breeding biology, behaviour or ecology.

The society's fifty years of bird work can be divided into two halves. For much of the period up to 1973, Lundy was classed as a national Bird Observatory and had resident ornithological wardens to carry out the objectives listed above, with valuable assistance from visitors and islanders such as the Gade family. Since then the wardens' tasks have not been primarily ornithological, though some important bird work such as seabird population monitoring has been carried out by them at times. Furthermore, none has had a ringing licence, so all of the ringing and much of the other bird work has been done by visitors and by other islanders, from Mick Rogers in the 1970s to Andrew Jewels in the 1990s, in their spare time.

Other changes have been evident. The ornithological wardens ringed large numbers of breeding seabirds and relatively few migrants, dependent as they were on Heligoland traps for the latter. From the 1970s, mist-nets have revolutionised the catching of passerines and so migrants have become the main target species. As illustrations of this change, the number of guillemots ringed up to 1973 was 2700, while only one has been ringed since then; equivalent numbers for willow warblers are 2859 and 6474. Early studies tended to concentrate on establishing the basic facts and figures of Lundy's birds: species, numbers, detailed descriptions of rarities (now adequately covered in modern bird identification guides, though still vital for the validation of records), and specific studies such as the ectoparasites on birds and the growth rate of shag chicks. Monitoring work remains vital, but detailed studies in the last twenty-five years have focused more on behaviour, including display flights of lapwing, the calls and mate selection strategy of kittiwakes and territoriality in skylarks.

Two of Lundy's bird wardens wrote important books on the status of the island's birds. "A List of the Birds of Lundy" by Peter Davis was published by the Society in 1954. By the time Nick Dymond wrote "The Birds of Lundy", published in 1980, he had a wealth of numerical data accumulated by him and his predecessors, so he was able to draw up detailed graphs and histograms showing how populations of breeding birds had fluctuated year by year and how the numbers of each regular migrant species varied through the seasons.

Breeding birds

The fortunes of Lundy's seabirds have been mixed. Fulmars have been the success story (Fig. 1), as elsewhere in the British Isles. They appear to have achieved this by exploiting the left-overs from human fishing activities. The only complete loss over the same period has been cormorants, with about ten or twelve pairs breeding in 1946 but none since 1959. Shags' numbers have fluctuated considerably but from consistently over a hundred pairs in the late 1950s they were reduced to twenty-two in 1992. The tendency, at least in the 1970s, for pairs in the Shutter Rock area to use sticks of cordite from the wreck of HMS *Montagu* in their nests is not, however, thought to have caused any fatalities.

Among the gulls, lesser black-backed appear to have increased significantly in recent years while herring and great black-backed have decreased. The fourth species, kittiwake, has perhaps shown the most worrying decline, from 2000 pairs in 1951 to 400 in 1992 (Fig. 2).

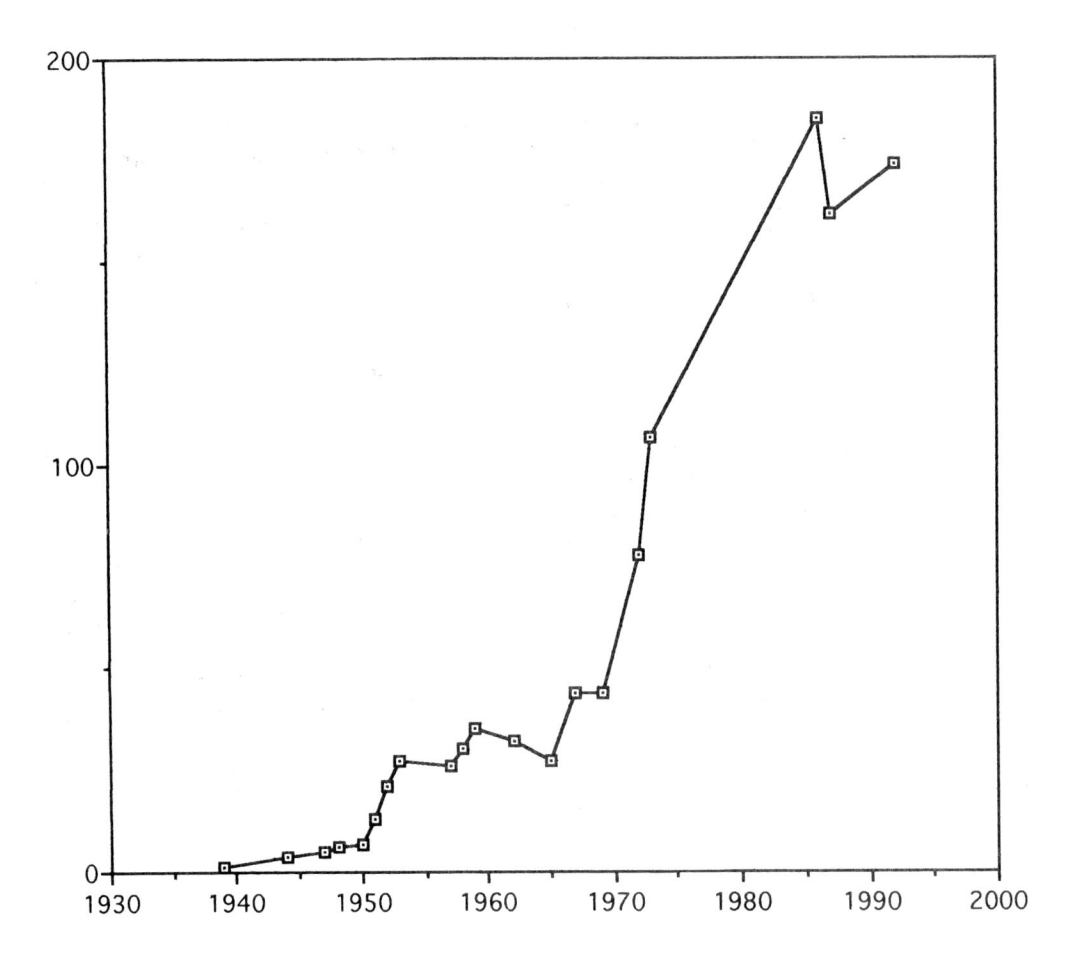

Fig. 1 Fulmar numbers (number of occupied sites)

The auks are difficult to census accurately but the evidence, from complete counts for the island and from the more detailed monitoring of selected sites, points to declines in all three breeding species until the mid-1970s. Since then guillemots have recovered significantly, razorbills continued to decline for another ten years but then stabilised, while puffins (Plate 8) have declined to a point where there has been no firm evidence of breeding for a number of years, though birds still visit the island: thirty-seven seen during the 1992 census work, for instance. As the species most closely associated with Lundy in people's minds, the downward trend in puffins is particularly sad.

Ringing on Lundy has contributed to an understanding of some of these changes, mainly by adding to the mass of data accumulated from ringing in Britain as a whole. Some of Lundy's seabirds have been found dead in fishing nets and others oiled. These factors are undoubtedly relevant to the declines, though others such as lack of food will not be so evident from ringing recoveries. Differences between species could be related to their wintering ranges, some going to higher-risk areas than others. As examples, shags from Lundy have been found frequently in southwest England and northwest France but rarely in the Irish Sea, while razorbills and particularly guillemots reach North Wales much more regularly. These two species also range further south than shags, with razorbill recoveries from as far as the western Mediterranean and guillemots in Portugal.

The colour-ringing of lesser black-backed gull chicks in 1995 brought quick results, with several sightings in the winter in Portugal.

In the 1970s, concern at the decline of auks on Lundy led to attempts to reduce predation by gulls, cutting down their reproductive rate by pricking eggs. However, detailed studies of a breeding group of guillemots in Jenny's Cove over four seasons showed that the problem was not that straightforward. In one year, a pair of herring gulls nested close to the guillemots. One of them specialised in taking guillemot eggs and chicks (Plate 9), causing considerable loss, but it also drove away other potential predators such as carrion crows and ravens (ironically the gull chicks died when small, almost certainly because they could not swallow the guillemot chicks brought to them). Another year, herring gulls nesting in the same area did not attempt predation and were highly beneficial in driving off other predators. In the third year, great black-backed gulls had an effect similar to the first herring gulls. In the fourth year, no gulls defended the area and the losses were greatest of all, because of the lack of protection. The same study showed an important indirect influence of humans, via gulls: when gull colonies on the slopes above guillemot breeding ledges were disturbed, the gulls' alarm calls prompted some guillemots to fly off, leaving their eggs or young vulnerable. Even greater losses were caused in a similar way when an osprey flew past on 18th July 1974. All the gulls in the area left their nests and mobbed it, calling loudly.

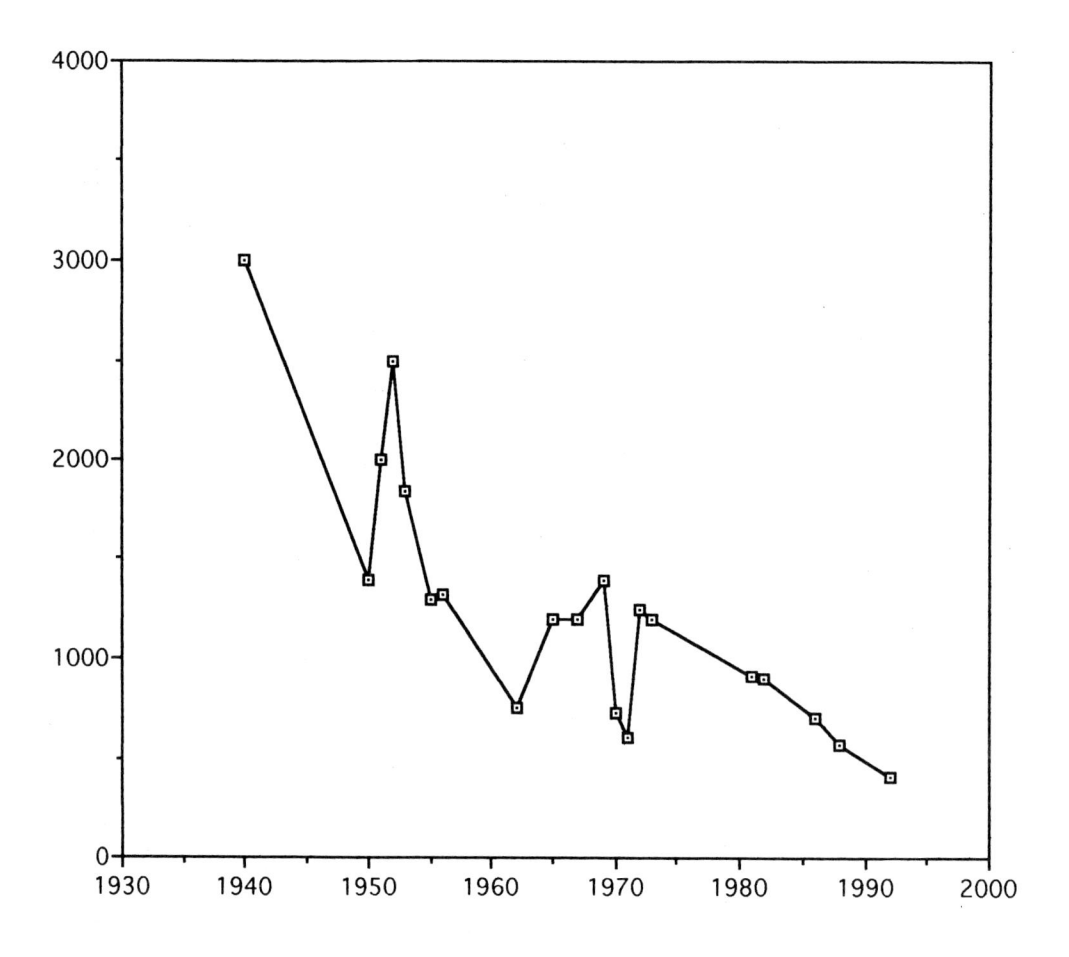

Fig. 2 Kittiwake numbers (counts of breeding pairs)

ISLAND STUDIES

Many guillemots left in response, even though the osprey, like the humans, was definitely not visible to them.

Among the land and wading birds, the two most obvious losses in the last fifty years have been buzzard (at the same time that myxomatosis affected the mainland buzzard populations, even though the disease did not reach Lundy then) and curlew. A number of other species have come and gone, always having bred on a sporadic basis only: examples include moorhen, house martin and song thrush. Regular breeders with apparently stable populations include common passerines such as wren, dunnock and blackbird, moor and grassland birds like meadow pipit and skylark, and – probably the most important species in terms of their scarcity in Britain – ravens. Lundy's peregrines, like buzzards, have reflected changes on the mainland, not breeding between the mid-1950s and late 1970s, the time when pesticide residues decimated the British population.

Migrants

Information on migrant birds travelling via Lundy is particularly significant when taken in conjunction with that of Britain's other Observatories and ringing stations. Together they provide a detailed picture of each species' strategy: their main routes, eventual destinations, timing and speed of movement, their survival rates and the particular hazards they face. The ways that weather conditions influence all these factors are also becoming better understood.

Spring migration on Lundy follows patterns that are familiar almost anywhere in Britain. For instance, among the earliest arrivals are wheatears; sand martins usually arrive before swallows, then house martins and finally swifts; chiffchaffs are generally earlier than willow warblers. In autumn, swifts, willow warblers and spotted flycatchers are among the earlier departures and blackcaps among the latest, at the same time that winter visitors such as redwings and fieldfares are beginning to move through.

In spring there is generally little direct evidence of migration in the form of birds visibly flying north. The main exceptions are swallows, martins and swifts and occasional larger species such as waders or birds of prey. Most passerines either work their way inconspicuously along the island, feeding as they go, or arrive overnight. Occasionally, when conditions are just right, hundreds or even thousands of new arrivals are found scattered across the island at first light. In late autumn, movements are much more conspicuous, with flock after flock of thrushes such as redwing, finches (mainly chaffinch) and starlings flying south, often without pausing on the island. Their combined daily totals can be in the thousands or tens of thousands.

Some migrants such as pied flycatchers, chaffinches and bramblings are seen in far greater numbers in autumn than spring, while a few, including turtle doves, are largely confined to spring.

Another group of species, most noticeably siskins and goldcrests, appear in highly variable numbers, with hundreds or thousands recorded one year and almost none the next. These variations reflect the severity of weather conditions the previous winter and the success of the breeding season, which together lead to large fluctuations in population size. On average, both goldcrest and siskin have increased markedly over the last fifty years on Lundy, probably as a result of the planting of conifer forests and warmer weather conditions in Britain. Perhaps the most spectacular success story reflected in the Society's records has been that of collared doves – though they are not showing migration so much as general dispersal of the species. Not seen on the island until 1961, records of twenty or more together are now commonplace. Some of the most obvious declines have been in trans-Saharan migrants such as whitethroats, apparently resulting from droughts, from the late 1960s onwards, in the African sahel regions where they winter.

Migrants ringed on Lundy have shown some spectacular movements; for example the woodcock found 2839 km away in Russia, one sedge warbler from Morocco and another to Senegal, a chiffchaff from Senegal, one pied flycatcher reaching Lundy from the Baltic island of Bornholm in twelve days and another travelling to Portugal, and redstarts found in Norway and Morocco. Other impressively quick movers include two goldcrests reaching Lundy a day after leaving the Scilly Isles and Great Saltee, Ireland, respectively and a chiffchaff doing so from Guernsey in two days. All of these are interesting, but without large numbers of ringing recoveries of the species it is not possible to know whether these are exceptional or the norm. Thus such data gain value enormously when they have been pooled with all other British ringing information and analysed centrally. Nevertheless for some species there is sufficient evidence from Lundy alone to draw some conclusions. An example that surprises many people is the extent to which blackbirds migrate. Our own familiar garden blackbirds are mainly residents but Britain receives many extra from abroad in autumn, when they move out of countries with more severe winters, as shown by a number of Lundy ringing recoveries to or from France, the Netherlands, Germany, Denmark and Norway.

Another species that has produced a good deal of information is willow warbler. Their British movements to or from Lundy are shown in Fig. 3. In those cases where the dates suggest they had reached their summer destinations, the great majority were to the north and northwest of Lundy, though one spring bird had presumably overshot its intended target because it returned south to spend the summer in Devon. Foreign records for this species include one from Denmark, one from Capri, Italy, and one to Morocco. Their speed of movement is indicated by the times of various journeys such as from Capri in seventeen days, and to Bardsey, North Wales, in three.

Rarities

There are several British islands and headlands with seabird colonies and migrants to match Lundy's but only the Scilly Isles and Fair Isle have better records for producing species never seen in Britain before. Lundy's list includes seven between 1952 and 1966: american robin, yellowthroat, rufous-sided towhee and northern oriole from North America; bimaculated lark from Asia and sardinian warbler and spanish sparrow from southern Europe. These have been followed by two more North American birds: eastern phoebe in 1987 and ancient murrelet in 1990, the murrelet being particularly remarkable because the species is normally confined to the Pacific coast.

Many other rare species have been seen on Lundy, ranging from veery (Plate 10) and ruppell's, bonelli's and yellow-rumped warblers, all making their second British appearances, to others like woodchat shrike which are seen in Britain annually.

It could be argued that finding rarities is the least important aspect of ornithological work on Lundy: exciting but not much more. However, it does have some scientific value because it is difficult to predict which species might be of significance in the future. Some, such as little egret and scarlet rosefinch, were regarded as rare vagrants until quite recently, but their numbers have now built up to a point where little egrets seem to be on the verge of establishing themselves as regular British breeders and scarlet rosefinches have already bred on several occasions. Collared doves were once rarities too. Without a reliable recording system, their spread, which has been reflected in their increasing frequency on Lundy, would not have been documented properly. Rarities also encourage careful, accurate observation by birdwatchers, highlighting identification problems and their solutions. Michael Jones, Lundy warden in 1962, and his assistant Richard Carden, were thorough and objective enough in their description of a bird they thought was a calandra lark – itself a major rarity – for it to be clear in retrospect that it was in fact a bimaculated lark, very similar but at the time totally unknown to British birdwatchers.

If the prospect of finding a rarity encourages birdwatchers to stay on Lundy, their daily input in recording commoner species is valuable even if their hopes of icing on the cake are sometimes unfulfilled.

Future work

The monitoring of Lundy's bird populations, whether breeding species, regular migrants or vagrants, needs to be continued into the future because of the importance of noting any changes, for conservation reasons. Species can only be protected effectively if people are alerted, through firm evidence rather than impressions, when numbers start declining seriously. The more detailed our understanding of their biology, the more likely it is that causes can be pinpointed and

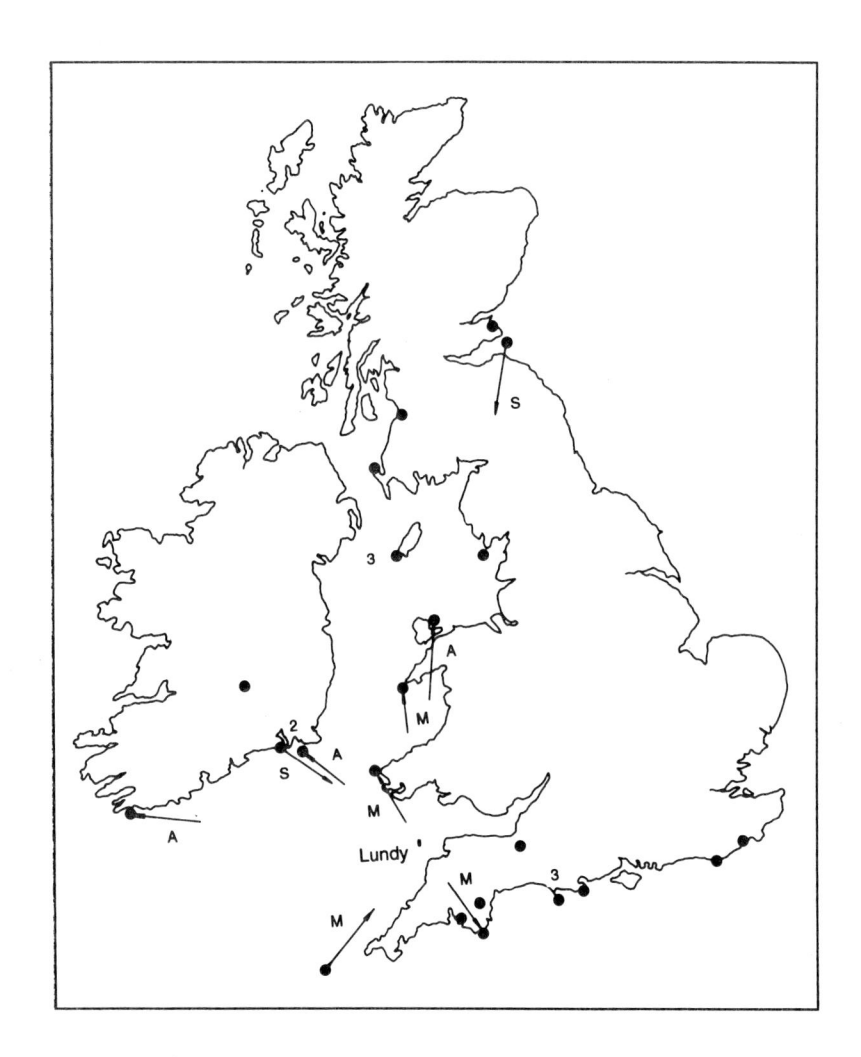

Fig 3 Movements of willow warblers to and from Lundy from within the British Isles. Numbers indicate how many ringed birds have moved between Lundy and a given site. Arrows show direction of movement and letters show the month (A=April, M=May, S=September), when recapture was less than 2 weeks after ringing.

effective action taken to solve the problems. Ringing provides an important means of obtaining this understanding.

There are still gaps in our knowledge of Lundy's birds, such as the breeding status of manx shearwaters (Plate 11) which are difficult to study because they nest down burrows and only enter or leave them at night. There is evidence for at least attempted breeding, in addition to extensive visiting at night by immatures. Ringing studies suggest that these non-breeders may originate from the large Pembrokeshire colonies on Skomer and Skokholm rather than from Lundy. Estimates of how many pairs lay eggs on Lundy vary enormously. There is evidence that when they do lay, the great majority of chicks do not survive to the fledging stage, since none are found in autumn. Rats have been suggested as a reason for this, but while it has been demonstrated that they are unlikely to be significant predators of eggs, the more important question of whether they take unguarded chicks remains unanswered. So Lundy's significance as a shearwater breeding colony is poorly understood in several respects.

There are plenty of opportunities on Lundy for other, specialised studies of birds, whether into their behaviour, ecology, population dynamics or other aspects of their biology. The birds themselves, the undisturbed conditions and the magnificent surroundings on the island could scarcely be bettered for fieldwork.

Landing Beach & South Light

Wild Mammals of Lundy

Ian Linn

As is normally the case with small islands, Lundy has an impoverished natural fauna of terrestrial mammals. Perhaps, when the sea engulfed the land bridge from Hartland Point to Lundy, at about the same time as the English Channel finally broke through to isolate Britain from continental Europe, most of the mammals which were at that time still migrating northwards into land becoming habitable once again after the last Ice Age simply had not got as far as the peninsula which was to become Lundy. Or perhaps some at least got there, only to become extinct later. Even the smallest of mammals is big compared with, say, a small insect such as an aphid. Consequently, in the case of mammals, the population density in terms of individuals per unit area tends to be small, so that on a small island where total numbers of any mammal species will be relatively small, a natural catastrophe which might only cause local extinction in a large land mass, can wipe out the entire population; so perhaps it is no accident that the only indigenous Lundy mammal is the smallest British mammal, and one of the smallest mammals known - the pygmy shrew *Sorex minutus* (Plate 13). The idea that these tiny mammals may have held on while larger species perished is supported by the fact that pygmy shrews are the only shrews, sometimes the only small mammals, present on a number of the small offshore islands scattered up the west side of mainland Britain (Arnold 1978).

Or possibly the pygmy shrew is just a fast mover, better able despite its small size to withstand the rigours of a sub-arctic climate. Thus, by pursuing the retreating ice more closely that some other species, it may have got to some outlying regions before other, less hardy species, and before rising sea levels cut off the areas of land on which they found themselves. It has been suggested that the rapid spread of the pygmy shrew was facilitated by the presence on the land bridges to Lundy and other islands which existed briefly some 8000 years ago, when sea levels were at their lowest, of the kind of wet, peaty moorland which particularly suits this little mammal (Yalden 1981, 1982). Such a scenario would be a possible explanation for the presence of pygmy shrews on the mainland of Ireland, an island large enough to support populations of larger mammals, which yet lacks any other shrew species. Natural populations of some other mammals found on mainland Britain, such as the bank vole and the brown hare, are also absent from Ireland.

So, for some thousands of years this tiny beast seems to have reigned alone on Lundy, the sole representative of the mammals apart from bats which could fly over the intervening sea and seals which frequented the beaches and sea caves. In recent times the very small pipistrelle *Pipistrellus pipistrellus* and the remarkable brown (common) long-eared bat *Plecotus auritus* have been observed fairly frequently (Anon. 1992; and several earlier records in Lundy Field Society Annual Reports). The large noctule bat *Nyctalus noctula* has also been seen (Dymond 1973), and a bat seen in 1995 may possibly have been a Daubenton's bat *Myotis daubentoni* (Anon. 1995). Grey seals *Halichoerus grypus* can often be seen today in the water or hauled out on the rocks of the east side. Beaches here are used for breeding, and pups are also born in Seal's Hole and other caves, perhaps as many as 25 in any one year (Clark 1977). Natural mortality among pups is high, however, and not all are able to survive.

During the time that the pygmy shrew was probably the only terrestrial mammal on Lundy, climatic changes must periodically have caused considerable modifications to the vegetation and microfauna of the island, but the tiny shrew has always been able to find good shelter and an adequate supply of the small invertebrates which provide its food. Today it is still common, particularly in Millcombe and on the terraces of the east side where, sheltered from the prevailing west wind, the vegetation is more luxuriant than elsewhere on the island. In due course our own species joined the fauna of Lundy; and it is *Homo sapiens* which has so dramatically enriched Lundy's wild mammal fauna.

Although human settlements on Lundy are of great antiquity (see Thackray, this volume), no written records remain of the animals which prehistoric man might have brought to the island. We cannot be certain, but it is very likely that the first new mammal to be introduced by man to Lundy was the common house mouse *Mus domesticus*. This rodent, an originally Asiatic species which has been a human commensal for a very long time, has been recorded from pre-Roman Iron Age deposits in Dorset and the Peak District (Yalden 1977), so it is entirely possible that it could have reached Lundy with the prehistoric human inhabitants. This must, however, remain speculation. What is certain is that house mice have been quite a problem on Lundy in recent times. Loyd (1925) reports "common" mice as numerous (he also thought that there were one, or even perhaps two, kinds of vole on the island, but this has never been confirmed by any other observer). More recently Gade (1978), who managed Lundy as agent for the owners from 1926 to 1971, records an extermination campaign against a heavy infestation of house mice around the farm, the hotel and the island stores. Although this campaign was temporarily successful, permanent extermination of mice is very difficult to achieve, and in any case can be quickly nullified by reinfestation. Mice have travelled all over the globe as unwilling passengers in material freighted by human carriers, and Gade saw them from time to time emerging from consignments of the thatching straw which was imported to Lundy from the mainland up to 1939. To this day mouse droppings are occasionally found in buildings on the island (G. Key and others, *in litt.*).

Felix Gade was an excellent naturalist, well able to distinguish between the commensal house mouse and the wild wood mouse *Apodemus sylvaticus*, and in addition to seeing house mice emerging from imported straw, he noticed on two occasions wood mice, and also recorded a wood mouse having been electrocuted in the compressor motor of a refrigerator (Gade 1974, 1978). Add to this the fact that the flea *Typhlocerus poppei poppei* collected from a common rat *Rattus norvegicus* on Lundy normally requires a wood mouse as a host in order to complete its life cycle (Couatarmanac'h & Linn 1988), and an intriguing possibility presents itself. Although extensive trapping campaigns by several different groups of biologists have never discovered any wood mice living wild on the island, is it possible that one or more transient populations of this rodent have existed on Lundy in the past? Speculation again!

The earliest recorded exotic mammal to arrive on Lundy was the rabbit *Oryctolagus cuniculus*. There is a record from Kent of rabbits in the last interglacial, about 250 000 BC (Stuart 1974), but it was long absent from Britain until reintroduced in more recent times. Although the Romans considered rabbit foetuses *(laurices)* a great delicacy, and it would not have been unlikely for them to have brought rabbits to Britain, there is no direct evidence that they ever did. Marcus Terrentius Varro reports in his *Rerum Rusticarum* that rabbits had been brought from Spain to Britain during the first century BC (Lever 1977), but if they did, the rabbits had died out by the time of the Norman Conquest, as there are no records of rabbit warrens in the Domesday Book. One of the earliest written records mentioning rabbits in Britain states that between 1183 and 1219 the tenant of Lundy was entitled to take 50 rabbits a year "from certain *chovis* (coves?) on the island" (Exeter City Archives, Misc. Deeds D.614). Earlier Latin translations of the Forest Laws of King Canute appear to refer to the taking of rabbits, but this is probably an error resulting from a poor grasp of mammal taxonomy by mediaeval scribes, who confused rabbits with the indigenous brown hare *Lepus europaeus*.

When rabbits were first brought to Britain they were highly esteemed as a source of fur and meat. Consequently they were kept closely guarded in enclosures – 'warrens' or 'coneygarths'. Many of these were situated in the south-west of England, particularly on Dartmoor where the wild country made their protection easier. The common Devon surname Coneybeare (Coneybeer, Conabeare, Conabeer, Conbeer, Conibear, Conibeer, Conibere, Connabeer) comes down to us from those times. Offshore islands were also greatly favoured as sites for warrens, being even easier to defend than a Dartmoor combe, which explains the early establishment of rabbits on Lundy.

Before too long, however, the rabbits escaped from their enclosures, and established what we think of today as warrens, namely groups of burrows which form the nucleus of a group territory, in the surrounding countryside. On Lundy the rabbit warrens are today mostly around the fringes of the flat plateau which forms the top of the island, but in earlier times they also lived in the dense thickets of gorse which covered much of the plateau. Ponies, which were introduced to the island in 1928, and bush fires greatly reduced the gorse over a period of years, but the rabbits remained plentiful. Many thousands were killed each year by the professional trapper employed in an attempt to control rabbit numbers, nearly 11,000 being taken in 1929 (Gade 1978). On the whole they have done very well on Lundy, but the fact that they compete with the ponies, domestic stock and wild ungulates for the available herbage means that they are regarded as a serious pest on the island, as they are on the mainland. Although the flea-borne disease myxomatosis was introduced to mainland Britain in the early 1950s, it was not until the early 1980s that it first appeared on Lundy (Parsons 1983).

The Harman family, who owned Lundy from 1925 to 1969, and ran it as a private estate, were keen to 'enrich' the island's fauna by introducing various new animals. Now that we know the regrettable results of some animal introductions to small islands, such actions are rather frowned on, but this was not always so - after all, the Zoological Society of London was first formed as an Acclimatisation Society to bring 'useful' new species to Britain. So, despite the pest status of the rabbit, various attempts were made to 'improve' the stock. Wild buck rabbits from the mainland were released, and individuals of domestic strains were introduced from time to time. On observing that some of the trapped wild rabbits had remarkably shaggy coats, Martin Coles Harman introduced Angora and Chinchilla rabbits, with no noticeable effect. His son Albion Harman later released some Rex rabbits which did not last long as they were very tame, and were soon shot, but which may have had some effect on the indigenous population, as a local increase in the proportion of dark-coloured individuals was observed (Gade 1978).

The rabbit was brought to Britain as a prized domestic animal, but a less welcome visitor from Asia arriving at about the same time, or perhaps even earlier, was the black or ship rat *Rattus rattus* (Plate 14). The name 'black rat' is something of a misnomer, since some 'black' rats are quite brown, so the alternative 'ship rat' is to be preferred. The precise date of this rodent's arrival in Britain is a bit vague, to some extent because, as with the rabbit and many other animals, naming of species was imprecise in the Middle Ages, and the exact distinction between rats and mice far from clear. As a result, contemporary written records are unreliable on this matter. Legend has it that ship rats reached Britain with returning Crusaders, some time in the eleventh or twelfth centuries, but they may have arrived as early as Roman times (Lever 1977; Armitage *et al.* 1984). Today the ship rat has a very limited distribution in Britain, having been almost totally superseded by the common or 'brown' rat *Rattus norvegicus* (which can sometimes be quite black! Plate 15).

The common rat is, like the ship rat, of Asiatic origin, and a widespread commensal of man. The date of its arrival in Britain is better documented, and was probably around 1720 (Twigg 1975). Although, like the rabbit, the spread of the common rat into the remoter parts of northern Scotland was slow, over most of Britain it quickly became the dominant species, reducing the population of the ship rat to relict status (Matheson 1962).

On mainland Britain common rats are now ubiquitous, while the ship rat clings on precariously in a few, mainly dockside, locations, with the common rat being largely blamed for its decline; yet on Lundy populations of both kinds of rat coexist, the two species apparently having carved up the territory in a more or less amicable manner. This is a situation of considerable biological interest, which has been the subject of several studies (Anon. 1950; Pearson *et al.* 1962; Perrin & Gurnell 1971; Smith 1985; Smith *et al.* 1991).

It appears that the rats are found only in the southern regions of the island; the common rat concentrated near, but by no means limited to, the hotel, the farm and the rubbish tip, while the ship rat is found mainly in the walled gardens in the lower reaches of Millcombe, and among the boulders above high water mark on the sea shore. But the range of the common rat extends down Millcombe as far as the Landing Beach, so that there is considerable territorial overlap. Nevertheless it seems that the ship rats, though fewer in numbers, are well able to persist in their preferred habitats, and reports of their recent decline in numbers may be exaggerated. The rats, like rats everywhere, are not the best-loved of creatures, and tend to become convenient scapegoats when a cause is sought for the decline of some of the more attractive denizens of the island, particularly the sea birds. But such accusations are usually founded on quite flimsy evidence, and seldom stand up to careful scrutiny.

Exactly when these rats, ship and common, reached Lundy is by no means clear. As on mainland Britain, the ship rats got there first. In 1775, by which time the common rat was well established on the mainland, Lundy was reported to have no common rats, although ship rats had been present since 1630 at least. By 1877, however, common rats were numerous, and the ship rat very much in decline (Willcox 1988; Loyd 1925). The rats could have travelled, like the mice, in man's baggage, or possibly have deserted the sinking ship in the time-honoured manner, ie. scrambled ashore from some of the many ships which have been wrecked on the rocks of Lundy's coast over the years.

A mammal which poses a much more serious potential threat to the smaller wildlife of Lundy is the common domestic cat *Felis catus*. Cats can easily become feral and cause serious problems on islands where nesting birds provide easy prey (Lever 1985). Gade (1978) tells of problems on Lundy in the 1920s with feral cats menacing ground-nesting birds. A more recent report of a lactating female feral cat on Lundy (Parsons 1984) is therefore a serious cause for concern.

So far only the smaller mammals have been considered, but what of the larger species? Ponies have been mentioned, but these are domestic stock, not wild mammals. At present three species of wild ungulates live on Lundy; goats *Capra hircus*, Soay sheep *Ovis aries* and sika deer *Cervus nippon*. Of these three, the first two are what is known technically as 'feral'; that is to say, they are descendants of animals which were once kept by man in captivity, or as domestic stock, but have escaped and reverted to a truly wild existence.

Goats have never been native to Britain, but have been kept as domestic animals since Neolithic times, and many herds of feral animals, so-called 'wild goats', are to be found in the less accessible regions and off-shore islands of Scotland, Wales and Ireland. Although these herds enjoy no legal protection, they are of considerable biological interest, as the animals are small, shaggy and well equipped with horns, much resembling the ancient domestic breeds descended from the bezoar goat *Capra aegagrus*, a wild species from eastern Europe and Asia (Lever 1977). It is reasonable to assume that Lundy's earliest human inhabitants kept goats, and that some of these escaped and lived wild on the island. Loyd (1925) reported wild goats on Lundy in 1752, but by 1802 they had disappeared (unpublished report by Britton quoted by Bathe *et al.* 1984). Escaped individuals from stocks of domesticated goats brought to the island by farmers, lighthousekeepers and quarrymen during the 19th century formed the nucleus of a new feral herd which was augmented by Martin Coles Harman in 1926 and subsequently (Gade 1977; Bathe *et al.* 1984). Although these more modern introductions were large, short-haired, 'improved' dairy goats, the Lundy goats of today show few obvious signs of their domesticated origin (e.g. hornlessness, throat tassels), and are typical wild goats in appearance (Plate 16). This may be thought surprising, but as Lever (1977) points out, "when goats escape from domestication they revert to this wild form within a few generations, and sometimes within ten years." The present-day feral goats of Lundy are small, agile, well adapted to their habitat, and well worth preservation, if only for the gene for hardiness which they undoubtedly carry. Despite considerable culling, they have maintained for many years an active and healthy herd of around 40 to 50 head. Today, however, their numbers are much reduced, a fact which is a cause for concern. They are not secretive, and can be observed demonstrating the traditional sure-footedness of the species on the cliffs and sidings of the island.

Soay sheep are of an ancient, primitive domestic stock which was brought to Britain about 5000 years ago, and persisted to mediaeval times. These sheep closely resemble their wild ancestors, probably *Ovis orientalis*, the Asiatic mouflon, and survived on the islands of St Kilda, in the Atlantic Ocean off northwest Scotland, because of the extreme isolation of the archipelago. In recent times they were limited to the island of Soay, where they lived ferally, but in 1932 they were introduced to Hirta, the largest island in the group, and some were later brought to mainland Britain. Several herds of these interesting animals exist in parks in Britain and elsewhere, but the Lundy herd is the largest outside St Kilda, and the only one living wild in a situation similar to the original Hebridean location. It is therefore of particular biological importance. The sheep were introduced to Lundy in 1942, with a further addition in 1944, and have found the island very much to their liking, the herd building up to over 100 head, despite culling. In appearance the Soay sheep are small, brown and agile, quite unlike the domestic sheep of today (Plate 17). The rams carry large curved horns. Like the feral goats, they are very much at home on the cliffs and steep sidings of Lundy, where they can readily be seen, although they do not like to be approached too closely (Bathe *et al.* 1984; Jewell & Bullock 1991).

Sika deer *Cervus nippon* are handsome animals, the summer coat a bright chestnut colour with light spots (Plate 18). The stags carry branched antlers similar to those of the red deer *Cervus elaphus*. Originally from Japan, Taiwan and the eastern Asiatic mainland, sika deer have been widely introduced to many countries including Britain, where they were brought to Regent's Park in 1860. Seven sika deer were introduced to Lundy in 1927. Sika deer hybridise freely with red deer, and apparently have done so on Taiwan and the Chinese mainland for a very long time. Only the two Japanese island races of sika deer are uncontaminated by red deer genes, and the fact that the Lundy deer are from one of these races, *Cervus nippon nippon*, and appear not to have interbred with the red deer with which they shared Lundy from 1927 to 1962, makes them of considerable biological importance. Unlike the feral goats and Soay sheep, the sika deer can only be seen in the early morning or the evening when they are out feeding. During the day they shelter in the dense rhododendron thickets of the east side. When caught in the open they express alarm by moving off with the stiff-legged, bouncing gait known as 'stotting' or 'pronking', erecting the hairs on the white rump patch ('flaring') and giving short, sharp whistling calls. Like red deer, sika deer are more grazers than browsers, although in the hard times of winter their tastes become perforce more catholic, eating poor quality foods such as the coarse rush *Juncus effusus*, and digging for bluebell bulbs and bracken rhizomes. The last food item is particularly interesting because all parts of the bracken plant are very toxic, and bracken is generally avoided by herbivorous mammals. The influence of the sika deer on plant diversity and soil erosion on Lundy has been studied by Eaton & Boddington (1987).

The Lundy sika started off well, the herd building up to about 90 head in 1961 despite frequent culling. Since then they have done less well, showing poor condition and high mortality in the 1970s, and by the 1980s the numbers had dropped to single figures. Today the deer numbers are slightly higher, but the persistent low population level is a cause for concern about the future of this species on the island (Bathe & Scriven 1974; Bathe *et al.* 1984; Ratcliffe 1991).

Two other species of deer were introduced to Lundy by Martin Coles Harman - fallow deer *Dama dama* and red deer. Fallow deer existed in Britain during the last interglacial, about 250 000 to 100 000 BC, but became extinct during the last glaciation until reintroduced (Chapman & Putman 1991). This may have been done by the Romans, but as with the rabbit, the possibility rests upon hearsay evidence. Jennison (1937) quotes a list in the *Augustan History* which states that in about 238 AD the Emperor Gordian I exhibited in Rome 200 stags of *cervi palmati* (referring to the distinctive palmate antlers of the fallow deer), some from Britain. Be that as it may, the Domesday Book records 31 parks in Southern England holding 'bucks', so it seems that fallow deer had arrived by the Middle Ages, and they are now widespread in Britain both in parks and in the wild. The first record on Lundy is of 16 deer in 1752, but in 1882 they were not doing all that well, being down to 12 animals, one of which when killed provided 'very thin meat'. It appears that the Lundy herd became extinct until 30 animals were reintroduced in 1927. At first they did well, peaking at 50 head in 1939, but during World War II they were over-culled, as the island tried to be self-sufficient in meat, and the fallow were the easiest deer to shoot. The herd never recovered from this over-exploitation, and became extinct in 1954 (Bathe & Scriven 1975).

The red deer is a species indigenous to the British Isles. Neither it nor the other indigenous British deer, the roe deer *Capreolus capreolus*, has ever occurred naturally on Lundy as far as is known. Fifteen red deer were introduced in 1927, three of which were hybrids with the North American wapiti *Cervus canadensis*. These cross-bred imdividuals had been hand-reared, and were very aggressive and unafraid of human beings, to the extent that several attacks on visitors took place, and the two most dangerous stags had to be destroyed. Like the fallow deer, the red deer did very well at first, building up by 1949 to a herd of 33 animals. By 1953 severe over-culling had reduced the herd to 11 animals, from which the red deer never recovered, becoming extinct in 1962 (Bathe & Scriven 1975; Gade 1978).

The history of ungulates on Lundy makes depressing reading. Only the Soay sheep are doing well. All the others, despite their intrinsic biological interest, have either been allowed to become extinct, or are hanging on at dangerously low levels. It is to be hoped that a comprehensive management plan which will assess objectively the food resources available, and the requirements of both domestic stock and wild undulates, will be initiated to address this problem and ensure a secure future for the sika deer and wild goat herds.

Finally, a brief mention must be made of the introduced mammals whose sojourn on Lundy was relatively short and ill-fated, as reported by Gade (1978). Two early attempts by Martin Coles Harman to introduce brown hares were unsuccessful, although one male lived for some years in a rhododendron thicket, and grew to an enormous size. A later attempt by Albion Harman in about 1960 was temporarily successful. Gade (1978) quotes a report of five hares having been seen 'recently' in the Lighthouse Field. These mammals do not feature in any recent reports of mammals seen on Lundy, however. Two 'rock' wallabies, probably red-necked wallabies *Macropus rufogriseus*, a species which has established one or two small colonies in Britain, were released into a poultry pen in St John's Valley in 1928, but unfortunately were drowned in St John's Well, one immediately, the other a couple of weeks later. Several attempts were made to introduce red squirrels *Sciurus vulgaris*, all ending in failure until the last, in 1935 or 1936. This colony of ten animals survived largely due to the devoted efforts of Felix Gade, who hand-fed them early each morning. The squirrels never bred, however, and the last one disappeared in the winter of 1943.

In conclusion, it must be emphasised that, although all but one of the terrestrial mammals of Lundy, and certainly all the obvious ones, have been introduced to the island by our own species, this does not mean that they are devoid of interest and importance, and that their conservation can be ignored. If it is accepted that the larger mammals are worthy of conservation, this is no easy task. The inherent instability of limited populations of these species on small islands means that enlightened and careful management is essential if they are to have any prospect of long-term survival. In the case of Lundy, the indiscriminate harvesting of the past should be replaced by a culling programme based on a sound scientific assessment of resources and requirements. The fact that Lundy's ungulates have survived so well in spite of their tribulations suggests that they are well suited to life on the island, and with enlightened management would have an excellent prospect of survival.

References

Anon. 1950. Terrestrial and freshwater ecology: interim notes. *Annual Report of the Lundy Field Society* 4, 28-33.

Anon. 1992. Mammals on Lundy, 1992. *Annual Report of the Lundy Field Society* 43, 117.

Anon. 1995. Mammals on Lundy, 1995. *Annual Report of the Lundy Field Society* 46, 94.

Armitage, P West, B & Steedman, K 1984. New evidence of black rats in Roman London. *London Archaeologist* 4, 375-383.

Arnold, H R, 1978. *Provisional atlas of the mammals of the British Isles*. Natural Environment Research Council, Abbots Ripton.

Bathe, G M, & Scriven, N,. 1974. The Japanese sika deer (*Cervus nippon nippon*) of Lundy with notes on the now extinct red and fallow populations. *Annual Report of the Lundy Field Society* 26, 19-27.

Bathe, G.M., Pulteney, D.J. & Pulteney, C.M. (1984). A survey of the Lundy ungulates. *Annual Report of the Lundy Field Society* 35, 16-18.

Chapman, N G, & Putman, R J, 1991. Fallow deer *Dama dama*. In Corbet, G.B. & Harris, S. (eds), *The Handbook of British Mammals* (3rd edit.), 508-18. Oxford: Blackwell.

Clark, N A, 1977. The composition and behaviour of the grey sea (*sic!*) colony of Lundy. *Annual Report of the Lundy Field Society* 28, 32-38.

Couatarmanac'h, M D, & Linn, I J, 1988. Two fleas (Siphonaptera) new to the Lundy list: were there once woodmice *Apodemus sylvaticus* on the island? *Reports and Transactions of the Devonshire Association for the Advancement of Science* 120, 145-153

Dymond, J N,1973. Bats. *Annual Report of the Lundy Field Society* 24, 27.

Eaton, A, & Boddington, S, 1987. Ecological effect of the sika deer on Lundy's east sidelands. *Annual Report of the Lundy Field Society* 38, 41-46.

Gade, F W, 1978. *My Life on Lundy*. Myrtle Langham, Reigate.

Jennison, G, 1937. *Animals for show and pleasure in ancient Rome*. Manchester University Press.

Jewell, P A, & Bullock, D J, 1991. Feral sheep *Ovis aries*. In Corbet, G.B. & Harris, S.(eds), *The Handbook of British Mammals* (3rd edit.), 547-552. Oxford: Blackwell.

Lever, C, 1977. *The Naturalized Animals of British Isles*. London: Hutchinson.

Lever, C, 1985. *Naturalized Mammals of the World*. London: Longman.

Loyd, R.W. 1925. *Lundy, Its History and Natural History.* London: Longmans.
Matheson. C. 1962. *Brown rats.* Animals of Britain 16. London: Sunday Times Publications.
Parsons, AJ, 1983. Notes on some mammals on Lundy. *Annual Report of the Lundy Field Society* 34, 40.
Parsons, AJ, 1984. Lundy 1984. *Annual Report of the Lundy Field Society* 35, 29-31.
Pearson, AD, Greenwood, J.J.D., Sinclair, G.R., Hemsley, C.C. & Billings, A.J. (1962).
    Oxford Lundy expedition 1962. *Annual Report of the Lundy Field Society* 15, 17-22.
Perrin, MR, & Gurnell, J, 1971. Rats on Lundy. A report 1971. *Lundy Field Society Annual* Report 22, 35-40.
Ratcliffe, PR, 1991. Sika deer *Cervus nippon* In Corbet, G.B. & Harris, S. (eds),
    The Handbook of British Mammals (3rd edit.), 504-508. Oxford: Blackwell.
Smith PA, 1985. Ship rats on Lundy. 1983. *Annual Report of the Lundy Field Society* 36, 35-38.
Smith, PA, Smith, JA, Tattersall, FH, Natynczuk, SE, Seymour, R, & Lancaster, V, (1991)
    The Lundy ship rat expedition 1991. *Annual Report of the Lundy Field Society* 42, 95-98.
Stuart, AJ, 1974. Pleistocene history of the British vertebrate fauna. *Biological Reviews* 49, 225-266.
Taylor, KD, 1991. Ship rat *Rattus rattus.* In: Corbet, G.B. & Harris, S. (eds), *The Handbook of British Mammals* (3rd edit.), 255-259. Oxford: Blackwell.
Willcox, N, 1988. Land mammals and other introductions. *Lundy Field Society Leaflet.*
Yalden, D, 1977. Small mammals and the archaeologist. *Bulletin of the Peakland Archaeological Society* 30, 18-25.
Yalden, DW, 1981. The occurrence of the pygmy shrew *Sorex minutus* on moorland,
    and the implications for its presence in Ireland. *Journal of Zoology* 195, 147-156.
Yalden, DW, 1982. When did the mammal fauna of the British Isles arrive? *Mammal Review* 12, 1-57.

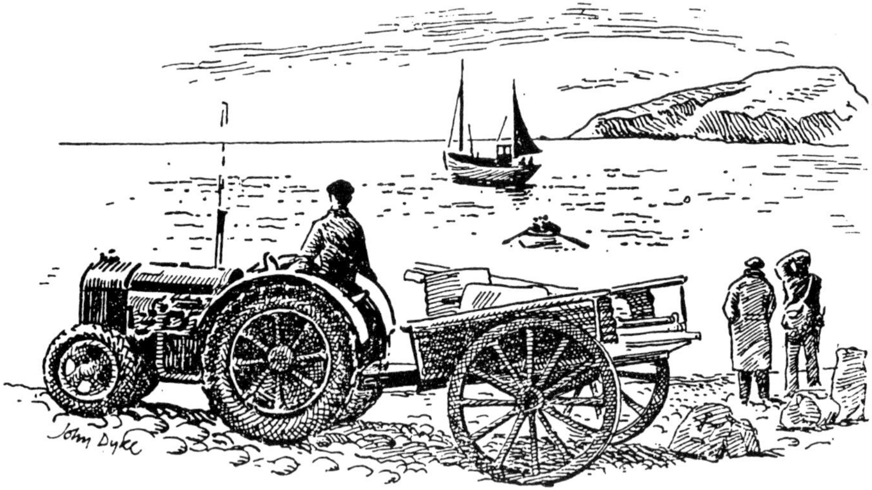
John Dyke

Animal Psychology and Behaviour

Hayley Randle

Psychology is the study of the mind and behaviour, with behaviour being manifest as actions which can be objectively measured or precisely defined. For example, providing there is a clear working definition of head shaking (ie. lateral movement of the head from side to side) any number of observers can use it to decide and agree on whether an individual is head shaking or not. Studying the mind, however, is not as straightforward as there is a tendency towards subjectivity. This is inevitable owing to those aspects of the mind which are usually studied: perception, sensation, memory and thought. One fact is true nonetheless: with animals we cannot simply ask them about themselves; instead we have to devise ways of finding out about them and how they function, and it is only through behaviour that we can obtain such information.

Animal behaviour is diverse and there are a number of scientific disciplines devoted to its study. Such studies can be undertaken virtually anywhere, but of all possible locations, small islands are perhaps among the best suited to research of this kind, with an isolated population and field conditions conducive to close examination of the animals; whether birds, wild mammals or the domestic stock, islands represent natural field laboratories. Over the last few years, the potential for such work on Lundy has been realised. Here a general framework describing aspects of animal psychology is presented, along with some examples of recent work conducted on Lundy.

Studying animal behaviour

Ethology has been defined as, "the study of animal behaviour in the natural environment, which uses evolutionary adaptation as its primary explanatory principle" (Gray 1991). Some regard animal behaviour as one of the most important aspects of biology, and the following section will examine briefly the history, emergence and subsequent development of ethology. This will include a summary of its growth and an examination of its subdisciplines.

Ethology and evolution

Early work on animal behaviour was set against an evolutionary background, as is evident from the definition of ethology. Evolution depends on *natural selection*, a process by which some individuals are preferred over others. Natural selection can be thought of as selective breeding by nature and parallels the artificial breeding programmes seen with domestic species, for example the selective breeding of Friesian cows for high milk yield when kept under intensive conditions. The immediate environment in which an individual lives is referred to as the ecological niche and this niche imposes selective pressures on the individual.

Natural selection is based on the fact that not all individuals in a population will survive and reproduce. The determination of who does and who does not depends partly on the individual's inherited characteristics. It follows then that any characteristics which increase the likelihood of survival are selected *for* in nature, whilst those characteristics which decrease the chances of survival are selected *against*. If this is the case, so long as there are heritable differences between individuals which have a direct bearing on their chances of survival, evolution will occur. If there are no changes in the environment then a species can become adapted to it, can cope with the pressures exerted on it and have no need to evolve further. However, environments change continually. Species living in them, therefore, must continue to evolve in order to remain adapted to their environment. (Fig.1 provides definitions of the terms used.)

The growth and diversification of ethology
Since its development in Europe in the 1930s ethology has grown considerably as a scientific discipline and although it invokes some evolutionary explanation, has expanded and diversified in many ways, for example into comparative, social and behavioural ethology. The two most famous ethologists largely responsible for establishing comparative ethology were Konrad Lorenz (1903-1989) and Niko Tinbergen (1907-1988), both of whom were originally zoologists interested in the biological aspects of behaviour. Comparative ethologists study individuals, relate differences in different animals' behaviour to the ecological pressures of the environments that they live in, maintain that the behaviour of animals could be studied in exactly the same way as other factors such as their morphology, and believe that the more closely related two species are, the more likely they are to share behaviours. Unlike comparative ethologists, social ethologists focus their attention on groups of individuals or societies. Their primary concern is to understand the society as a whole and then to consider the individual within it. A social ethologist would maintain that the most important selective pressures impinging on an animal would be those arising from its society.

So far we have examined disciplines in which behaviour is studied. However, other scientific disciplines are concerned with animals' ability to learn. There are two main approaches to the study of animal learning: behaviourism and cognitivism.

An early form of behaviourism stated that learning could be accounted for completely by simple Stimulus-Response (S-R) connections. However, by the 1960s a new kind of behaviourism, methodological behaviourism, arose. Here it was suggested that all that could be observed about an animal is its behaviour, which can then be used to infer thought. Methodological behaviourists infer internal mental (cognitive) processes, represented by an intervening 'O' in the S-O-R relationship, where 'O' represents organism variables. Organism variables might include the individual's emotion, motivation, past experience and personality, amongst other things. In other words, between the Stimulus (S) and Response (R) something happens within the animal which has a determining role on the observed response (see Fig.2). Methodological behaviourism provided the foundations for a new approach to the study of animal learning: the study of cognition or knowledge: "the study of the ability to acquire, organise, store, access and use information" (Gray 1991,16).

Ethologists and behaviourists thus had much in common. Indeed, by the 1960s they began to co-operate. Behaviourists started to take into account biological constraints on learning and admitted that learning was subject to evolution according to imposed environmental constraints and pressures. Meanwhile, ethologists were discovering that the behaviour of mammals in particular was much more flexible than that of the birds which they had traditionally studied, and that prior experiences, including learning, played an important role in the determination of behaviour. This 'merging' to some extent culminated in cognitive ethology, otherwise referred to as the study of cognition in animals. Cognitive ethology has undergone rapid growth over the last fifteen years and a large amount of evidence has been gathered showing that animals possess awareness and consciousness and are able to employ their cognitive skills and strategies to solve problems (eg Randle 1995).

In order to study farm animals, and in particular their welfare, another branch of ethology arose, applied ethology. Applied ethology differs from the pure ethology practised by Lorenz and Tinbergen (mainly on birds) in two ways: first, the greater use of quantitative methods, and second, the integration of information from other disciplines. Whilst pure ethologists study behaviour for its own sake, describing what behaviours a species performs and how much of each behaviour there is, applied ethologists formulate and statistically test hypotheses, studying behaviour as a means of examining why behaviours and behavioural problems and abnormalities do or do not occur.

Applied ethologists employ both descriptive and manipulative methods. Much of the early work was devoted to comparisons of farmed animals' behavioural repertoires with their natural or *wild* counterparts. Another approach was to monitor the occurrence of abnormal behaviours, such as crate chewing by veal calves. The occurrence of vices such as weaving in stabled horses and stereotypes, such as pacing in caged animals, were also examined. Their causes were determined (often boredom owing to inadequate environmental stimulation) and measures put in place to rectify them. Disrupted patterning of behaviour was also studied; for example it was found that if overcrowded, dairy cows increased the amount of time they spent chasing and jostling one another (Wierenga 1980). The manipulative approach makes use of comparisons between 'control' and 'experimental' conditions, in which differences can be related to the conditions

Figure 1.   **Definitions associated with the process of Evolution**

Term	Definition
Evolution	A process of gradual change.
Natural Selection	The selective breeding that results from the obstacles to reproduction that are imposed by the natural environment. The driving force of evolution.
Ecological Niche	The precise environment in which the individual lives and reproduces.
Selective Pressure	An aspect of the environment in general, or more specifically the Ecological Niche, which might render some individuals 'fitter' than others.
Adaptedness	An indication of how well suited an individual is to the environmental conditions in which he/she lives.
Fitness	The ability to leave behind descendents, where a 'fit' individual leaves more than a 'less fit' individual.

Note. These definitions are derived from Lea (1984, pp5-6) and Gray (1991) being examined, for example of two different calf rearing conditions, where a number of calves were group reared whilst the same number of calves were reared in partial isolation (Broom and Leaver 1978).

It has been suggested that psychology is an important aspect of animal welfare research. This view is particularly salient given the current interest in the animal mind. Much of the applied ethology research published in the early 1980s was devoted to animal choice in which an attempt was made to assess animals' preferences by giving them the opportunity to make choices. Another focus of applied ethology, stemming from developmental psychology, is the relative role of genetics and the environment (physical and social) in determining an animal's behaviour.

Much work has been undertaken and is underway within the branches of animal psychology described here. Some of that work has been undertaken on islands, with the control (even laboratory) conditions they provide giving the results particular significance. The majority of the research carried out on Lundy is documented in the Lundy Field Society's Annual Report. Inspection of the contents of the Report demonstrates that a large number of studies have been carried out on many species over the last fifty years. Some of these fall under the realm of pure ethology, some ecology and others, more recently, applied ethology. Almost all of Lundy's species have been studied to some extent. Some examples illustrate the range.

Island studies, Lundy studies

"Islands have been recognised as important 'field laboratories' for many years, the physical isolation making them ideal for research. Because of this, the results of research conducted on Lundy have an importance which extends beyond the island's immediate environs."

LFS introductory leaflet

Perhaps the single most important advantage of islands for the types of research described in this contribution, is the physical, geographical isolation they provide. Such isolation means that researchers are removed from the hurly-burly of mainland life and can commit themselves fully to the research in hand. For those, including students who are unfamiliar with the species under study, islands provide an ideal environment in which to gain familiarity and confidence. Two of the physical attributes of Lundy render it particularly suitable for carrying out research into animal behaviour. First, the small size means that, on the whole, it is relatively easy to locate the species under study. Second, and particularly for those interested in birds and marine life, there is a relatively large amount of coast per unit area. Habitats around Lundy are also varied, each coast having a different aspect and influenced by different winds. In 1925 Loyd referred to

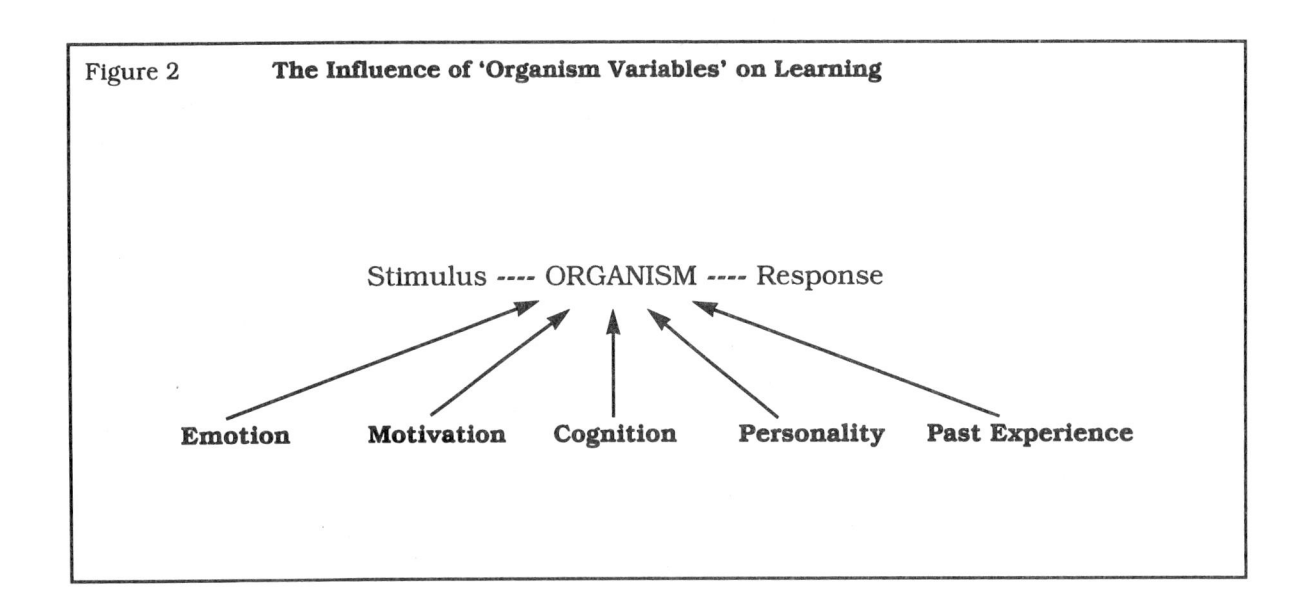

Figure 2 **The Influence of 'Organism Variables' on Learning**

Stimulus ---- ORGANISM ---- Response

Emotion   **Motivation**   **Cognition**   **Personality**   **Past Experience**

Lundy's climate as 'peculiar', with prevailing winds from the West and a sheltered East side. Lundy also boasts a range of species (see Linn, this volume). As well as the birds, there are wild mammals such as Soay sheep, goats and deer, rabbits and rats, and a number of domestic farm animal species including sheep, ponies, until recently cattle and at times different pig species. Over the years a number of species have been introduced to Lundy, with little success, including squirrels, red necked wallabies, barbary sheep, red deer, fallow deer (Bathe *et al* 1984), peafowl and swans (Langham and Langham 1984,44). Earlier, Loyd (1925, 77) attributed many of these failures to birds of prey. The only species successfully introduced to Lundy (by M. Coles Harman in the 1940s) were goats, Soay sheep and sika deer (Bathe *et al* 1984). All three species were suited to the Lundy environment and their populations expanded rapidly.

Whilst it can be argued that having populations of wild or feral animals contained on an island is an advantage, Bathe *et al* (1984) highlight a number of drawbacks associated mainly with culling policies. In 1955 there were 100 deer, 45 goats and 85 soays which were substantially reduced to 30 deer, 12 soays and 27 goats by a cull carried out in 1957 (Langham and Langham 1984, 44). Culls are generally haphazard and indiscriminate affairs and result in a population of individuals which does not have a natural population structure. However, Bathe *et al* (1984) conclude that culls can be carried out satisfactorily if proper planning and control is exercised (see Gulland 1992 for an example of good culling strategy used on the Soay sheep). As a consequence animal populations on islands can be intrinsically less stable than those on the mainland. Instability is further enhanced if the population is 'closed', that is, there are no incomers bringing new genes with them. But, so long as groups are managed appropriately, islands can provide an excellent opportunity for monitoring population changes.

One of the main problems with studying groups of wild animals is their wariness of humans. However, the presence of many visitors on Lundy renders the animals relatively used to human movement all over the island. As a result, they are fairly easy to study and with little disruption of their typical behaviour and daily patterns.

Since 1963 there have been a number of studies of the grey seal on Lundy. Hook (1963) noted how the number of individuals hauling out onto the shores of Lundy peaks in August, followed by a steep drop. Numbers then increase again sharply in November as individuals arrive from breeding groups elsewhere. Seals typically haul out on the side of the island with the least swell (Clarke 1977). A series of studies carried out by Clarke and Baillie (1973; 1974) suggest that individual seals show some loyalty to the island returning for at least two consecutive years, and furthermore that some individuals show preference for particular haul-out and pupping sites (Clarke

1987). It has been possible to identify individuals, most frequently using small cuts and hair patterns (Clarke 1977), a project now being developed by John Heath. Clarke concluded that a core of individuals use Lundy and that there is little movement between Lundy and the mainland. Heath's work will no doubt shed more light on this.

A number of studies have been carried out to assess the behaviour and activity of the rats on Lundy. Many of these investigated whether or not rats have been responsible for the infamous decline of the puffin population (eg. Perrin and Gurnell 1971). Allen (1974) examined two aspects of the social behaviour of the feral goats on Lundy: communication and hierarchy. This work uncovered a complex of startle reactions, comprising different combinations of snorts and movements. Many aspects of the Lundy sika deer behaviour have also been studied (see Bathe and Scriven 1974), including vigilance (Boddington 1987), their ecological effect on Lundy (Boddington and Eaton 1987) and their perceptual processes (Eaton 1988).

Since 1990 a number of studies have been carried out on the farm animal species. These include an assessment of the social behaviour and personality of the North Devon cattle (Randle 1992) and the Lundy ponies (Randle 1994a) and an investigation into the ecological influences on lamb play behaviour (Randle 1993). Other unpublished work carried out on Lundy includes association and neighbour preferences in steers and Friesian heifers, suckling behaviour of single and twin lambs and a comparison of mother-young behaviour in the soay and domestic sheep. Further work might focus on how typical farming practices work on an island; practices peculiar to farming on an island (for example transporting livestock by boat) could also be examined.

Two further points should be made: First, Lundy's inhabitants have generally been supportive of such studies, as they are keen for the behaviour and ecology of 'their' species to be understood, and to integrate findings into their management. Of course, the support of organisations such as the Lundy Field Society is also invaluable. Another great attribute of Lundy is that it can accommodate field trips, and in doing so a good atmosphere is generated and individual's motivations for engaging in research increased. Second, the implications of work carried out on Lundy are not restricted to the island itself. Work carried out on Lundy often serves as pilot material leading to other research both on and off the island. For example, Stephen Lea started investigating the diving behaviour of the European shag on Lundy in 1990. This work then continued both on Cormorant on the Exe estuary and on Little and Pied shags on South Island, New Zealand (Lea *et al* in press). Another regular visitor to the island over many years is Denver Daniels, who has carried out a series of ethological studies of the Kittiwake on Lundy, which have been continued elsewhere in Europe (Daniels 1983, 1992; Daniels *et al* 1984). Research carried out on Lundy can also be used to confirm findings of studies carried out elsewhere. For example I have used the cattle on Lundy to back up conclusions reached in research on the mainland (Randle 1994b).

Summary

The study of animal behaviour is not straightforward; rather it is multi-faceted and to be done properly must be multidisciplinary. This contribution has described the growth of ethology, the area of study devoted to animal behaviour. Applied and cognitive ethology were highlighted as currently fashionable areas of research which enable questions to be answered about animal welfare and the animal mind respectively. Examples of such work undertaken on Lundy were presented.

Lundy provides a wonderful opportunity for carrying out a wide range of research projects in a stimulating environment. This has been attributed to a number of factors, including its physical attributes, the range of wild and domestic species present, and the interest and support of the islanders, those who visit Lundy regularly, and the Lundy Field Society. However, in my view, the real attraction of Lundy is the atmosphere, whether attributable to geographical isolation or social, or a mixture of the two, which makes it a refreshing, stimulating place to engage in research of all kinds, at any level, whether plain discovery and wonderment at how a particular animal behaves, or in-depth research of international credibility.

References

Allen, K, 1974. Some aspects of the social behaviour of Lundy goats. *Annual Report of the Lundy Field Society* 25, 62-66.

Bathe, G M & Scriven, N J, 1974. The japanese sika deer (*Cervus nippon nippon*) of Lundy with notes on the now extinct red and fallow populations. *Annual Report of the Lundy Field Society* 26, 19-27.

Bathe, G M, Pultney, D J & Pultney, C M 1984. A survey of the Lundy ungulates. *Annual Report of the Lundy Field Society* 35, 16–18.

Boddington, S, 1987. Factors affecting vigilance in the japanese sika deer (*Cervus nippon nippon*) of Lundy Island. *Annual Report of the Lundy Field Society* 38, 33-40.

Boddington, S, & Eaton, A, 1987. Ecological affect of the sika deer on Lundy's east sidelands. *Annual Report of the Lundy Field Society* 38, 41-46.

Broom, D M, & Leaver, J D, 1978. Effects of group-rearing or partial isolation on later social behaviour of calves. *Animal Behaviour* 26, 1255-1263.

Clarke, N A, 1977. The composition and behaviour of the grey seal colony of Lundy. *Annual Report of the Lundy Field Society* 28, 16–42.

Clarke, N A, 1987. Grey seal pupping on Lundy in 1987. *Annual Report of the Lundy Field Society* 38, 47.

Clarke, N A, & Baillie, C C, 1973. Observations on the Grey Seal (*Halichoerus grypus*) populations of Lundy. *Annual Report of the Lundy Field Society* 24, 41-42.

Clarke, N A, & Baillie, C C, 1974. Observations on the Grey Seal (*Halichoerus grypus*) populations of Lundy. *Annual Report of the Lundy Field Society* 25, 57-59.

Daniels, D, 1983. Vocal behaviour in the Kittiwake Gull (*Rissa tridactyla*). *Annual Report of the Lundy Field Society* 34, 3–15.

Daniels, D, 1992. Evidence for pair-bond formation in Kittiwakes (*Rissa tridactyla*) prior to occupation of the breeding sites on Lundy. *Annual Report of the Lundy Field Society* 43, 36–41.

Daniels, D, Heath, J, & Rawson, W, 1984. A declaration of intent in the Kittiwake Gull (*Rissa tridactyla*). *Animal Behaviour* 35, 81–93.

Eaton, A D, 1988. The organisation of perceptual processing in sika deer (*Cervus nippon nippon*). *Annual Report of the Lundy Field Society* 39, 50-58.

Gray, P, 1991. *Psychology*. New York: Worth Publishers Inc.

Plate 1 Metamorphosed sedimentary rocks on Lundy, near the landing beach. (Jill Lang)

THE GEOLOGY OF LUNDY — SANDY SMITH AND CLIVE ROBERTS

Plate 2 The Lundy granite; white alkali feldspar megacrysts in a groundmass of alkali and plagioclase feldspar, quartz, biotite and muscovite. (Jill Lang)

THE GEOLOGY OF LUNDY — SANDY SMITH AND CLIVE ROBERTS

Plate 3   Dykes intrude the Lundy granite. (Jill Lang)

THE GEOLOGY OF LUNDY — SANDY SMITH AND CLIVE ROBERTS

Plate 4   One of the best preserved prehistoric hut circles at North End. (National Trust)

THE ARCHAEOLOGY OF LUNDY — CAROLINE THACKRAY

Plate 5   Keith Gardner, standing by the early Christian stones, explaining the 1969 excavations at Beacon Hill to LFS members.   (CJ Webster, 1996)

THE ARCHAEOLOGY OF LUNDY — CAROLINE THACKRAY

Plate 6   Diver with recording slate.

MARINE ARCHAEOLOGY —PHILIP ROBERTSON AND JOHN HEATH

Plate 7

Stepway leading to the cargo hold on the MV Robert.

MARINE ARCHAEOLOGY
PHILIP ROBERTSON AND JOHN HEATH

Plate 8   Puffin in Jenny's Cove

THE BIRDS OF LUNDY — TONY TAYLOR

Plate 9   Three breeding guillimots, one defending its chick against predation by a herring gull.

THE BIRDS OF LUNDY — TONY TAYLOR

Plate 10   Whitethroat

THE BIRDS OF LUNDY — TONY TAYLOR

Plate 11

Veery: a North American species, ringed on Lundy in 1987.

THE BIRDS OF LUNDY — TONY TAYLOR

Plate 12   Manx shearwater.

THE BIRDS OF LUNDY — A M TAYLOR

Plate 13   Pigmy shrew *Sorex minutus*

WILD MAMMALS OF LUNDY — IAN LINN

Plate 14   Black rat *Rattus rattus*

WILD MAMMALS OF LUNDY — IAN LINN

Plate 15   Brown rat *Rattus norvegicus*

WILD MAMMALS OF LUNDY — IAN LINN

Plate 16   Feral goats *Capra hircus*

WILD MAMMALS OF LUNDY — IAN LINN

Plate 17   Soay sheep *Ovis Orientalis*

WILD MAMMALS OF LUNDY — IAN LINN

Plate 18
Sika deer *Cervus nippon*

WILD MAMMALS OF LUNDY
IAN LINN

Plate 19   *Cteniopus sulphureus*

NON-MARINE INVERTEBRATES — TONY PARSONS

Plate 20   Damselfly *Calopteryx virgo*

NON-MARINE INVERTEBRATES —TONY PARSONS

Plate 21   Green hairstreak *Callophrys rubi*

NON-MARINE INVERTEBRATES — TONY PARSONS

Plate 22   Ichneumon *Eniscospilus ramidulus*

NON-MARINE INVERTEBRATES —TONY PARSONS

Plate 23

Lundy cabbage
Coincya wrightii

(Lorna Gibson)

BOTANICAL STUDIES — ELIZABETH HUBBARD

Plate 24

Flowers of the Lundy cabbage
Coincya wrightii

(Lorna Gibson)

BOTANICAL STUDIES — ELIZABETH HUBBARD

Plate 25   Flowers of the balm-leaved figwort *Scrophularia scorodonia*   (Lorna Gibson)

BOTANICAL STUDIES — ELIZABETH HUBBARD

Plate 26

Bog asphodel
Narthecium ossifragum

(Lorna Gibson)

BOTANICAL STUDIES — ELIZABETH HUBBARD

Plate 27

Heath spotted orchid
Dactylorhiza maculata subsp. *ericetorum*

(Lorna Gibson)

BOTANICAL STUDIES — ELIZABETH HUBBARD

Plate 28   Bog pimpernel *Anagallis tenella* (Lorna Gibson)

BOTANICAL STUDIES — ELIZABETH HUBBARD

Plate 29   Carpet of thrift *Armeria maritima* on the west sidelands (Lorna Gibson)

BOTANICAL STUDIES — ELIZABETH HUBBARD

Plate 30   View of Pondsbury in August 1979

FRESHWATER HABITATS OF LUNDY — JENNIFER J GEORGE

Plate 31   The Rocket Pole pond

FRESHWATER HABITATS OF LUNDY — JENNIFER J GEORGE

Plate 32   View of the larger pond at Quarter Wall

FRESHWATER HABITATS OF LUNDY — JENNIFER J GEORGE

Plate 33 The Quarry Pool in June 1996

FRESHWATER HABITATS OF LUNDY — JENNIFER J GEORGE

Plate 34 A ballan wrasse swims through the kelp forest in shallow water at Montagu Bay. The kelp stipes are colonised by a distinctive assemblage of red algae. Picture width c. 2m.

MARINE BIOLOGICAL RESEARCH — KEITH HISCOCK

Plate 35   Animal dominated rocks with a red algae at 20m depth on the sheltered east coast off the Knoll Pins. The rocks are dominated by a turf of sea firs and branching sea mats with sea fans and red sea fingers present. Picture width c. 1.5m.

MARINE BIOLOGICAL RESEARCH — KEITH HISCOCK

Plate 36 A concentration of rare species under an overhang at the Knoll Pins. The sunset cup coral, carpet coral (scarcely visible), brown cup coral, pink sea fingers and the white sponge are nationally rare or scarce species. Picture width c. 60cm.

MARINE BIOLOGICAL RESEARCH — KEITH HISCOCK

Plate 37   Community off the Hen and Chickens at 25m depth typical of tide-swept underwater rocks and including jewel anemones, oaten pipes hydroid and yellow cushion sponge. Picture width c. 20cm.

MARINE BIOLOGICAL RESEARCH — KEITH HISCOCK

Plate 38

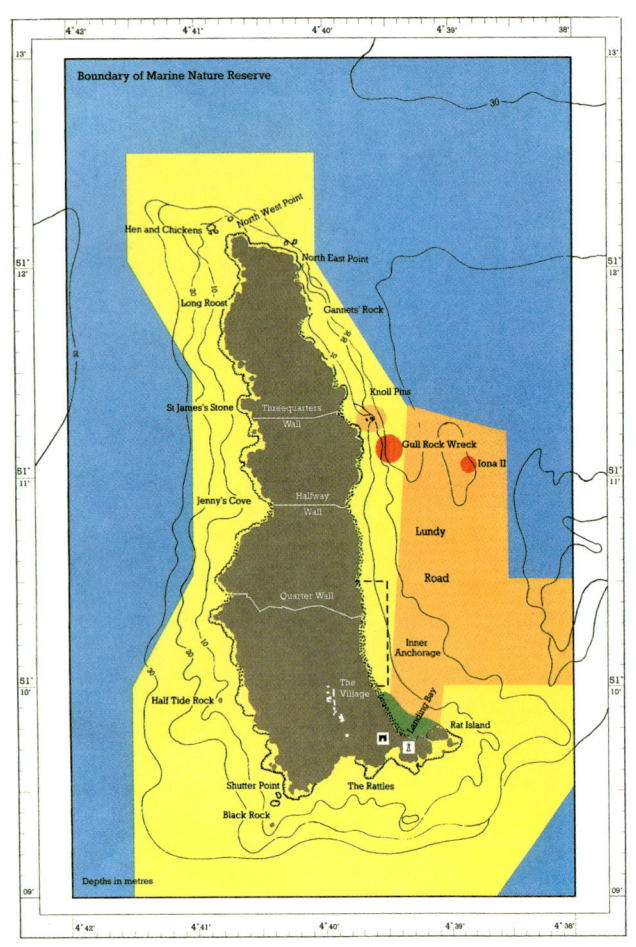

The Zoning Scheme (revised version 1995)

**MARINE NATURE RESERVE
ROBERT IRVING AND PAUL GILLILAND**

This map is illustrative not definitive

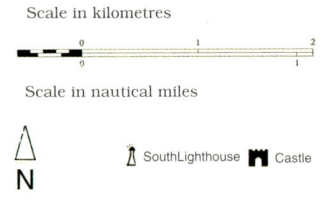

Scale in kilometres

Scale in nautical miles

N   South Lighthouse   Castle

Based upon Admiralty Chart 1164 with the permission of the controller of Her Majesty's Stationery Office ©Crown Copyright

Activity		General Use Zone	Recreational Zone	Refuge Zone	Sanctuary Zone	Archaeology Protection Zone
Recreational	Diving	Yes	Yes	Yes	Yes	No
	Snorkelling[1]	No	Yes	No	No	No
	Swimming[1]	No	Yes	No	No	No
	Spearfishing	No	No	No	No	No
Commercial	Trawling	Yes	No	No	No	No
	Dredging	Yes	No	No	No	No
	Potting	Yes	Yes	Yes[2]	Limited[3]	No
	Tangle nets	Yes	No	Limited[4]	No	No
	Fixed nets	Yes	No	Limited[4]	No	No
Collecting	Group educational excursions	Permit	Permit	Permit	Permit	No
	Scientific research	Permit	Permit	Permit	Permit	Permit

Plate 39   Key to Zoning Scheme

MARINE NATURE RESERVE — ROBERT IRVING AND PAUL GILLILAND

Plate 40   Snorkelling

LUNDY WARDENS — EMMA PARKES

Gulland, F M D, 1992. The soay sheep of Lundy. *Annual Report of the Lundy Field Society* 43, 50-51.
Hook, O, 1963. Grey seals (*Halichoerus grypus*) at Lundy. *Annual Report of the Lundy Field Society* 16, 24-25
Langham, A & M. 1984. *Lundy*. Second Edition. Newton Abbot: David and Charles.
Lea, S E G, 1984. *Instinct, Environment and Behaviour*. London: Methuen.
Lea, S E G, Daley, C, Boddington, P J C, & Morison, V, in press. Diving patterns in shags and cormorants (*Phalacrocorax*): tests of an optimal breeding model. *IBIS*.
Loyd, L W R, 1925. *Lundy: its History and Natural History*. London: Longmans, Green and Co.
Parsons, E, 1972. Lundy Ponies. *Annual Report of the Lundy Field Society* 23, 59.
Perrin, M R, & Gurnell, J, 1971. Rats on Lundy: a report. *Annual Report of the Lundy Field Society* 22, 35-40.
Randle, H D, 1992. The Lundy North Devon cattle: an insight into their social behaviour. *Annual Report of the Lundy Field Society* 43, 52-67.
Randle, H D, 1993. Lamb play behaviour: behavioural and ecological influences. *Annual Report of the Lundy Field Society* 44, 36-43.
Randle, H D, 1994. The Lundy ponies: the importance of personality. *Annual Report of the Lundy Field Society* 45, 35-42.
Randle, H D, 1994b. *Adaptation and Personality in Cattle*. Unpublished PhD thesis. University of Exeter.
Randle, H D, 1995. Can cattle think? In S M Rutter, J Rushen, H D Randle & J C Eddison (eds), *Proceedings of the 29th International Congress of the International Society for Applied Ethology*, 17-18.
Wierenga, H K, 1990. Social dominance in dairy cattle and the influences of housing and management. *Applied Animal Behaviour Science* 27, 201-229.

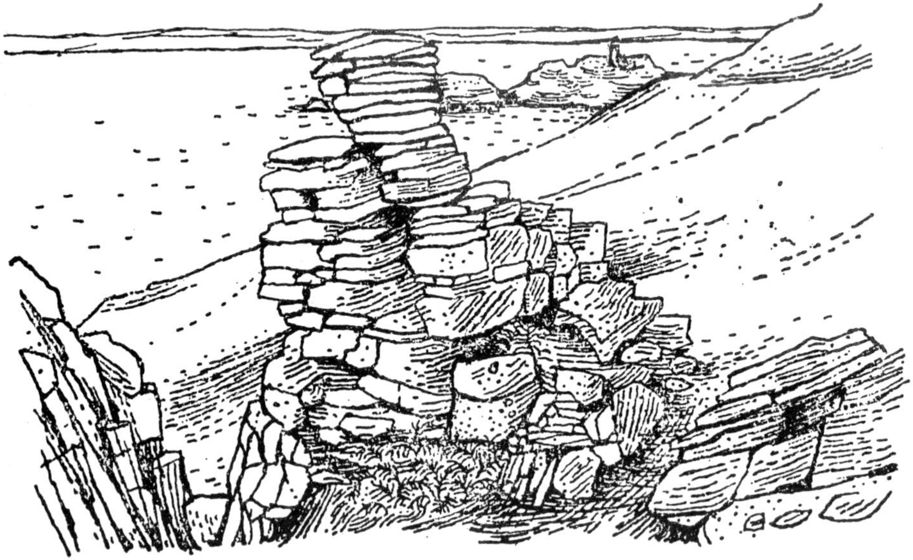

Lundy's Non-marine Invertebrates

Tony Parsons

Introduction

The invertebrates include insects and a great many other groups such as Arachnida (spiders, harvesters, mites and their allies), Mollusca (slugs and snails), Myriapoda (centipedes and millipedes), Crustacea (woodlice) and Annelida (earthworms and leeches). The term 'non-marine' reminds us that there are also many marine invertebrates (see also Hiscock, this volume). There are a number of reasons why a knowledge of the invertebrates of Lundy is important:-

1. Studies on the invertebrates may help in understanding the local history of individual species.
2. Many flying insects arrive regularly on the island and studies of these may advance our knowledge of insect movements.
3. In the case of some species which are scarce and/or localised elsewhere but have strong populations on the island, conservation is of particular importance.
4. Conservation requires knowledge of the biology of the species and knowledge of the island's invertebrates may assist specialists in such studies.
5. Most of the island is a Site of Special Scientific Interest (SSSI) and management policies need to reflect the requirements of species which are generally local or scarce or are important on the island.
6. There is a small number of people who will willingly travel to the island to see good populations of scarce insects (in the same way that larger numbers come for the birds); hence the invertebrates may help, in a small way, in the financial viability of the island.

Residents and visitors

At the end of the last Ice Age sea-levels were much lower than they are today, due to the amount of water locked up in ice and snow, and Lundy was most probably connected to the mainland. As the ice melted and the sea rose (very gradually, in a series of fluctuations), some invertebrates which were gradually moving north, following the retreating ice, had an opportunity to reach the island. Other species, moving north at later dates, would have failed to cross to the island before its insulation. For example, the centipede *Lithobius borealis*, widespread under heather on the island, is likely to have been a fairly early arrival. This is probably true, also, of its relative *L. forficatus* but we cannot be certain because this common species is often found associated with man and could possibly have been carried to the island with materials or supplies at a later date.

It seems likely that insulation occurred around 8,000 years ago, although the critical time would have varied for different species (the environment around the island would have changed over the years as the sea advanced). One species which is common on the island is the field grasshopper *Chorthippus brunneus* which can fly well. However, its flightless relative the meadow grasshopper *C. parallelus*, which is also abundant on the mainland, does not occur and this suggests that these grasshoppers arrived too late to use the land bridge. With some flightless species, there were still possibilities for natural arrival on the island after insulation. For example, many spiders disperse by casting a silken thread into the air and using this as a 'hang-glider'. Evidence from such islands as Krakatoa and Surtsey suggests that such spiders are often amongst the first colonists. Other species may have arrived, on occasion, on natural flotsam although this is not likely to have been a major factor in colonisation. Much more likely is the carriage of species by man, as hitch-hikers in supplies or associated with introduced plants (perhaps as larvae, in galls or leafmines, or associated with soil around the roots). It is a reasonable assumption that numerous species have been carried to the island in this fashion.

On warm days between April and October, the air over southern England carries vast numbers of flying insects. Some are strong fliers, deliberately dispersing in a particular direction. Others are weak fliers, virtually drifting on the wind. Huge numbers of these insects arrive on Lundy each year but most pass unnoticed, either because of their small size, or because they fly at night. Some may find the island suitable for habitation (and may reinforce an existing population) while, to others, it may be totally unsuitable, perhaps because a specific host or larval habitat is absent. Single records of conspicuous species are likely to fall into the latter category, such as the damselfly *Calopteryx virgo* in 1985.

Even with relatively conspicuous species such as the butterflies, problems arise which are difficult to solve. The green hairstreak *Callophrys rubi* was only recorded for the first time in 1983 but has been seen since and undoubtedly is resident on the island. Has it always been an inconspicuous resident or is it a recent colonist? The brown argus *Aricia agestis* was recorded before the Second World War then one appeared in 1989. This butterfly breeds on rock-rose but is also known to be able to use storksbills. Has there been a tiny population on the island, unnoticed for over 50 years, or is this merely a rare vagrant?

The woodlouse-like 'pill millipede' *Glomeris marginata* was found in the Quarries in 1983. It usually occurs on calcareous soils and is a surprising denizen of a granite island but, presumably, has a viable population. When and how did it arrive on the island and why can it survive here but not in similar conditions elsewhere?

Some species which are widespread in south-west England are not as common as they used to be on the mainland (through habitat degradation or other changes). Lundy, however, holds particularly good populations of a few of these. The thrift clearwing *Bembecia muscaeformis* is a small moth which is restricted to the habitat of its food plant and is localised on the mainland. Lundy, however, has an exceptionally strong population of this species. Similarly, there are thriving populations of the grayling butterfly *Hipparchia semele*, the green tiger beetle *Cicindela campestris*, the ground beetle *Carabus granulatus*, the rose chafer *Cetonia aurata*, the sulphur beetle *Cteniopus sulphureus* and the very large fly *Tachina grossa*. The latter is a parasitoid (the accepted term, nowadays, for such a 'parasitic' species) of large moths, particularly the oak eggar *Lasiocampa quercus* and the fox moth *Macrothylacia rubi*, both of which are common on the island, and is a local species only found consistently in Devon and Cornwall. The solitary wasp *Ancistrocerus oviventris* is common on the island and is parasitised by a large, black ichneumon *Acroricnus stylator* which is also common on Lundy but is very scarce elsewhere.

Many insects live in association with particular plants. Lundy has an exceptionally rich flora for a granite island, and some plant/insect associations are of paramount importance. Balm-leaved figwort *Scrophularia scorodonia* is a relatively rare plant in Britain and is home to a tiny moth *Nothris congressariella* which has now been looked for (and immediately found) in the plant on Lundy. It is known, otherwise, only from the Scillies. Lundy cabbage *Coincya wrightii* occurs nowhere else in the world and has its quota of 'hangers-on'. The ecology of this plant's invertebrates has been the subject of a special study for the past three years, not least because one tiny species of leaf beetle, *Psylliodes luridipennis*, only occurs on this cabbage and, therefore, Lundy has the entire world population of this beetle.

Other scarce species probably have established populations on the island but are either difficult to identify, have limited flight periods, or are inconspicuous because of their habits or habitat. One such is the large rove beetle *Staphylinus dimidiaticornis* which appears to be established on the island but has only been recorded on one day (when several were present). A female of the very rare ichneumon *Dicaelotus fitchi* was found in 1983, there being only five known specimens of this species at that time; then, in 1986, a male of the same species was found. It seems reasonable to assume that there is a resident population of this little parasite on the island but it is so rare that nothing whatsoever is known about its biology. Similarly, Lundy provided the first British record of the tiny ichneumon *Polyblastus nanus*. All *Polyblastus* species are parasitoids of sawflies and it is safe to include *P. nanus* in this but there is undoubtably a viable population of this species on the island which cannot be included, at present, in any conservation regime since nothing is known about it.

Research: past, present and future

In the past twenty years or so, the study of invertebrates has been advanced considerably by the use of more sophisticated equipment, such as light traps which have been used on Lundy in recent years. Actinic ultra-violet, mercury-vapour and mercury-vapour / tungsten-halogen ('blended') lights have all been used, although the catches from the first-named tend to be lower. Not only are moths attracted to these traps. Many caddis-flies, night-flying parasitic hymenoptera and beetles are regularly caught, with smaller numbers of other orders. Unfortunately, the use of such traps does require a generator and, on Lundy, this considerably increases the effort required to record in areas beyond the south-east corner. Two previously unrecorded pyralid moths, *Catoptria pinella* and *C. margaritella*, both uncommon wetland species, were located in St John's Valley in 1995 by the use of a blended light. This demonstrates the potential for finding new and important species and also indicates the importance of the small wetland of St John's Valley.

To the best of my knowledge, very little work has been undertaken with pit traps and none at all with Malaise traps. The former are pots sunk into the ground to monitor terrestrial invertebrates and the latter are large, tent-like structures used to monitor flying insects. One problem with the use of Malaise traps is that very large samples of insects can be captured in a short time. This means that the user must have the time and expertise (or contacts) to be able to sort out and identify the catch. Massive samples are only of value once the contents are identified and excessive use of such traps could damage the populations which are being studied. Nevertheless, work on the mainland indicates that a small number of species are unlikely to be located without the use of such equipment.

Another technique which is beginning to be used on the island is that of rearing insects. Collecting eggs, larvae, pupae or apparently parasitised adults will add considerably to our knowledge in due course. Rearing is not particularly difficult in most cases but does require a degree of self-discipline in feeding and caring for one's charges. Often, even the simplest rearing, that of hatching out a pupa, will provide interesting results. Pupal cases of a small braconid parasitoid of the cream-spot tiger *Arctia villica* collected on the island produced not only the parasitoid *Apanteles villanus* but also two 'hyperparasites' which are parasitoids of the *Apanteles*, the ichneumons *Lysibia nana* and *Gelis instabilis*. A small pupa collected in St Helen's Copse in 1995 produced a hoverfly, *Meliscaeva auricollis* which had been recorded on only one previous occasion.

One candidate for study could be the night-flying ichneumon *Enicospilus ramidulus* which is a regular visitor to light traps on the island. Little is known about this large, orange-brown 'ophion' with a black end to its abdomen. Old records from elsewhere suggest that it is a parasitoid of various medium-sized moths but it is so frequent on Lundy that either its host must be abundant or it must have a range of hosts. Rearing identified moth larvae might provide the answer.

For those who might wish to conduct further research on the invertebrates of Lundy, there are many possibilities. The distribution of most species on the island is imperfectly known. The numbers of many species vary from year to year, either as a result of variable breeding conditions on the island or of variable rates of immigration. Census work on many species, particularly some of the more conspicuous ones such as the butterflies, bumble-bees and social wasps, might help eventually in the correlation of climatic conditions and populations. Ecological work could take two main directions. Firstly, studies on the communities of certain habitats, whether of individual plant species such as turkey oak or creeping willow, or of wider communities such as short turf or wet heath, would be invaluable. Secondly, as has already been mentioned, the rearing of early stages can be very productive. Even the simple counting of butterflies, dragonflies and damselflies, rose-chafers and other species in a given area will always be of historical interest and may be of use in long-term population studies.

Around 1,600 species of invertebrates have been recorded on the island so far and, undoubtedly, very many more will be found. With some groups, there are papers published in the Field Society's Annual Reports which collate existing records up to a certain date and which form a strong basis for future studies. Examples are the beetles (Coleoptera) in Welch's paper in 1969 and in Brendell's synopsis in 1975; the flies (Diptera) in Lane's synopsis in 1977; the bugs (Hemiptera) in Alexander's synopsis in 1991; and the spiders (Araneae) in Howes' paper in 1968 (which includes harvesters and pseudoscorpions) and in Alexander's synopsis in 1989, with an addendum covering the Hemiptera and the Araneae in the 1992 Report (Alexander 1992). The freshwater biology has been covered in a series of papers by George and others; these include George (1978), George & Stone (1979), George & Stone (1980) and George & Sheridan (1986).

Unfortunately, information on some groups is scattered throughout the literature both within the Society's Annual Reports and also, on occasion, in equally obscure, specialist books and journals. For example, the earliest records of moths and butterflies (Lepidoptera) from Lundy known to me are in a note in *The Entomologist* in 1894 (referring to a small collection made by Chase), and in the 1907 paper by Longstaff in *The Entomologist's Monthly Magazine* and in his book about the Morthoe area. The next major lists of Lepidoptera are those of Dymond (1972 & 1973) and a note by Sherwood on the butterflies in 1974 (Sherwood 1974). Since 1985, the Lepidoptera have been listed separately in the Society's Annual Report each year. Early records of ants and species associated with ants are to be found in Donisthorpe's two books, both published in 1927. The excellent book on the Fauna and Flora of the Ilfracombe District, edited by Palmer (1946), contains many Lundy records (although most of these are also covered by other references). The maps produced by the Biological Records Centre (BRC), often used in publications such as *The Moths and Butterflies of Great Britain and Ireland* (edited by Heath 1976) and editions of *The Provisional Atlas of the Insects of the British Isles* (published by the BRC), sometimes indicate Lundy records which do not appear elsewhere and which were presumably passed direct to the BRC.

Amongst the references to invertebrates should be mentioned those on the ectoparasites and one on the endoparasites. I would emphasise that these are the papers of which I am personally aware and that others may also exist. The main articles are by Gordon Thompson which, apart from his papers in the 1952, 1953, 1954 and 1956 Annual Reports, consist of several papers in *The Entomologist's Monthly Magazine* during 1955 to 1957. They refer to ticks, fleas, lice and flat-flies. Arthur's papers published in *Parasitology* (Arthur 1955 & 1957) relate to a species of tick then believed to be new to science, *Ixodes thompsoni* Arthur (= *I. festai* Rondelli), which was found on Lundy; and Thompson and Arthur published a joint paper in 1955 on ticks from birds which included many Lundy records (Thompson & Arthur 1955). Mead-Briggs' 1967 paper also relates to *I. festai*, from Lundy. A valuable study which is unlikely to be repeated or expanded soon is the work of Barbara Cole in the 12th Annual Report (Cole 1959) on the endoparasites found on the island.

Conclusion

The study of invertebrates on Lundy is progressing gradually from a series of lists of species found (which, in themselves, are of great importance) to a multi-disciplinary study involving the flora, the geology, the climate and land management. Straight identifications of species are still of great importance but ecological studies have now taken their rightful place alongside these. One point worthy of mention here is that any information which is not published and therefore not accessible to future workers, is lost. I would plead for publication, within the *Annual Report of the Lundy Field Society*, of either the results of any work or, at least, a resumé, with relevant references.

References

The following list of references to the invertebrates of Lundy includes major items and some which are relatively obscure. It does not include references to all articles on invertebrates in the Reports. Since 1983, there have been many notes and lists published in this journal which should be accessible to anyone who is interested. Students of Lundy should also be aware of the Index to Lundy Field Society Reports 1947-1990, by Chris Webster, published by the Society in 1991. I believe it is worth mentioning here that any branch of the Public Library Service can provide any reference held by the British Library (providing an absolutely accurate reference is given) on payment of a small fee.

Alexander, K N A, 1989. The spiders of Lundy. *Annual Report of the Lundy Field Society* 40, 60-64.

Alexander, K N A, 1991. The Hemiptera of Lundy. *Annual Report of the Lundy Field Society* 42, 101-105.

Alexander, K N A, 1992. Some additions to the spiders & Hemiptera of Lundy. *Annual Report of the Lundy Field Society* 43, 113-114.

Arthur, D R, 1955. *Ixodes thompsoni* sp.n. from Lundy [= *I. festai* Rondelli]. *Parasitology* 45, 131-140.

Arthur, D R, 1957. The male of *Ixodes thompsoni* Arthur [= *I. festai* Rondelli]. *Parasitology* 47, 347-349.

Brendell, M, 1975. Coleoptera of Lundy. *Annual Report of the Lundy Field Society* 26, 29-53.

Cole, B, 1959. A report on the endoparasites found on Lundy, 1956-7. *Annual Report of the Lundy Field Society* 12, 31-34.

Dymond, J N, 1973. Butterflies in 1972. *Annual Report of the Lundy Field Society* 23, 38.

Dymond, J N, 1974. Butterflies and moths. *Annual Report of the Lundy Field Society* 24, 24-27.

George, J J, 1978. The freshwater fauna of Lundy. *Annual Report of the Lundy Field Society* 29, 46-48.

George, J J, & Sheridan, S P, 1986. Further investigations of the flora and fauna of the Lundy freshwater habitats. *Annual Report of the Lundy Field Society* 37, 35-46.

George, J J, & Stone, B M, 1979. The flora and fauna of Pondsbury. *Annual Report of the Lundy Field Society* 30, 20-31.

George, J J, & Stone, B M, 1980. A comparative investigation of the freshwater flora and fauna of the Lundy ponds. *Annual Report of the Lundy Field Society* 31, 19-34.

Howes, C A, 1969. A report on the arachnids of Lundy. *Annual Report of the Lundy Field Society* 19, 33-36.

Lane, R P, 1977. The Diptera (two-winged flies) of Lundy Island. *Annual Report of the Lundy Field Society* 28, 15-31.

Mead-Briggs, A R, 1967. *Ixodes festai* – an ectoparasite of wild rabbits on the islands of Herm, Tresco and Lundy. *Entomologist's Monthly Magazine* 103, 115-119.
Palmer, M G, (Ed.), 1946. *The fauna and flora of the Ilfracombe District of North Devon*. Exeter: James Townsend & Sons.
Sherwood, B R, 1975. Outline survey of the Rhopalocera of Lundy. *Annual Report of the Lundy Field Society* 25, 70 & 72-73.
Thompson, G B, 1953. Ectoparasites. *Annual Report of the Lundy Field Society* 6, 35-36.
Thompson, G B, 1954. Ectoparasites. *Annual Report of the Lundy Field Society* 7, 24-27.
Thompson, G B, 1955. Ectoparasites. *Entomologist's Monthly Magazine* 91, 4-6.
Thompson, G B, 1955. Ectoparasites. *Entomologist's Monthly Magazine* 91, 43-45.
Thompson, G B, 1955. Ectoparasites. *Annual Report of the Lundy Field Society* 8, 30-1.
Thompson, G B, 1956. Ectoparasites. *Annual Report of the Lundy Field Society* 9, 21.
Thompson, G B, 1957. Ectoparasites. *Annual Report of the Lundy Field Society* 10, 40-41.
Thompson, G B, 1957. Ectoparasites. *Entomologist's Monthly Magazine* 93, 189-190.
Thompson, G B, 1957. Ectoparasites. *Entomologist's Monthly Magazine* 93, 213-216.
Thompson, G B, and Arthur, DR, 1955. Records of ticks collected from birds in the British Isles – 2. *Annals and Magazine of Natural History* series 12, 8, 57-60.
Webster, C J, 1991. *Annual Reports 1947-1990: Index and Contents*. Taunton: Lundy Field Society.
Welch, R C, 1970. Coleoptera of Lundy and additions to the Coleopterous fauna of Lundy. *Annual Report of the Lundy Field Society* 20, 33-43.

Additional Reading

Anon. 1894. [A few Lepidoptera collected on Lundy by R.W.Chase]. *Entomologist* 27, 203.
Anon. 1987. A note on woodlice on Lundy, 1986. *Annual Report of the Lundy Field Society* 37, 56.
Bristow, CR, Mitchell, S.H. and Bolton, DE, 1993. *Devon Butterflies*. Tiverton: Devon Books.
Bristowe, WS, 1929. The spiders of Lundy Island. *Proceedings of the Zoological Society* 2, 235-244.
Cleave, J, 1981. Vyne School biology field trip – July 1979 [dragonflies]. *Annual Report of the Lundy Field Society* 31, 67-69.
Couatarmanac'h, A & Linn, IJ 1988. Two fleas new to the Lundy list. *Report of the Transactions of the Devon Association for the Advancement of Science* 120, 143-153.
Donisthorpe, HSt.JK, 1927. *British ants*. London: George Routledge & Sons.
Donisthorpe, HSt.JK, 1927. *The guests of British ants*. London: George Routledge & Sons.
Garrett-Jones, C, 1969. Early July on Lundy: butterflies and moths recorded. *Annual Report of the Lundy Field Society* 19, 30-33.
Jones, M, 1965. Invasion of dragonflies. *Annual Report of the Lundy Field Society* 16, 22-23.
Longstaff, GB, 1907. First notes on the Lepidoptera of Lundy Island. *Entomologist's Monthly Magazine* 44, 241. [This is reprinted within the following reference.]
Longstaff, GB, 1907. *Lepidoptera and other insects observed in the parish of Mortehoe, N.Devon.* (Third edition). London: Mitchell, Hughes & Clarke.
Marshall, FR, 1970. Orthoptera on Lundy. *Annual Report of the Lundy Field Society* 20, 33.

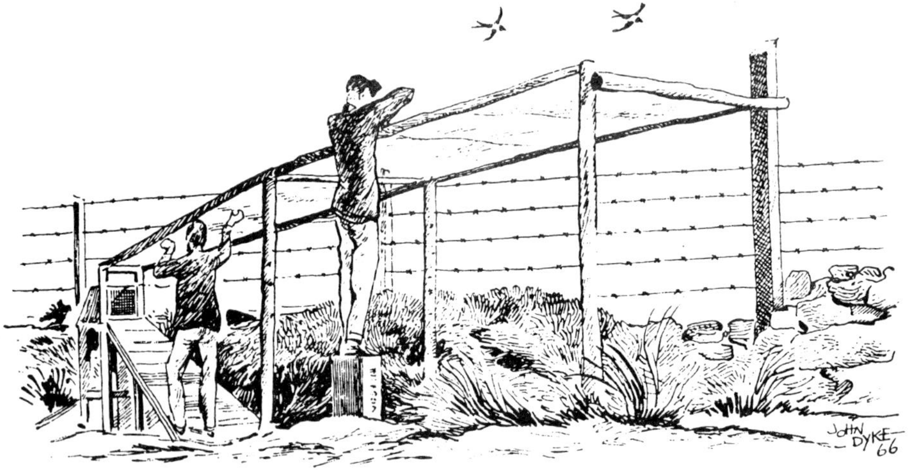
JOHN
DYKE
66

Botanical Studies

Elizabeth Hubbard

The natural history of Lundy has been extensively studied in the fifty years of the Lundy Field Society's existence. Understandably most emphasis has been on the fauna – especially the bird life – but the flora has not been totally neglected, with the result that 517 species have been recorded at some time or another. Some of these are ephemeral and some may have been misidentified, so that the resident plant population is rather less than this figure and it is these that the visitor is most likely to see.

Lundy's flora

For those unfamiliar with the island, a brief descriptive tour of the flora is perhaps in order here, to provide one with a feeling for what is on offer. From the Landing Beach, the way to the island plateau is by the Beach Road and, as one ascends, it is apparent that, broadly speaking, the island's floral habitats fall into two distinct categories: the vegetation of the sidelands and that of the plateau.

The Beach Road has been hewn out of the shale and the dip of the laminated rock makes it prone to rock fall and soil slippage. In this area grows the Lundy cabbage *Coincya wrightii*, unique to the island and all the more remarkable that a brassica should find a home on such an acid soil. Also noticeable are wall pennywort *Umbilicus rupestris*, sheepsbit *Jasione montana*, ivy-leaved toadflax *Cymbalaria muralis* and kidney vetch *Anthyllis vulneraria*, which grow on the inland side of the road. On the seaward side, balm-leaved figwort *Scrophularia scorodonia*, another rarity, grows and the margin of the road is bordered with English stonecrop *Sedum anglica*.

The lower levels of the sidelands are characterised by the growth of maritime halophilic (salt tolerant) plants such as sea campion *Silene maritima*, common and early scurvy grass *Cochlearia officinalis* and *C. danica*, cliff spurrey *Spergularia rupicola*, sea beet *Beta vulgaris*, Oraches *Atriplex patula* and *A. hastata*, thrift *Armeria maritima* and rock samphire *Crithmum maritimum*.

The eastern sidelands (of which the Beach Road forms a part) show the richest and most diverse of the island's flora. Here in the spring before the growth of the all-enveloping bracken, grow primrose *Primula vulgaris*, ground ivy *Glechoma hederacea*, celandine *Ranunculus ficaria* and bluebell *Hyacinthoides non-scripta*. Bracken *Pteridium aquilinum* is not exclusively a sidelands species and neither is foxglove *Digitalis purpurea*, but both are prominent here. Though the rhododenron thickets are attractive when in flower, their nature ensures the total exclusion of other plants.

On the rock faces of the Quarries grow broom

Sarothamnus scoparius, royal fern *Osmunda regalis* and gorse *Ulex europaeus*, while a feature of Gannets' Coombe further north is the growth of tussock sedge *Carex paniculata*. Crossing over to the west side of the island, the sidelands are exposed to the salt-laden prevailing winds and are less interesting to the botanist but can still be rewarding to the visitor: in mid summer there is often a spectacular growth of thrift *Armeria maritima* here, which may form an almost continuous pink carpet, especially in Jenny's Cove.

The island plateau, uncultivated north of Quarter Wall, is exposed, gently undulating and mostly covered by a very thin peaty soil; indeed, the North End is chiefly bare rock. Here the main plants are heather *Calluna vulgaris*, bell heather *Erica cineraria*, cross-leaved heath *Erica tetralix*, and tormentil *Potentilla erecta*. Creeping willow *Salix repens* grows in the southern part alongside heath bedstraw *Galium saxatile*, heath milkwort *Polygala serpyllifolia*, birdsfoot trefoil *Lotus corniculatus* and sheep's sorrel *Rumex acetosella* growing in the shorter turf. The exposed nature of the North End has led to impressive stands of waved heath, the plants' growth form adapting to the strong westerly winds.

An important area on the plateau is Pondsbury, the largest area of open fresh water on the island. This is surrounded by sphagnum moss *Sphagnum cuspidatum* which forms a bog-like habitat. Here can be found the common sundew *Drosera rotundiflora*, bog asphodel *Narthecium ossifragum*, heath-spotted orchid *Dactylorchis maculata*, bog pimpernel *Anagallis tenella*, water forget-me-not *Myosotis scorpioides*, and lesser spearwort *Ranunculus flammula*, all of which flower in this particular habitat. Besides these, mention should be made of Marsh St John's wort *Hypericum elodes*, which grows more peripherally. The rare fern, dwarf adders tongue *Ophioglossum azoricum*, has been found at a number of sites in the grass/heath habitat north of Pondsbury.

Botanical studies in perspective – a brief overview

Two comprehensive lists of the island's flora have been published in the Lundy Field Society's Annual Reports. The first of these was in 1971 when the 22nd Annual Report published my attempt at providing a definitive list by placing my own list, compiled between 1960 and 1971 (Hubbard 1971), in a synoptic comparison with a number of others. These were *The Atlas of British Flora* (Anon 1962); *Lundy, its History and Natural History* (Loyd 1925); *Ilfracombe Flora and Fauna* (Palmer 1946) with additions listed in the Society's 2nd Annual Report; and *Lundy* (Langham & Langham 1970), whose list was supplemented by a personal communication from Professor Harvey of Exeter University. The second list, published in the Society's 42nd report (Gibson 1991), was made by Lorna Gibson between 1989-1991. She, being an island resident over that period of time, had the advantage of observing the whole flowering season. She also attempted to photograph all of the flowers on the island. Despite some additions and some losses, the two lists tally well.

In 1979, I had access to lists made by Dr F.R. Elliston Wright made in 1933-1935, and published in the *Journal of Botany*. In his preface Dr Wright says that he considers Loyd's list, which was itself mainly derived from an earlier list made by Chanter, to be "wholly unreliable". Nevertheless it is interesting that most of the plants listed are still to be found there.

Dr Wright's outstanding contribution to the study of the Lundy flora was, of course, the identification of that primitive brassica, a fertile hybrid, the Lundy cabbage, successively named in the scientific terminology *Brassicella wrightii* in 1936 by Professor O.E. Schultz, and then amended subsequently to first *Rhyncosinapis* and then *Coincya wrightii*. A number of articles have appeared in the Annual Reports on the Lundy cabbage (Marren 1971; Cassidi 1980; Irving 1984), all of which demonstrate convincingly how the plant has extended its range from its original locality on the metamorphic Devonian slate northwards along the granite sidelands as far as Knight Templar Rock. A note in the 1993 Annual Report suggests a total of 3,000 plants between the Landing Bay and Quarter Wall.

In the 1982 Annual Report, an important article on the Lundy vegetation appeared, written by Trudy A. Watt and K.J. Kirby (Watt & Kirby 1982). This took the form of a systematic survey of the whole island with sampling of one metre squares at 200 m intervals on an E-W axis and 500 m intervals on a N-S axis. There were 45 sampling plots in all. The survey demonstrated the differences in vegetation between the east and the west sides. It is a valuable addition to the study of the island flora but because of the limitations of the sampling method, many prevalent species went unrecorded. In the 30th Annual Report (Watt 1979), Trudy Watt reported a survey of the grass growth on Lundy. This was followed a few years later by R. Takagi-Arigho publishing a list of the grasses found on the island between the months of May and October (Takagi-Arigho 1986).

Preliminary work by Mr P.D. Garbutt and Professor and Mrs Harvey, quoted in the 5th Annual Report (1951), on the differences in plant population between the east and west coasts, was followed in the following year by a more detailed study of the slopes on the northern aspect of Jenny's Cove on the west side, and the north flank of Brazen Ward on the east side. The gradients of the slopes and the pH and chloride content of the soil were measured, with the frequency of various species being noted against these parameters.

A vegetation survey was carried out in 1971 by Alice Dunn and Helen Bristow (Dunn & Bristow 1971) with the aim of helping Colin Taylor complete a map of the island vegetation. He had already surveyed the south end and the cultivated fields. They studied Ackland's Moor, Pondsbury, Middle Park and the North End.

In 1973, Paul Wilkins and Julian Debham undertook a survey of the recolonisation of the North End after the fires there in the 1930s (Wilkins & Debham 1973). They found there was little difference in soil depth or plant variety between the burned and unburned areas. Heather *Calluna vulgaris*, bell heather *Erica cineraria* and thrift *Armeria maritima* were the most common flowering plants and of the non-flowering plants, lichens, sedges, rushes and grasses dominated. They believed that lichens played a significant part in soil development.

In 1974, Dr H.C. Dawkins surveyed the fescue blanket on the east end of Rat Island, which he found to be very deep (Dawkins 1974a). He then surveyed the west end, which had been burned by a flare and noted the plants which were recolonising that area. These were important observations since Rat Island is the only part of Lundy left ungrazed. In the same year, Dr Dawkins also studied the southern slopes of Hangman's Hill below the Ugly, which he likened to a small scale version of a forest with a canopy layer of blackthorn, gorse and hawthorn, and a basal layer of shade-loving plants (Dawkins 1974b).

Rhododendron *Rhododendron ponticum* was a plant introduced by the Heaven family into the Millcombe area in the nineteenth century and it soon began to spread. J.R. Chanter in 1877 comments in his book *Lundy Island* that the plants had become naturalised and were spreading. A fire in 1926 destroyed most of the vegetation between the northernmost quarry and St Helens Coombe, but the rhododendron regenerated from the surviving underground roots and rapidly recolonised the whole area. P.R. Marren conducted a survey in 1972 and recorded the spread of seedlings to the island plateau. Since then much has been done to check the plant's spread and cut back established plants.

Other deliberately introduced species include *Escallonia* and *Hebe* bushes beside the path leading to Millcombe. It is clear from the study of photographs of the house and from early written records that many trees have been introduced to the island. Perhaps the most unexpected of these is the Japanese spindle *Euonymus japonica*. It is possible that birds may be responsible for the arrival of some of the berried species.

In 1978 and 1979, Dr J.J. George and others studied the flora of the Lundy ponds and the results were published in the 30th and 31st Annual Reports. There is a further study in the 37th Report. The plants found had already been included in the main lists.

Additional notes and flower lists have appeared over the years starting with the 1st Report when a permanent quadrat was staked out in a deeply burned area west of Middle Coombe. A list in the second report compiled by a number of Field Society members was added to the list in *Ilfracombe Flora and Fauna*. Since then lists have been contributed by Mrs Ann Westcott (e.g. Westcott 1969 & 1971) and others. One particularly interesting note was made in 1968 by Canon J. Stafford Wright who found honewort *Trinia glauca* –

unrecorded elsewhere (Wright 1968).

A report in 1980 by Mr Rob Randall tells how he failed to find purple spurge *Euphorbia peplis* (Randall 1980). He also examined the status of balm-leaved figwort *Scrophularia scorodonia*, which was becoming rare on the north coasts of Devon and Cornwall, but which was still flourishing on the east coast of Lundy.

Fungal species are listed in the 14th, 21st, 22nd, 23rd, 38th, and 43rd Annual Reports. Lichen species are listed in the 3rd, 13th and 23rd Reports, with a major lichen survey currently being undertaken by Peter James and Anne Allen. Liverworts are reported in the 13th and 26th Reports; and freshwater diatoms in the 3rd Annual Report.

Trees

With the help of Mr W.H. Dyer I surveyed the trees found growing on the island in 1969 and 1970. 433 trees were counted in the eight main wooded areas, which were all on the east side. Sycamore *Acer pseudoplatanus* was by far the most successful species and showed the most signs of regeneration. Elder *Sambucus nigra*, willow *Salix atrocinerea* and *S. caprea* and ash *Fraxinus excelsior* were the next most numerous. All trees showed signs of wind damage where they were unprotected by the bulk of the island. During the summer of 1970, beech *Fagus sylvatica*, sessile oak *Quercus petraea* and three species of pine *Pinus* spp., were planted on the north side of Millcombe in the memory of Albion Harman.

Tree planting has taken place since then and there are two reports of this. Further planting was undertaken in 1983 in Millcombe Valley, St John's Valley, north of the Ugly, and St Helen's Copse. Trees have been planted to replace mature and dying trees and also in new areas in the hope that they will support wildlife and the expectation that they will enhance the beauty of the island. The species chosen were mainly those already growing on the island, but field maple *Acer campestre*, aspen *Populus tremula* and a strawberry tree *Arbutus unedo* were also planted. A.J. Parsons questioned the wisdom of planting trees in St John's Valley, holding that its ecological importance lay in its open nature. P. de Groot replied to this in 1984 saying that the *Pinus muricata*, which had been planted close to the edge of the road to provide shelter, had not fared well and many had died. The aspen and alder had been planted to provide shelter for birds.

Management studies

In 1988, the then warden Neil Willcox, in conjunction with the Committee of the Lundy Field Society, produced the first draft of A Management Plan for Lundy (Willcox 1988); this was developed over the next few years. In 1994, English Nature published a management plan for the Marine Nature Reserve together with the island's Site of Special Scientific Interest, entitled Managing Lundy's Wildlife (English Nature 1994).

An important addition to the botanical studies mentioned above was the survey of the island's flora and fauna undertaken in 1986 by the National Trust, owners of the island since 1969. The ensuing report (National Trust 1991) was based on the observations of a team of scientists during a visit to the island, combined with references to previously published studies and consultations with involved organisations and specialist journals. The report is divided into a number of sections describing the different vegetative communities which occur on Lundy. It highlights the presence of a number of rare plants on Lundy such as the Lundy cabbage *Coincya wrightii*, balm-leaved figwort *Scrophularia scordonia*, dwarf adders tongue fern *Ophioglossum azoricum*, and hay-scented buckler fern *Dryopteris aemula*. Mention is made too of the records of plants which have appeared from time to time in disturbed ground, such as thorn apple *Datura stramonium*, henbane *Hyoscyamus niger* and small-flowered catchfly *Silene anglica*. The report includes useful comments on the accuracy of some species identifications which have been included in floral lists. In addition to flowering plants, mosses, liverworts, lichens, fungi, sedges, rushes and grasses were included in the survey. Besides reporting on what was found, the report comments on the interaction between the vegetation, the grazing of farm animals, and the fauna. It also contains some suggestions for improving the island's overall ecological balance.

In conclusion

Lundy provides opportunities for further botanical studies and it may be that, because these can be carried out in a circumscribed geographical area, comparisons can be made and lessons learned which can be applied elsewhere in what is, on the whole, inhospitable terrain.

References

Anon. 1962. *The Atlas of British Flora*.

Cassidi, M D, 1981. Status of the Lundy Cabbage *Rhyncosinapis wrightii*. *Annual Report of the Lundy Field Society* 31, 64-67.

Chanter, J R, 1877. *Lundy Island – a monograph*.

Dawkins, H C, 1974a. The fescue blanket of Rat Island. *Annual Report of the Lundy Field Society* 25, 53-55.

Dawkins, 1974b. The Ugly nanodrymion. *Annual Report of the Lundy Field Society* 25, 55-56.

Dunn, A, and Bristow, H, 1971. Vegetation survey – Lundy 1971. *Annual Report of the Lundy Field Society* 22, 42-43.

English Nature. 1994. *Managing Lundy's Wildlife: a Management Plan for the Marine Nature Reserve and the Site of Special Scientific Interest*. Okehampton: English Nature.

Garbutt, P D, 1952. A study of the vegetation of the coastal slopes of Lundy. *Annual Report of the Lundy Field Society* 6, 36-49.

Gibson, L, 1992. Lundy flora, 1989-1992. *Annual Report of the Lundy Field Society* 43, 104-112.

Hubbard, E M, 1971. A contribution to the study of the Lundy flora. *Annual Report of the Lundy Field Society* 22, 13-24.

Irving, R A, 1984. Notes on the distribution of the Lundy cabbage *Rhyncosinapis wrightii*. *Annual Report of the Lundy Field Society* 35, 25-27.

Langham, A & M 1970. *Lundy*. Newton Abbot: David & Charles.

Loyd, L R W, 1925. *Lundy, its history and natural history*. London: Longmans.

Marren, P R, 1971. The Lundy Cabbage. *Annual Report of the Lundy Field Society* 22, 27-31.

National Trust. 1991. *Biological survey – Lundy, Devon. 1986 survey*. Spitalgate, Cirencester: National Trust Biological Survey.

Palmer, M G, 1946. *Ilfracombe flora and fauna*.

Randall, R, 1980. The purple splurge [sic]. *Annual Report of the Lundy Field Society* 31, 70.

Takagi-Arigho, R, 1986. Notes on Lundy Graminae. *Annual Report of the Lundy Field Society* 37, 47-50.

Watt, T A, 1979. Grass growth on two areas of Lundy in June 1978. *Annual Report of the Lundy Field Society* 30, 37-38.

Watt, T A, & Kirby, K J, 1982. The vegetation of Lundy Island. *Annual Report of the Lundy Field Society* 33, 14-28.
Westcott, A, 1969. Some notes on the Lundy flora. *Annual Report of the Lundy Field Society* 20, 18-22.
Westcott, A, 1969. Further notes on the Lundy flora. *Annual Report of the Lundy Field Society* 22, 25-26.
Wilkins, P, and Debham, J R, 1973. Some preliminary observations on the recolonisation of the north end of Lundy. *Annual Report of the Lundy Field Society* 24, 42-50.
Willcox, N, 1988. A Management Plan for Lundy.
Wright, JS, 1968. Botanical note. *Annual Report of the Lundy Field Society* 19, 49.

The Freshwater Habitats of Lundy

Jennifer J George

Introduction

Although the natural history of Lundy has been fairly well-documented over the last 50 years, the emphasis has mainly been on the terrestrial flora and fauna, particularly the birds, and on the rich and varied marine life in the waters surrounding the island. In comparison, until the late 1970s the freshwater habitats had received little attention.

Organisms from the mainland often have great difficulty reaching islands and consequently habitats such as ponds and streams have a restricted fauna and flora when compared to similar habitats on the mainland. However, islands – because of their isolation – provide unique opportunities for species to evolve as there are usually fewer of their parasites, predators and competing species present. It should be emphasized that adaptation to, and hence survival in, a new environment is often very difficult for an organism; and island populations are more susceptible to changes in the environment and more likely to become extinct than mainland populations which characteristically possess greater genetic variation.

Ponds and streams

Lundy's ponds and streams are governed by the weather, with several drying up during prolonged drought periods and many temporary ponds, pools and streams appearing after periods of intense rainfall. Nearly all of the larger ponds are artificial, being formed from dammed-up springs or from flooding of quarries and depressions in the rock. Since 1945, one detailed classification of the freshwater habitats has been carried out, by Langham in 1967 and 1968 (Langham 1968), who listed all of the permanent (including reservoirs) and temporary habitats present at that time. Previous to 1978, when a study of Pondsbury was undertaken (George and Stone 1979) there had been no detailed investigation of the freshwater flora and fauna, but individual groups of freshwater organisms have been studied since 1945 by various workers: for example, aquatic Hemiptera (Morgan *et al* 1947), diatoms (Fraser-Barstow 1949), Crustacea and Rotifera (Galliford 1953) and the isopod *Asellus* (Williams 1962). Some aquatic organisms have been listed in the mainly terrestrial surveys of specific animal groups: for example, Coleoptera or beetles (Brendell 1975), Diptera (Lane 1977), Hemiptera or water bugs (Alexander 1991) and adult aerial stages of aquatic insects have often been recorded in the list of invertebrates/insects in the Lundy Field Society's Annual Reports since 1982. The fish, mainly carp, that occur in some of the ponds, were introduced by previous island owners, such as Martin Coles Harman, and have been detailed in two small reports (Baillie and Rogers 1976; George 1981). Further to the 1978 survey, additional work has been undertaken at Pondsbury (George and Sheridan 1986, Clabburn 1993a), the other ponds (George and Stone 1980, George and Sheridan 1986) and the Lundy streams (Long 1993).

This review will consider the flora and fauna of the five major ponds (Pondsbury, Quarry Pool, Rocket Pole pond and the two main ponds at Quarterwall), and six of the more permanent streams on the island, as well as raising some more general points relating to this aspect of island ecology.

Pondsbury

Pondsbury, which is the largest body of freshwater on the island, is surrounded by *Sphagnum bog*, heathland and rough grazing pasture (Plate 30). It is probably of natural origin although damming on the west side has increased its size and depth. It receives surface runoff from the surrounding land and has an outlet stream that flows down the Punchbowl Valley and into the sea at Jenny's Cove. During dry periods, the pond becomes reduced in size and very occasionally can dry up altogether (as it did in 1976).

The detailed surveys of Pondsbury, all carried out in the months of July and August, by George and Stone (1979), George and Sheridan (1986) and by Clabburn (1993a), not only give a comprehensive account of the habitat at a particular time, but also allow conclusions to be drawn on the colonisation and disappearance of species and therefore the stability of the ecosystem over a period of fourteen years. All three surveys employed similar sampling techniques thus allowing meaningful comparisons to be made.

The detailed mapping of the pond shows that it regularly changes shape due to varying water levels, macrophyte encroachment, silt deposition and human activity. To illustrate this, during the 1993 survey, Pondsbury covered an area of 3,900 m^2 with 92% of open water, whereas fourteen years earlier it had an area of approximately 3,300 m^2 with only 20% of open water, the rest being covered by emergent beds of *Juncus* and *Hypericum* and a carpet of *Sphagnum*.

Maximum depths of 1 - 1.2 m have been recorded in the north and east regions of the pond, which became progressively shallower to the west and south. The recording of water temperatures over a 24 hour period by Clabburn (1993 a & b) showed that considerable temperature fluctuations occur with depth, and that surface daytime temperatures were only a few degrees below ambient air temperatures.

Maximum dissolved oxygen levels are found near to the pond's surface and the 24 hour recording in 1993 showed that periods of deoxygenation occur just above the sediments in parts of the pond. However, Clabburn also showed that in these regions considerable oxygen fluctuations take place with maximum levels occurring at night, the opposite to what is normally expected. He suggests that these fluctuations relate to a daily overturn of water brought about by the wind. A small pond can become thermally stratified during the warmer day period which prevents mixing and the transference of oxygen to the deeper areas. Deoxygenation may occur in the deeper water. At night the water temperature drops and this, together with an onshore wind, would cause an overturn of water in the pond, allowing the oxygen to penetrate into water overlying the sediments.

The water chemistry of Pondsbury relates to the geology of the island which is composed of tertiary granite. All three surveys recorded an average pH of 4.8 indicating an acidic body of water. Such a constant pH over fourteen years is probably due to the large amount of *Sphagnum* moss in and around the water (Sphagnum has the ability to bind cations and release hydrogen ions in their place thus maintaining the acidity). The 1993 survey also showed a mean total hardess of 9.4 mgl^{-1} thus classifying Pondsbury as a 'soft' water body. Levels of magnesium and calcium are therefore low, but surprisingly the conductivity readings are high. Conductivity also relates to sodium and chloride levels and the closeness of the pond to the sea may be an explanation for these high levels of 420-439mμs, more typical of chalk streams (Clabburn 1993a & b).

In all three surveys, 1979, 1986 and 1993, the same twelve species of **plant** were found, with the moss *Sphagnum cuspidatum* completely dominating the entire area. However, relative abundance of the plants varied and Table 1 shows a generalised summary of species and their abundance as different sampling techniques were used. In 1979 general vegetation mapping of the entire pond was carried out followed by the detailed examination of species and their abundance along a 40 m transect line extending from the southern bank through the central area of the pond (George and Stone 1979). In 1993 the fringing macrophytes and their abundance were assessed using a quadrat 50 x 50 cm along each of the banks of the pond (Clabburn 1993a). All data were converted to the Domin scale which records abundance on a scale of 1-10, where 10 represents 91-100%, 5 is 11-25%, and 1 is just a few individuals present.

In 1979 the dominant plant on the southern side was Marsh St. John's Wort *Hypericum elodes* being present on *Sphagnum* islands in the open water as well as around the edge of the pond (Plate 30). It grew in association with Marsh Pennywort *Hydrocotyle vulgaris* and Water Forget-me-not *Myosotis scorpioides*, both of which it shaded. In 1993 two plants dominated the south side: Common Spike Rush *Eleocharis palustris* and Soft Rush *Juncus effusus* with Bog Pondweed *Potamogeton polygonifolius flora* and *Hypericum elodes* also abundant. The Soft Rush *Juncus* also dominated the north, south and eastern sides of Pondsbury in both years. A few isolated patches of the Waterwort *Elatine hexandra*, a species fairly rare in Britain, was found in 1979 and the Marsh Bedstraw *Galium palustre* was recorded on the pond fringes in 1993.

The macrophytes of Pondsbury, with the exception of *Juncus effusus* which is found in many types of wet habitat, are typical bog plants, often occurring widely on mainland Britain.

In all these surveys only a superficial examination of the **plankton** was carried out. Regular sampling throughout a year is required as populations of both phyto– and zooplankton in ponds are very variable with often one species dominating for a short period. In 1979 and 1986 plankton was sampled by taking two 10 m hauls across the open water area and in 1993, chlorophyll content (giving an indication of algal biomass present) was measured at different depths in the NE corner of Pondsbury.

In 1979 the plankton was completely dominated by a 'bloom' of the green flagellate *Euglena viridis* with the zooplankton cladocerans *Chydorus sphaericus* and *Alonella nana* (also recorded by Galliford in 1953), and the copepod *Cyclops* reasonably abundant. Several rotifers were recorded with the spiny *Keratella serrulata*, a common inhabitant of bog waters, being present in fairly large numbers. Seven years later, the dominating species was the cladoceran *Daphnia obtusa* with also *Chydorus sphaericus* and *Cyclops* fairly abundant. Chlorophyll analysis in 1993 indicated that the greatest algal biomass occurred in the surface waters with a progressive decrease with depth.

The **macroinvertebrate fauna** in all three surveys was sampled by sweep-netting through the beds of

Table 1

Relative abundance of plant species in Pondsbury

Species	Abundance using Domin Scale	
	1979	1993
Sphagnum cuspidatum Ehrh ex Hoffm emend	10	10
Hypericum elodes L.	8	4
Hydrocotyle vulgaris L.	7	3
Callitriche stagnalis Scop.	5	4
Lythrum (Peplis) portula L.	4	4
Juncus effusus L.	4	6
Juncus articulatus L.	3	3
Myosotis scorpiodes L.	4	3
Potamogeton polygonifolius (Pourret)	3	3
Eleocharis palustris (L)	3	5
Ranunculus flammula L.	2	3
Ranunculus omiophyllus Ten.	1	1
Elatine hexandra (Lapierre)	1	–
Galium palustre L.	–	2

(Domin scale: 10 = 91-100%; 9 = 76-90%; 8 = 51-75%; 7 = 34-50%; 6 = 26-33%; 5 = 11-25%; 4 = 4-10%; 1,2,3 = <4% (3 with many individuals, 2 several individuals and 1 few individuals)

vegetation for a specified period, and grabs were used for sampling the bottom sediments. Results (Table 2) showed a greater diversity of macroinvertebrates in the vegetation in 1993 than fourteen years earlier. However, this conclusion must be treated with caution as the 1993 survey was more comprehensive than the earlier surveys and consequently probably collected more of the rarer species (abundance rating 1).

However, trends can be seen concerning the more abundant species. For instance, Pondsbury is dominated by the isopod *Asellus meridianus* being particularly abundant in 1986 and 1993, where it was recorded in every sample taken. *Asellus* feeds on organic detritus that is plentiful in the bottom of the pond. The closely-related species *Asellus aquaticus* that often coexists with *Asellus meridianus* on the mainland, does not occur on Lundy, and this is in agreement with the findings of Williams (1962, 1979) who found *Asellus meridianus* on offshore islands only.

Another abundant species from 1979-93, is the common mainland flatworm *Polycelis nigra* which is predatory, feeding on worms, insect larvae and small *Asellus*. Other well-represented groups are the Hemiptera, Coleoptera and Chironomid Diptera, all invertebrates with aerial adult stages.

An interesting record is the water spider *Argyroneta aquatica* that dominated the extensive *Hypericum* beds in 1979 and was still fairly abundant fourteen years later. Also recorded as "quite abundant" by Galliford (1953), it is obviously a long-standing member of Lundy's freshwater fauna. It is an air-breather and quite capable of withstanding drought conditions.

Fewer species were found living upon and in the bottom sediments, but again, *Asellus meridianus* was dominant in the samples in all three surveys. Only one species, the oligochaete worm *Limnodrilus hofmeisteri*, was restricted to the sediments, the others occurring also in the vegetation. The bivalve mollusc *Pisidium personatum* was not found in 1979 and 1986, but it occurred in both the vegetation and sediments in 1993. This mollusc that was very abundant (over 5,000 individuals) in the sediments in 1993, appears to be a recent immigrant to the Lundy freshwater fauna.

There have been no major surveys of **fish** populations in Pondsbury. Crucian carp *Carassius carassius* have been recorded in the pond, and several were transferred to the Quarry Pool when Pondsbury dried out completely in 1976 (Baillie and Rogers 1976). In January 1977, Pondsbury was restocked with thirty carp of varying sizes and ages from Quarry Pool, and several fish were observed in Pondsbury in the summer of 1986 (George and Sheridan 1986).

In conclusion, Pondsbury can be classified as a 'soft' water body with an acidic pH that is maintained by the luxuriant growth of *Sphagnum* moss that dominates the pond. The plant species present have remained remarkably stable since 1979 and can generally be found in similar habitats on the mainland.

The fauna present is influenced by the water

Table 2   **Macroinvertebrates recorded from the vegetation in Pondsbury**
(Rare species (Scale I) found only on one occasion, not shown here)

Macroinvertebrates	1979	1986	1993
PLATHYHELMINTHES	3	5	4
Polycelis nigra (Müller)			
ANNELIDA: OLIGOCHAETA			
Lumbriculus variegatus (Müller)	2	2	4
CRUSTACEA			
Daphnia obtusa Kurz	–	3	–
Chydorus sphaericus (Muller)	2	2	–
Alonella nana (Baird)	2	–	–
Cyclops sp.	2	2	–
Asellus meridianus Racovitza	3	5	5
ARACHNIDA			
Argyroneta aquatica L.	4	2	2
Hydracarina (water mites)	2	2	2
INSECTA: ODONATA			
Sympetrum striolatum (Charpentier)	1	1	2
Enallagma cyathigerum (Charpentier)	–	–	2
INSECTA: HEMIPTERA			
Notonecta glauca L.	1	–	1
N. obliqua Thunb	2	2	2
Immature notonectids	1	2	2
Plea leachii (McGregor & Kirkaldy)	–	–	2
Callicorixa praeusta (Fieber)	1	2	3
Hespercorixa linnaei (Fieber)	–	–	2
Sigara spp.	–	–	2
Immature corixids/cymatids	1	3	3

Macroinvertebrates	1979	1986	1993
INSECTA: COLEOPTERA			
Gyrinus substriatus Stephens	2	–	–
Ilbyius quadriguttatus L.	2	–	–
Agabus bipustulatus L.	2	3	2
Hygrotus inequalis (Fabricius)	2	2	2
Hydroporus pubescens Gyllenhal	1	1	1
INSECTA: TRICHOPTERA			
Limnephilus vittatus (Fabricius) larvae	2	–	–
INSECTA: CHIRONOMIDAE			
Tanypodinae	3	2	4
Chironominae	2	2	3
MOLLUSCA			
Pisidium personatum Malm	–	–	3
TOTAL NUMBER OF SPECIES/GROUPS	23	16	36

Note: Abundance scale of 1-5   5 = over 500 individuals, 4 = 200-199, 3 = 59-199, 2= 5-49, 1 below 5.

chemistry, periodic drying up of the pond and the isolation of Lundy from the mainland. There appear to be no endemic species. Coleoptera (beetles) and Hemiptera (water bugs) are the most diverse groups in the pond, and these are characteristic of acid waters. The crustacean isopod *Asellus meridianus* has been an abundant member of the fauna for over fourteen years, and the water spider *Argyroneta aquatica* has maintained its population since 1953 when it was first recorded.

Other freshwater habitats

The other bodies of standing freshwater that have been studied in detail are the Quarry Pool, Rocket Pole pond, and the two main ponds at Quarterwall (George and Stone 1980; George and Sheridan 1986).

Quarry Pool (Plate 31)

This is a true quarry pool, a deep body of water overshadowed by steep rocky walls and some trees. It has a maximum depth of 1.7 m, and there is an outlet at the eastern side of the pool.

Rocket Pole pond (Plate 32)

This is the deepest pond on the island with a depth of 2.2 m. It has been formed from an excavation in the rock and has no through drainage.

Quarterwall pond 1 (Plate 33)

This is the larger of the two ponds and is an open body of water with fairly steep rocky banks and only a few weed beds. A maximum depth of 0.8 m was recorded in 1986. It is situated at a fairly high level on the island and probably receives little surface drainage.

Quarterwall pond 2

This is a shallow pond (maximum depth 0.4 m) with a fairly dense weed cover in the summer months. Although there are a few large rocks, the edges are marshy, and the pond has no through drainage.

All four ponds are acidic with pHs ranging from 5.0 to 5.9. At the time of sampling (summer period) the water temperatures were closely related to the ambient air temperature, and there was evidence of temperature stratification, with lower temperatures in the deeper parts of the Quarry pool and Rocket Pole pond. Light penetrates furthest in the clearer Quarry Pool and the shallower Quarterwall pond 1, whereas light penetration is poor in Rocket Pole pond which frequently has dense algal blooms in the summer. The surface waters of all four ponds appear to be well-oxygenated, but in both 1979 and 1986 the oxygen content dropped off markedly in the deeper regions of Quarry Pool and Rocket Pole pond.

Ten different **plant species** are found growing in

Table 3   Relative abundance (Domin scale) of plant species at the four ponds

Species	Quarry Pool	Rocket Pole pond	Quarterwall 1	Quarterwall 2
Fontinalis sp	4	–	–	–
Juncus effusus L.	4	4	4	9
Eleocharis palustris L.	4	7	9	4
Potamogeton polygonifolius (Pourret)	8	–	4	10
Hydrocotyle vulgaris L.	–	6	9	3
Callitriche sp	3	–	–	–
Peplis portula L.	3	–	7	8
Myosotis scorpioides L.	–	–	2	6
Anagallis tenella (L)	–	–	–	2
Ranunculus flammula L.	5	–	–	2
Total number of Species	7	3	6	8

the ponds with the most diverse flora occurring in the small Quarterwall pond 2 (Table 3). Rocket Pole pond contained the lowest numbers of plant species in both 1979 and 1986. Quarterwall pond 2 is normally completely covered with vegetation in the summer with no open water present. Quarry Pool possesses some reasonably-sized plant beds, but the least vegetation cover occurs in the Quarterwall 1 and Rocket Pole ponds that both have large stretches of open water.

Two rushes, the Soft Rush *Juncus effusus* and the Common Spike Rush *Eleocharis palustris* occur at the margins of all of the ponds, with *Juncus* being particularly abundant at Quarterwall pond 2 where it almost surrounds the whole pond. The bog pondweed *Potamogeton polygonifolius* completely dominates the small Quarterwall pond 2 and is also fairly abundant in the Quarry Pool. It is a plant characteristic of upland oligotrophic acidic waters, and there is evidence that it prefers sheltered conditions, and this may be a reason for its absence from the more exposed Rocket Pole pond.

The absence of the Marsh Pennywort *Hydrocotyle vulgaris* from the Quarry Pool may be due to the depth of the water and the lack of muddy regions in this pond. The Water Purslane *Peplis portula* is another plant restricted by depth, and this may explain its absence from Rocket Pole pond and its occurrence only in the shallow muddy area near the outflow of the Quarry Pool.

Plankton samples taken in 1979 and 1986 show that the Rocket Pole pond is very eutrophic with blooms of blue-green algae (*Microcystis, Arthrospira*) frequently occurring. This pond is used by birds, and their droppings obviously contribute nutrient to the water, thus allowing these 'pea-soup blooms' to develop. Evidence of eutrophy in the summer is also seen in the larger Quarterwall pond which is used by cattle and ponies: fairly large populations of filamentous and green algae and the desmid *Closterium* frequently occur in this pond.

Cyclopoid copepods are present in all the ponds, but appear to be particularly abundant in the larger Quarterwall pond and Quarry Pool where they dominate the zooplankton. Calanoid copepods, which are common in mainland ponds, appear to be absent on Lundy. Cladocera are reasonably abundant in the weedy Quarterwall pond and species of Rotifera are found in the open water of the other three ponds.

Macroinvertebrates found in the four ponds are listed in Table 4. The small pond at Quarterwall (Quarterwall pond 2) possesses the greatest diversity and numbers of macroinvertebrates, due mainly to the prolific plant growth in this pond. Very large numbers of the isopod crustacean *Asellus meridianus*, occur here where the decaying vegetation provides an ideal habitat for this detritus-feeding animal.

The large Quarterwall pond with its open water, appears to be an excellent habitat for water boatmen (Hemiptera) and beetles (Coleoptera) which dominate in this pond, while the sheltered waters of the Quarry Pool provide suitable conditions for the surface-dwelling forms, pond skaters (*Gerris*) and whirligig beetles (*Gyrinus*), whose presence demonstrate the importance of exposure as an environmental factor in pond ecology. The Rocket Pole pond has the smallest number of species and organisms probably due to the recurring blooms of blue-green algae which occur there.

The bottom sediments of the ponds are not rich in animal species, and only two groups are represented in all four ponds: oligochaete worms and red chironomid larvae, both tolerant of low oxygen conditions. In 1986 the pea-mussel *Pisidium*, not previously recorded, was found in the smaller pond at Quarterwall.

There have been no detailed surveys of fish in the ponds. Golden carp *Carassius auratus* are often

Table 4 Species and numbers of macroinvertebrates in the plant beds and openwater of the four ponds
(Abundance scale as in Pondsbury data)

Species	Quarry	Rocket Pole	QW1	QW2
ANNELIDA				
Lumbriculus variegatus (Müller)	---	---	2	2
CRUSTACEA				
Daphnia obtusa Kurz	---	2	---	2
Simocephalus vetulus (Müller)	---	---	---	2
Harpacticoid copepods	---	---	---	1
Asellus meridianus Racovitza	2	1	3	5
ARACHNIDA				
Hygrobatid mite	---	---	---	2

Species	Quarry	Rocket Pole	QW1	QW2
INSECTA				
Cloeon dipterum (L.)	---	1	---	2
Ischnura elegans (Van de Linden)	1	1	---	1
Sympetrum striolatum (Charpentier)	1	---	---	---
Gerris gibbifer Schum.	2	---	2	---
Notonecta obliqua Thunb.	---	---	2	2
Corixa panzeri (Fieb)	---	---	3	---
Callicorixa praeusta (Fieb.)	---	---	2	---
Sigara nigrolineata (Fieb.)	---	---	1	---
Immature corixids	---	1	2	2
Gyrinus substriatus Stephens	2	---	---	---
Hydroporus pubescens (Gyllenhal)	---	---	----	1
Ilybius quadriguttatus L	1	---	1	2
Dytiscid larvae	2	---	2	1
Helophorus grandis Illiger	---	---	---	2
Limnephilus vittatus (Fieb.)	---	---	2	1
Chironomid larva	1	2	3	2
MOLLUSCA				
Lymnaea truncatula (Muller)	---	---	---	1
TOTAL NUMBER OF SPECIES/GROUPS	8	6	12	17

ISLAND STUDIES

observed in Quarry Pool (over 100 in 1986) and Crucian carp *Carassius carassius* have also been recorded in this pond. A very large population of the mirror carp *Cyprinus carpio* occurs in the Rocket Pole pond (George 1981), and it is difficult to see how this pond with its sparse macroinvertebrate fauna and plant life can support these fish. Feeding by visitors in the summer and cannibalism of the young forms are probably contributing factors to the apparent success of this population.

Streams

Only one major survey, by Long in the summer of 1993, has been carried out on the Lundy streams. He examined the water quality and macroinvertebrate composition of six streams, four on the west side of the island and two on the east side (Fig.1).

Various physico-chemical parameters were measured, such as flow/discharge, dissolved oxygen, temperature, pH, hardness, conductivity, suspended solids, Biochemical Oxygen Demand, and these together with macroinvertebrate data were used to assess water quality. The Extence method of classifying streams into 'Excellent' to 'Unsuitable' (Extence *et al* 1987) showed that four of the streams (West 2, 3, 4 and East 2) are in the 'Good' category and that West 1 and East 1 are classified as 'Moderate'. The pH of the streams ranges from 4 – 6, and all are poor in nutrients. There is no evidence of organic pollution that may result from livestock farming; however, the lower

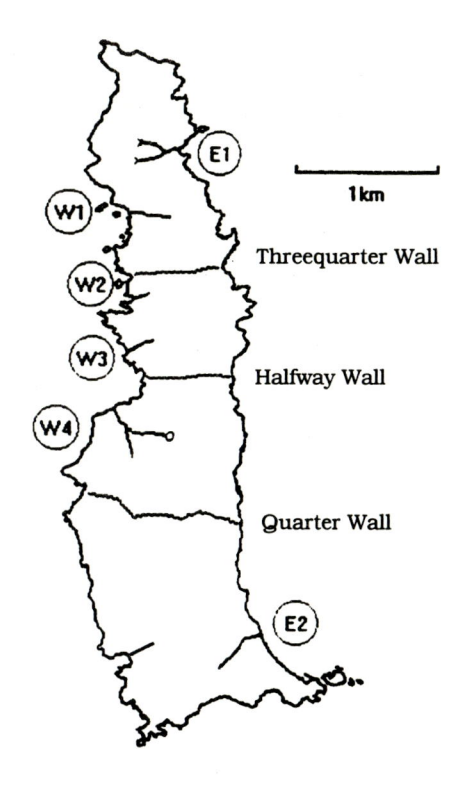

Figure 1 Location of streams (after Long 1993a)

W1 – St. Peter's Shore Stream	MR 1333 4697
W2 – St. Marks Bay stream	MR 1329 4634
W3 – Pyramid stream	MR 1330 4609
W4 - Punchbowl stream	MR 1318 4548
E1 – Gannets Bay stream	MR 1332 4570
E2 – St. John's stream	MR 1385 4384

Table 5 Summary of macroinvertebrate sampling data from the streams

	E1	E2	W1	W2	W3	W4
TRICHOPTERA						
Beraeidae	---	*	---	---	---	---
Hydroptilidae	---	---	---	*	*	*
Limnephilidae	---	*	---	---	---	---
Philopotamidae	---	*	---	*	---	*
Polycentropodidae	*	*	*	*	*	*
Psychomyidae	---	*	*	*	*	---
DIPTERA						
Ceratapogonidae	*	---	---	*	*	---
Chironomidae	*	*	*	*	*	*
Culicidae	---	*	---	---	---	---
Dixidae	---	*	---	---	---	---
Psychodidae	---	*	---	---	---	---
Simuliidae	*	*	---	*	*	*
Tipulidae	*	*	*	*	*	*
COLEOPTERA						
Dryopidae	---	---	*	*	*	---
Dytiscidae	---	*	---	---	---	---
Elmidae	*	---	---	---	---	---
Hydrophilidae	---	*	*	*	*	*
Hygrobiidae	---	---	---	---	---	*

	E1	E2	W1	W2	W3	W4
HEMIPTERA						
Corixidae	---	---	---	---	*	*
Veliidae	*	*	---	---	---	*
CRUSTACEA						
Asellidae	*	*	*	*	*	*
Crangonictidae	---	---	---	*	---	*
Cyprididae	---	*	---	*	*	---
Gammaridae	---	---	---	---	*	*
MOLLUSCA						
Hydrobiidae	---	*	*	*	*	*
Lymnaeidae	---	*	*	*	---	---
Sphaeriidae	---	*	*	*	---	---
OLIGOCHAETA	*	*	*	*	*	*
HIRUDINEA	---	---	---	*	---	---
HYDROZOA	---	---	*	*	---	---
PLATYHELMINTHES	---	*	---	---	---	*

KEY * PRESENT   --- ABSENT   (After Long 1993a&b)

half of St. John's stream (East 2) appears to be influenced on occasions by organic pollution of domestic origin.

In terms of **flora**, samples of Bryophytes were collected by Long along the length of each stream, but there was no attempt at quantitative assessment. Four species were present in all six streams: *Pellia epiphylla, Scapania undulata, Fontinalis antipyretica* and *Sphagnum* sp.

Samples of **plankton** taken at each stream's point of discharge with a FBA plankton net (0.96 mm mesh) show that there is a reasonable plankton community present with the copepod *Cyclops* and cladoceran *Daphia* predominating. A more diverse community appears to exist in the streams that have large areas of bogland in their catchments, such as Punchbowl Stream (West 4).

The comprehensive **macroinvertebrate** survey undertaken by Long (1993a & b) shows that different groups occur in different streams on the island. However, Dipteran and Trichopteran larvae are dominant in all six streams with the midge (Chironomid) larvae and the net-spinning caddis (Polycentropid) larvae families being particularly abundant. Table 5 shows the main families present in the six streams.

Molluscs are fairly prominent in the streams with the exception of the Gannets Bay stream (East 1). Hydrobiids are very abundant in St. John's stream (East 2), and the Pyramid stream (West 3). Two species of crustaceans that are commonly found on small islands, *Asellus meridianus* and *Gammarus duebeni*, are dominant members of the community.

St. John's stream (East 2) has the greatest diversity and the greatest abundance of macroinvertebrates. It is a stream that rarely dries up, and obviously provides a fairly stable environment for its fauna. It rates as 'good' on the Extence water quality scale and has a near neutral pH.

As Long points out, the fauna of the Lundy streams is impoverished when compared to similar streams on the mainland, with the mayflies (Ephemeroptera) and the stone-flies (Plecoptera) notable absentees. Adult stone-flies (and mayflies to a lesser extent) are however weak fliers and may not be able to reach Lundy from the mainland. One mayfly larva *Cloeon dipterum*, found in running waters on the mainland, has been recorded in the ponds (1979, 1986, 1993) suggesting that the short steep streams on Lundy are not a suitable habitat.

On Lundy, the main factor affecting the survival of freshwater macroinvertebrates is the periodic drying up of streams (excluding St. John's). Some organisms have mechanisms for withstanding drought conditions, and there is obviously colonisation from other habitats on the island, such as Pondsbury and St. John's stream, when favourable conditions return.

Conclusions

The flora and macroinvertebrate fauna of the Lundy freshwater habitats is fairly typical of acidic waters on the mainland. There appear to be no endemic species or varieties present, which indicates a fairly frequent renewal of organisms from the mainland. Overall, however, the fauna is impoverished compared to mainland waters, but the isolation of Lundy is probably not a major limiting factor. An important environmental factor affecting the habitats is drought, with most of the streams and several of the ponds (including Pondsbury) drying up in past years. Research in Pondsbury over fourteen years shows a remarkable stability in the composition of the flora and fauna in spite of the periodic dredging and drought that have occurred. True holoaquatic organisms, that are unable to leave the water, such as Crustacea and Oligochaeta, are able to survive periods of desiccation by encystment or production of resistant eggs. Others, such as insect larvae and molluscs, can aestivate in the bottom sediments until favourable conditions return.

The ponds and streams do display interesting differences in their flora and fauna, and these can be related to factors such as position and exposure, water chemistry, vegetation cover, amount of decaying matter present and algal blooms.

The study of Lundy's freshwater habitats provides valuable information on the composition and evolution of small island flora and fauna. Unfortunately, there have only been two major surveys of the ponds (1979, 1993) and only one of the streams (1993) in the past 50 years, all of which have been in the summer months. In future years more survey work is required at different times of the year so that the nature and evolution of the island's freshwater flora and fauna can be discussed with confidence.

References

Alexander, K N A, 1991. The Hemiptera of Lundy. *Annual Report of the Lundy Field Society* 42, 101-105.

Baillie, C C, and Rogers, M, & W, 1976. Sizes and ages of some Crucian carp on Lundy. *Annual Report of the Lundy Field Society* 27, 65-66.

Brendell, M, 1975. Coleoptera of Lundy. *Annual Report of the Lundy Field Society* 26, 29-53.

Clabburn, P A T, 1993a. *Pondsbury, Lundy Island: the study of an acid pool.* Unpublished MSc thesis. University of Cardiff.

Clabburn, P A T, 1993b. Freshwater Biological Survey of Lundy 1993: Further studies of the fauna of Pondsbury. *Annual Report of the Lundy Field Society* 44, 73-83.

Extence, C A, Bates, A J, Forbes, W J, & Barham, P J, 1987. Biologically based water quality management. *Environmental Pollution* 45, 221-236.

Fraser-Bastow, R, 1949. Freshwater Diatom Flora. *Annual Report of the Lundy Field Society* 3, 32-41.

Galliford, A L, 1953. Notes on the freshwater organisms of Lundy with especial reference to the Crustacea and Rotifera. *Annual Report of the Lundy Field Society* 7, 29-35.

George, J J, 1981. The mirror carp, *Cyprinus carpio*, of the Rocket Pole pond. *Annual Report of the Lundy Field Society* 32, 38–39.

George, J J, and Sheridan, S P, 1986. Further investigations of the flora and fauna of the Lundy freshwater habitats. *Annual Report of the Lundy Field Society* 37, 35-46.

George, J J, and Stone, B M, 1979. The flora and fauna of Pondsbury. *Annual Report of the Lundy Field Society* 30, 20-31.

George, J J, and Stone, B M, 1980. A comparative investigation of the freshwater flora and fauna of the Lundy ponds. *Annual Report of the Lundy Field Society* 31, 19-34.

Lane, R P, 1977. The Diptera (two-winged flies) of Lundy Island. *Annual Report of the Lundy Field Society* 28, 15-31.

Langham, A F, 1968. Water courses and reservoirs on Lundy. *Annual Report of the Lundy Field Society* 19, 36-39.

Long, P S, 1993a. *A study into the effects of water quality, climate, and geographical isolation on the lotic environment of Lundy Island in the Bristol Channel.* Unpublished MSc thesis, University of Cardiff.

Long, P S, 1993b. A study into the macroinvertebrate fauna and water quality of Lundy Island's lotic environment. *Annual Report of the Lundy Field Society* 44, 59-72.

Williams, W D, 1962. The geographical distribution of the isopods *Asellus aquaticus (L.) and Asellus meridianus* Rac. *Proceedings of the Zoological Society of London* 139, 75-96.

Williams, W D, 1979. The distribution of *Asellus aquaticus* and *A. meridianus* (Crustacea, Isopoda) in Britain. *Freshwater Biology* 9, 491-501.

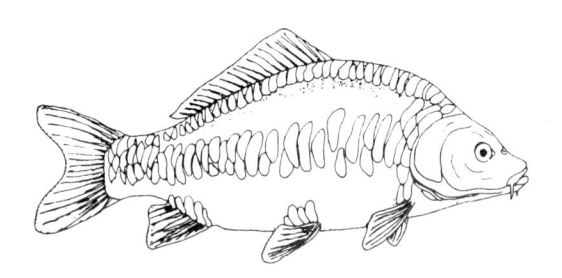

Marine Biological Research at Lundy

Keith Hiscock

Introduction

The earliest recorded marine biological studies near to Lundy are noted in the work of Forbes (1851) who took dredge samples off the east coast of the island in 1848. The first descriptions of the seashore wildlife on Lundy are those published in 1853 by the foremost Victorian marine naturalist and writer, P.H. Gosse, in the *Home Friend* (reproduced later in Gosse 1865). However, his descriptions are unenthusiastic, reveal nothing unusual and draw attention to the very few species found on the granite shores. There are further brief references to Lundy in the literature of other Victorian naturalists. Tugwell (1856) found the shores rich collecting grounds and cites the success of a collecting party who (with the help of "an able-bodied man with a crowbar") returned from Lundy in 1851 "laden with all imaginable and unimaginable spoils". However, Lundy never achieved the popularity of the nearby North Devon coast amongst Victorian sea-shore naturalists and significant published studies of the marine life of the island did not appear until the 1930s.

Each summer between 1934 to 1937, G.F. Tregelles visited Lundy to collect seaweeds. His records are summarised in Tregelles (1937) and are incorporated into the *Ilfracombe fauna and flora* (Tregelles, Palmer & Brokenshire 1946) and the *Flora of Devon* (Anonymous 1952).

The first systematic studies of marine ecology at Lundy were undertaken by Professor L.A. Harvey and Mrs C.C. Harvey together with students of Exeter University in the late 1940s and early 1950s (Anonymous 1949, Harvey 1951, Harvey 1952). These studies again emphasised the richness of the slate shores especially when compared to the relatively impoverished fauna on the granite shores. A later study (Hawkins & Hiscock 1983) suggested that impoverishment in intertidal mollusc species was due to the isolation of Lundy from mainland sources of larvae.

When marine biologists started to use diving equipment to explore underwater around Lundy at the end of the 1960s, they discovered rich and diverse communities and many rare species leading to a wide range of studies being undertaken, both underwater and on the shore, in the 1970s and early 1980s. Ecological studies resulted in a detailed knowledge of the inshore marine biology of the island and contributed significantly to understanding of sublittoral marine ecology in Britain. More recently, particularly as Lundy became Britain's first marine nature reserve, surveillance studies have revealed the great longevity of many species and their likely irreplacibility if damaged.

Intertidal marine ecology

As with any island, the different exposures of shores to wave action leads to the presence of a wide variety of communities. These range from those typical of wave-sheltered situations, especially in the Landing Bay, where dense algal dominated communities occur, to those exposed to the full force of Atlantic gales on the west coast where algae are sparse and colonisation is mainly by limpets, barnacles and low algal turfs. The granite shores also provide a harsh environment for intertidal species. Granite does not hold water and has few crevices in which species may hide or which may become enlarged into rockpools.

The only sediment shore on Lundy is in the Landing Bay and this is of very mobile coarse shingle devoid of species which can be seen with the naked eye except at the strandline where the sandhopper *Talitrus saltator* may be found. (The scientific names used in this paper are those in Howson & Picton in prep. where authorities can be found.). On the lowest tides, some sand is exposed below the jetty. This has not yet been sampled on the shore but probably contains an extension of the communities known from the adjacent subtidal sediments.

Harvey (1951) lists 141 algae and 226 animal species for Lundy shores and several other animal groups from which the species were not identified.

Rocky slopes

The great majority of the shoreline around Lundy is of steep bedrock or stable boulders. The character of these shores and the associated flora and fauna are described in the papers by Professor Harvey (cited earlier). The patterns of vertical zonation and the abundance of all of the conspicuous species present on four contrasting shores were described by Hiscock & Hiscock (1980). The main conspicuous species present on rocky shores and their zonation on exposed and sheltered coasts are illustrated in Figs 1 and 2. On exposed coasts, shores are dominated by limpets and barnacles with patches of small mussels. Turfs of erect coralline algae (*Corallina officinalis*) occur on the lower shore but other algae are very sparse. On sheltered shores, brown algae may be extensive and, on the most sheltered shores, there may be significant growths of red foliose algae.

Rockpools

When left by the tide, rockpools provide an oasis of life on an otherwise arid shore. The species present are mainly those characteristic of the damp lower shore but include some specialities. Three southern species of algae which occur at Lundy are especially notable: *Cystoseira tamariscifolia*, *Bifurcaria bifurcata* and *Jania rubens*. The pod-weed, *Halidrys siliquosa*, also occurs in pools but not elsewhere on the shore and the fine filamentous branching red alga *Ceramium nodulosum* (= *C. rubrum*) is especially abundant in

Yellow and grey lichens (species of *Xanthoria, Lecanora, Caloplaca*).

Black lichens (*Verrucaria maura*) and *Melarhaphe* (=*Littorina*) *neritoides*.

Porphyra linearis, *Lichina pygmaea*, *Littorina saxatilis*, *Melarhaphe* (=*Littorina*) *neritoides*.

Barnacles (*Chthmalus* spp.), limpets (*Patella* spp.), *Littorina neglecta*, *Melarhaphe* (=*Littorina*) *neritoides*, *Fucus vesiculosus* f. *linearis*, amphipods (*Hyale nilssoni*), small mussels (*Mytilus edulis*).

Encrusting coralline algae, *Corallina officinalis*, beadlet anemones (*Actinia equina*), limpets (*Patella ulyssiponensis*).

As above plus sparse *Mastocarpus* (= *Gigartina*) *stellatus*, *Alaria esculenta*, *Himanthalia elongata*, keeled tubeworms (*Pomatoceros triqueter*).

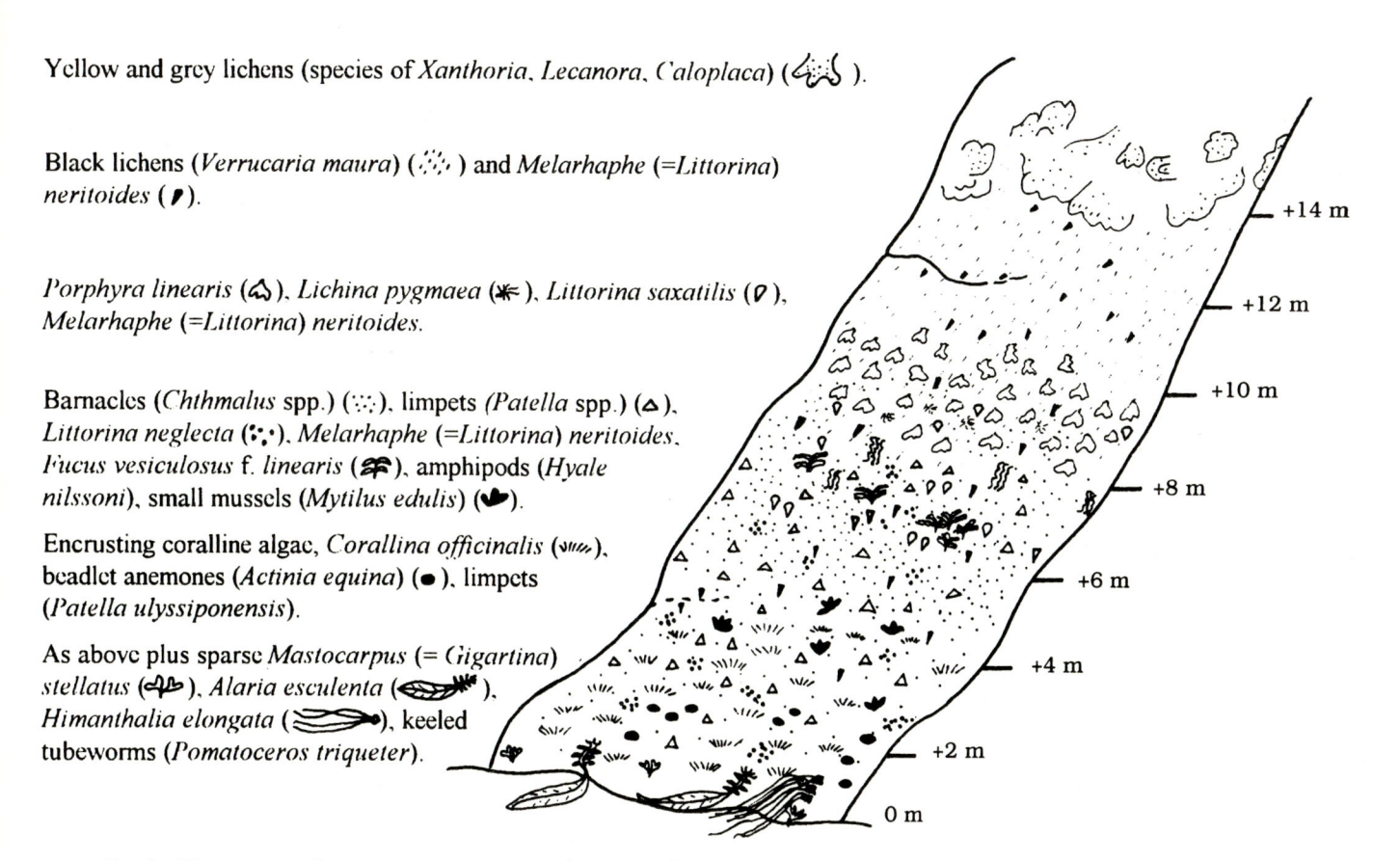

Fig 1. Illustration of zonation on an exposed granite shore on the west coast of Lundy. The descriptions of zonal communities are based on those for Dead Cow Point in Hiscock & Hiscock (1980) and are for major species only. There is overlap in the distribution of species between zones.

Flowering plants especially *Armeria maritima* (🌿).

Yellow and grey lichens (🔆), *Ramalina siliquosa*.

Black lichens (*Verrucaria maura*) (🌫) and *Lichina confinis* (❋), *Melarhaphe* (=*Littorina*) *neritoides* (▸).

Channelled wrack (*Pelvetia canaliculata*) (🐚), spiral wrack (*Fucus spiralis*) (🌿), barnacles (*Chthamalus* spp., *Elminius modestus*) (∴), *Littorina saxatilis* (♀).

Black lichen (*Verrucaria mucosa*), barnacles (as above), limpets (*Patella* spp.) (△), *Littorina saxatilis*, beadlet anemones (*Actinia equina*) (●), dogwhelks (*Nucella lapillus*) (▽), filamentous green algae (*Enteromorpha sp.*) (𝄃).

As above plus knotted wrack (*Ascophyllum nodosum*) (🌿), bladder wrack (*Fucus vesiculosus*) (▲), barnacles (*Balanus perforatus*), amphipod crustaceans (*Hyale nilssoni*).

As above plus sparse large mussels (*Mytilus edulis*) (♠), encrusting coralline algae, *Corallina officinalis* (ᗯ), dulse *Palmaria palmata* (♠), serrated wrack (*Fucus serratus*) (🌿), isopod crustaceans (*Idotea* spp., *Dynamene bidentata*).

As above plus *Osmundia* (= *Laurencia*) *pinnatifida* (🌿), *Mastocarpus* (= *Gigartina*) *stellatus* (🌿), thong-weed (*Himanthalia elongata*) (➤), flat periwinkles (*Littorina obtusata*) (∘), keeled tube-worms (*Pomatoceros triqueter*), kelp (*Laminaria digitata*) (☞)

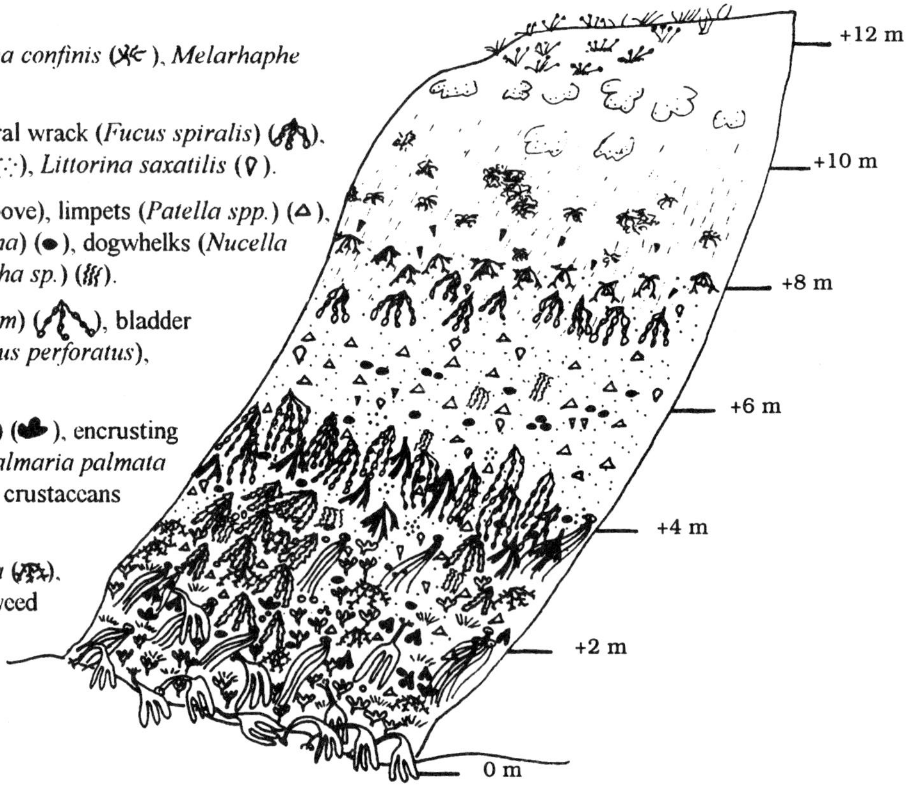

Fig 2 Illustration of zonation on a sheltered shore on the Landing Bay at Lundy. The descriptions of zonal communities are based those for the north shore of Rat Island in Hiscock & Hiscock (1980) and are for major species only. There is overlap in the distribution of species between zones.

pools. Pools, and the damp rocks around them, provide a habitat for high numbers of the snakelocks anemone *Anemonia viridis* in the Devils Kitchen and Landing Bay. Blennies (*Lipophrys* (= *Blennius*) *pholis*) and prawns (*Palaemon serratus*) also occur in the pools. The flora and fauna of rockpools at the Devils Kitchen has been surveyed as part of the programme of monitoring commenced in 1984 for the then Nature Conservancy Council and now continued by English Nature (Fowler & Pilley 1992).

Underboulders

Although there are many boulder shores around Lundy, few of the boulders are capable of being turned to discover the often rich communities which live under them. Indeed, turning and replacing boulders is only to be undertaken with utmost care as the fauna below is easily crushed. Professor Harvey (Harvey 1951) described the fauna of boulders based mainly on many visits to the shore at Ladies Beach. Boulders not embedded in sediment are usually colonised on their lower sides and undersides by encrusting sea mats (Bryozoa), tube worms (Serpulidae) and anemones including the strawberry anemone *Actinia fragacea*. Blennies are often present and the Cornish lumpsucker, *Lepadogaster lepadogaster*, may be found. Small edible crabs, *Cancer pagurus*, may be common together with swimming crabs, *Liocarcinus puber* and the characteristic porcelain crab *Porcellana platycheles*.

Caves

The flora and fauna of the many deep intertidal caves of Lundy is generally unremarkable being mainly of barnacles and encrusting calcareous tubeworms. Small caves around Rat Island do provide a habitat for sea anemones and bryozoans not generally seen elsewhere. The greatest importance from a wildlife point-of-view of the majority of caves is probably as pupping sites for seals.

Overhangs and shaded places

These occur on the slate shores where the dip of the strata and erosion creates hollows which are always shaded and, on a few granite shores, where deep gullies and sometimes very large boulders create shade and damp. Here are likely to be found the scarce scarlet and gold star coral, *Balanophyllia regia*, and the much more widespread Devonshire cup coral, *Caryophyllia smithii*, together with encrusting sponges such as the blood red *Microciona atrasanguinea*, white calcareous sponges such as *Leuconia nivea* and small branching sponges, *Stelligera rigida*, together with other species rarely found on the shore. Certain seaweeds are also characteristic of this habitat including *Plumaria plumosa* (= *P. elegans*) and *Lomentaria articulata*.

Underwater hard substrata

Diving has been required to observe and sample underwater rocky areas. In 1969, a party of botanists supported by divers undertook a thorough study of the marine algae of Lundy (Irvine et al. 1972). 1969 was also the year in which the author first dived on Lundy as part of a three-day student excursion, during which time he was impressed by the richness of the fauna on underwater rocks and, perhaps emphasising the importance of Lundy to him personally, he discovered the Mediterranean coral *Leptopsammia pruvoti* in great numbers at the Knoll Pins. This beautiful bright yellow cup coral was, at the time, unrecorded from Britain, and Lundy remains only one of five locations from which it is known in the British Isles.

In an early paper, Hiscock (1971) compared the fauna of submerged rocks on south and east coasts. This work contributed to a PhD thesis (Hiscock 1976) where the fauna of the west, south and east coasts were compared to assess the effects of strength of wave action and tidal streams in determining the composition of sublittoral animal communities. By the time this material was published, a wide range of studies were underway on Lundy with annual expeditions of experienced marine biologists visiting the island to undertake a wide range of ecological investigations and collect specimens for the preparation of lists of the Lundy marine fauna. Much of the ecological information was published in reports of wider studies in Great Britain (for instance, Hiscock 1983, 1985) or was published in limited circulation reports (for instance, Hiscock 1981).

Rocky slopes

Rocky surfaces extend to depths of about 40 m (all depths refer to below chart datum / Lowest Astronomical Tides level) around much of the island where they reach the level sediment or shingle plain. The depth is much less on the east coast south of the Knoll Pins where muddy sediments generally occur below depths of about 14 m. The presence of deep rocky surfaces afforded the opportunity to study the vertical zonation of species (related to light intensity and the severity of wave action, both of which are attenuated with depth) on very wave exposed to wave sheltered coasts. These studies contributed greatly to early understanding of the ecology of sublittoral rocky areas (for instance, Hiscock & Mitchell 1980; Hiscock 1983, 1985).

Some of the main species present and their zonation are illustrated in Fig. 3. In general, light around the island is sufficient to support the growth of a dense kelp (*Laminaria hyperborea* mainly) forest to a depth of about 8 m, followed by a kelp park and dense foliose red and brown algae to about 14 m, where upward facing rocks become dominated by animals (although some foliose red algae can be found to as deep as about 22 m).

Sublittoral fringe. Kelps (*Laminaria digitata* ( ), *Alaria esculenta*[1] ( ), *Saccorhiza polyschides*[2]), coralline algae (*Corallina officinalis*) ( ), and encrusting coralline algae (including *Mesophyllum lichenoides*[2]), encrusting bryozoan (*Umbonula littoralis*) ( ), anemones (*Sagartia elegans*[1]) ( ) in very shallow (< 2 m) depths.

Upper infralittoral to upper circalittoral. Kelp forest and park (*Laminaria hyperborea*) (c. 5 m to maximum c. 22 m). Foliose algae (*Bonnemaisonia asparagoides*, *Brongniartella byssoides*, *Antithamnion* sp(p), *Phyllophora crispa*, *Hypoglossum hypoglossoides*, *Haraldiophyllum* (= *Myriogramme*) *bonnemaisonii*, *Rhodymenia pseudopalmata* var. *ellisiae*, *Dictyopteris membranacea*, *Dictyota dichotoma*, *Carpomitra costata*[2]), snakelocks anemone (*Anemonia viridis*)[2], trumpet anemone (*Aiptasia mutabilis*[2]) ( ), erect bryozoans (*Scrupocellaria* spp.)[1].

Upper infralittoral to lower circalittoral. Kelp forest to deep water (c. 5 m to 40 m +). Sponge (*Leucosolenia botryoides*)[1], sea urchins (*Echinus esculentus*)[2] ( ), erect bryozoans (Crisiidae, *Bugula plumosa*, *Cellaria* spp.)[2] ( ), Devonshire cup coral (*Caryophyllia smithii*)[2] ( ), spiny starfish (*Marthasterias glacialis*)[1] ( ).

Upper infralittoral. Kelp forest (*Laminaria hyperborea*) ( ) and species abundant in shallow (< 8 m) depths with coralline algae (*Corallina officinalis*), erect bryozoans (*Scrupocellaria* spp.)[2] ( ), foliose algae (*Delesseria sanguinea*[1], *Plocamium cartilagineum*[2], *Kallymenia reniformis*, *Cryptopleura ramosa*, *Callophyllis lacineata*) ( ).

Lower infralittoral to circalittoral. Kelp park and dense foliose algae to deep water (c. 8 m to 45 m+). Devonshire cup coral (*Caryophyllia smithii*)[1], erect bryozoans (*Bugula plumosa*, *Cellaria* spp.), sea urchins (*Echinus esculentus*)[1], sea fan (*Eunicella verrucosa*)[2] ( ), branching sponges (*Homaxinella subdola*, *Axinella dissimilis*, *Raspailia* spp.)[2] ( ), cushion sponges (*Polymastia boletiformis* ( ), *Cliona celata*[2] ( )), hydroids (*Nemertesia* spp., *Aglaophenia tubulifera*, *Aglaophenia kirchenpaueri*[1]) ( ), colonial anemone (*Epizoanthus couchii*)[2], light-bulb sea-squirt (*Clavelina lepadiformis*)[2], ross (*Pentapora foliacea*) ( ), dead-mens fingers (*Alcyonium digitatum*) ( ), sea cucumber (*Holothuria forskali*) ( ), spiny starfish (*Marthasterias glacialis*)[2].

Circalittoral. Below algal domination (c > 12 m) or strong wave action into deep water. Encrusting bryozoan (*Parasmittina trispinosa*), cushion bryozoan (*Cellepora pumicosa*), sea squirts (*Stolonica socialis*[2] ( ), *Archidistoma aggregatum*[1]), hydroid (*Gymnangium montagui*)[1] ( ), red sea fingers (*Alcyonium glomeratum*)[2] ( ), sunset cup coral (*Leptopsammia pruvoti*)[2] ( ), colonial sea anemone (*Parazoanthus axinellae*)[2] ( ), branching sponges (*Homaxinella subdola*, *Axinella dissimilis*, *Raspailia* spp.)[1], cushion sponge (*Cliona celata*)[1], sea fans (*Eunicella verrucosa*)[1], hornwrack (*Flustra foliacea*) ( ).

Fig 3 Illustration of zonation on underwater rocks around Lundy. Only dominant or most characteristic seabed species are illustrated and captioned. Depictions of species are not to the same scale. [1] = characteristic of exposed coasts. [2] = characteristic of sheltered coast. Some species (for instance, the jewel anemone *Corynactis viridus*) do not show a consistent distribution with depth and wave exposure and are influenced by other factors.

The major turf-forming species in this animal-dominated zone are erect Bryozoa (sea mats), amongst which live encrusting and erect sponges, sea firs, sea anemones, sea fans and sea squirts. Samples of the bryozoan turf reveal a rich variety of small animals including bristleworms, amphipod crustaceans, small snails, bivalve molluscs and small crabs. In samples collected to study the distribution of small turf-living animals with depth at Dead Cow Point on the west coast and Brazen Ward on the east coast, 228 and 172 animal taxa were recorded from this turf on west and east coasts respectively. Some of the most beautiful creatures to be found on Lundy are the sea slugs, usually closely associated with the species on which they feed. Forty-seven species were recorded in Brown & Hunnam (1977) and more have been added to the list since. Fish living on the rocky seabed are well camouflaged and include the sea scorpion *Taurulus bubalis*. Wherever there are boulder holes or other sheltered places, cuckoo wrasse (*Labrus mixtus*) and goldsinny wrasse (*Ctenolabrus rupestris*) will be seen – the bright blue male cuckoo wrasse being particularly inquisitive.

The strength of wave action and tidal streams at a particular location are most important in determining which species survive and characterise particular areas. The turf of erect Bryozoa with scattered colonies of sea firs occurs at wave exposed locations. Where such conditions have, in addition, strong tidal streams (the south-west and north-west corners), rocks are dominated by the tubes of the sea fir *Tubularia indivisa* amongst sheets of jewel anemones, *Corynactis viridis*. In wave sheltered conditions, erect sponges and delicate sea anemones thrive. The richest animal communities are found where there is shelter from prevailing wave action but with fairly strong tidal flow bringing food and preventing siltation. Some species are characteristic of particular conditions other than water movement and depth. For instance, where sand covers rocks, the algae *Jania rubens*, the Falkenbergia-phase of *Asparagopsis armata* and *Furcellaria fastigiata* occur in shallow depths (the Landing Bay), whilst the sponges *Ciocalypta penicillus* and the nationally rare *Adreus fascicularis* are present in deeper water (for instance, Rattles Anchorage).

Canyons, cliffs and caves

Some of the most spectacular underwater scenery in Britain is found around Lundy. In shallow depths, the underwater gullies between Mouse Island and Rat Island provide vertical and overhanging surfaces covered by characteristic tide-swept communities of sponges and hydroids, often with rare or unusual sea slugs (and playful seals). Off the west coast, are granite gullies which, in the gloom and limited visibility, seem like canyons. The land-bound can best imagine these by going to the 'Earthquake' on the west coast of the island where topographical features are very similar. Off Gannets Rock is a submerged feature very similar to that of the Rock itself with extensive cliffs and overhanging surfaces on the north side and a gravel bank piled by the prevailing currents against the south side. Cliffs of creviced slate occur in massive underwater pinnacles off Black Rock, the south-west corner of Lundy. There are no true caves yet found underwater although many overhanging surfaces create cave-like features. It is on the vertical or overhanging shaded surfaces which these features create that some of the most fascinating and unusual species occur. Four of the five British shallow-water species of cup coral can be found on these shaded surfaces (the fifth, the scarlet and gold star coral, occurs in the kelp forest zone). Soft corals, including the spectacular red sea fingers *Alcyonium glomeratum* are often abundant, although careful searching is required to discover the much rarer pink soft coral *Parerythropodium coralloides*. Under overhangs and in fissures wherever there is shelter, the leopard spotted goby *Thorogobius ephippiatus* is likely to be found. Crawfish, *Palinurus elephas*, were once frequently observed in depressions on cliffs or broken rock slopes but are now very rarely seen. Sheets of highly coloured jewel anemones occur particularly in tide-swept areas whilst, in more sheltered locations can be found the beautiful yellow colonial anemone *Parazoanthus axinellae* and its much rarer white relative *Parazoanthus anguicomus*.

Wrecks

An account of the most conspicuous species colonising some of the wrecks is given by Heyes (1995). Very little is left of the vast majority and, in many cases (for instance, the wreck of the *Carmine Filomena* off Rat Island and of HMS *Montagu* off Shutter Rock) most of the remains are scarcely distinguishable from the surrounding rock. The wreck of the small coaster, the MV *Robert*, which sank off Tibbets Point in 1975, is an exception and provides a fascinating contrast to rock communities. The marine life colonising the *Robert* was described by Hiscock (1982) and the port side of the wreck was used in a programme of sampling undertaken to investigate the smaller fauna present in 1980 (K. Hiscock and D. Rostron, unpublished). The *Robert* is largely intact and lies on her starboard side with the port side at a depth of about 15 m. The marine communities are distinctly different to the coastal rocks about 1 km to the west and are visually dominated by the plumose anemone *Metridium senile*, erect Bryozoa and the sea fir *Nemertesia antennina*. By the time of the wreck's discovery in 1979, the port side had been colonised by the barnacle *Balanus crenatus* and the tube worm *Sabellaria spinulosa* together with other tube worms which provided a substratum blocking any effects of anti-fouling paints. This allowed for further colonisation by erect sea mats amongst which lived marine bristleworms, small snails, small bivalve molluscs and crabs. In total, 192 species were recorded from 1.4 m^2 sampled. The darker parts of the wreck provided a habitat for conger eel, *Conger conger*, and for the squat lobster *Munida rugosa*, whilst the still water in the hold created a habitat suitable for active suspension feeders with large numbers of the sea

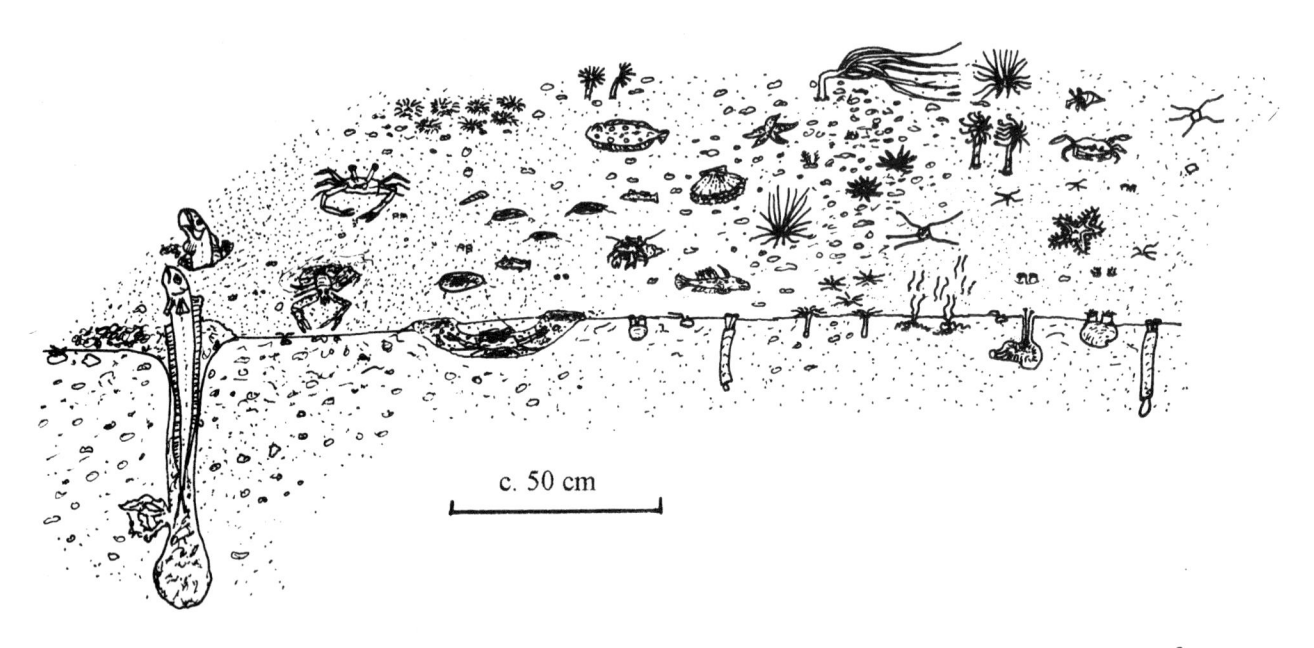

Fig 4   Illustration of sediment fauna from the east coast of Lundy. The illustration is a composite from widely separated types. Depictions of species are not to the same scale. The sediment type is from muddy gravel overlain by mud (typical of the seabed at about 15m depth off the Quarries) through tide-swept gravel (typical of the banks built-up against the south side of the Knoll Pins and Gannets Rock at 20 to 30m depth) to muddy sand typical of areas near to rocks (for instance adjacent to rock at about 20m depth on the north part of the east coast with elements of shallow – about 6m depth – sediments in the Landing Bay). Species are named (at first occurrence) from left to right.

Epibiota

daisy anemones *Cereus pedunculatus* ( )
squat lobster *Munida rugosa* in burrow ( )
fan worm *Sabella pavonina* ( )
plaice *Pleuronectes platessa* ( )
goby *Pomatoschistus* sp. ( )
hermit crab *Pagurus bernhardus* ( )
scallop *Pecten maximus* ( )
dragonet *Callionymus lyra* ( )
common starfish *Asterias rubens* ( )
burrowing anemones *Cerianthus lloydi* ( )
　　　　　Halcampoides elongatus ( )
　　　　　Mesacmaea mitchelli ( )
brittlestar *Ophiura ophiura* ( )
hydroid *Corymorpha nutans* ( )
brittlestar *Ophiura albida* ( )
swimming crab *Liocarcinus depurator* ( )
starfish *Astropecten irregularis* ( )

Burrowing fauna in section

Red band fish *Cepola rubescens* ( ) with burrow of the crustacea *Upogebia stellata* adjoining
angular crab *Goneplax rhomboides* ( )
bivalve mollusc *Lucinoma borealis* ( )
Bivalve mollusc *Abra nitida* ( )
razor shell *Ensis siliqua* ( )
burrowing anemone *Edwardsia claparedii* ( )
burrowing brittlestars *Amphiura filiformis* ( )
sea potato *Echinocardium cordatum* ( )
bivalve mollusc *Arctica islandica* ( )

Legend to accompany figure 4 (opposite)

squirt *Ascidia mentula*. The species present when the wreck was first investigated four and a half years after sinking provide an indication of those which are likely to (re)colonise rapidly in the event of disturbance. They included the cup coral *Caryophyllia smithii*, ross *Pentapora foliacea* and the feather star *Antedon bifida* which is rarely found elsewhere on Lundy. Wrecks may provide unusual substrata for species not often or not elsewhere recorded from Lundy. For instance, the limestone cannonballs on the Gull Rock wreck site (a protected site) off the east coast are colonised by the worm *Phoronis hippocrepia* (Heyes 1995, described as "Phoronida", identified by the author from photographs as *P. hippocrepia*).

Sediments

Although Lundy is surrounded by a wide variety of sediment types, very little has been done to sample them. Edward Forbes described the results of dredging off the east coast of Lundy in the Report of the British Association for the Advancement of Science (Forbes 1851) but it was more than one hundred years later that the seabed to the north and east of Lundy was sampled as a part of a study of the Bristol Channel and Severn Estuary (Warwick & Davies 1977) and nearshore sediments off the east coast were sampled by Hoare and Wilson (1977) using diver-operated cores.

Sediment communities

The sediment communities identified in these studies include examples of well-known assemblages dominated by the bivalve *Abra alba*, brittle stars *Amphiura filiformis*, the sea cucumber *Leptosynapta inhaerens* and, in more sandy sediments, the heart urchin *Echinocardium cordatum* and the bivalve mollusc *Timoclea* (= *Venus*) *ovata*. Those of the 'boreal offshore muddy-gravel association' (Holme 1966) are notable as they have a restricted distribution. However, some of the species present in sediments are infrequently recorded, especially in shallow depths. The most conspicuous and exciting find was of the red band fish *Cepola rubescens* in 1974. This eel-shaped orange-coloured fish up to 70 cm long excavates vertical shafts in muddy gravel and protrudes out of its burrows to snap at passing plankton. During 1977, the population was estimated to be about 14,000 individuals (Pullin & Atkinson 1978). In subsequent years the population has reduced enormously and only a few have been found in recent years even after intense searching. The muddy gravel also provides a habitat for the angular burrowing crab *Goneplax rhomboides* and for smaller burrowing crustaceans of the genus *Upogebia*. The nationally rare sea anemone *Halcampoides elongatus* was observed extending its long tentacles over the gravel bank at the Knoll Pins during a night dive in August 1982. The gravely substrate appear to provide the most interesting of habitats with some occupied by dense colonies of the daisy anemone *Cereus pedunculatus*, by the fleshy hydroid *Corymorpha nutans* and, less frequently, and on clean gravel, the burrowing sea anemones *Mesacmaea mitchellii* and *Peachia cylindrica*. Scallops *Pecten maximus*, are occasionally seen. Other burrowing anemones encountered in more sandy or muddy substrata are *Cerianthus lloydii* and *Edwardsia claparedii*. Several fish species are likely to be observed on sediments including small gobies *Pomataschistus* spp., plaice *Pleuronectes platessa*, dogfish *Scyliorhinus canicula*, and, often near to rocks, the anglerfish *Lophius piscatorius*.

Slate pebble plains

Much of the sedimentary rock south and south-east of Lundy has collapsed into the sea and now lies strewn over the seabed as a level plain of flat slates amongst occasional rock outcrops. The strong currents keep the slates clear of silt and they are colonised by distinctive assemblages of species. The algae in shallow depths include species not found in other habitats such as *Stenogramme interrupta*, *Scinaia turgida* and species of *Schmitzia*. In deeper waters, encrusting and erect bryozoans (sea mats), including the fleshy *Alcyonidium diaphanum*, may dominate the slates whilst, in depths greater than about 20 m, extensive beds of the brittle stars *Ophiothrix fragilis* and *Ophiocomina nigra* occur.

Open waters

This is the world of the plankton, unicellular algae and microscopic animals, predominantly crustaceans and the larvae of seabed species and the larger nekton such as jellyfish and fish. The only records of planktonic species are those collected as part of the large scale studies of the Bristol Channel and Severn Estuary (Collins & Williams 1982; Williams & Collins 1985), those of fish plankton (Townley & King 1980) and those collected in association with studies of the red band fish (Atkinson, Pullin & Dipper 1977). Plankton communities near to Lundy are consistently characteristic of fully saline marine waters whilst those off the North Devon coast to the south and east are often characteristic of variable salinity waters.

Some of the larger open water species can be spectacular and include the basking shark *Cetorhinus maximus* and the sunfish *Mola mola*. Porbeagle and blue sharks (*Lamna nasus* and *Prionace glauca*) occur to the west of Lundy but have not been seen inshore. Compass jellyfish *Chrysaora hysoscella* and the large white jellyfish *Rhizostoma octopus* are frequently seen. Every few years, there are strandings of the oceanic by-the-wind sailor jellyfish *Vellella vellella*. However, Lundy is not sufficiently close to deep oceanic waters to attract significant numbers of large gelatinous plankton.

Species

The most comprehensive collection of algae was made in 1969, 1970 and 1971 by Irvine et al. (1972). They recorded 298 species (11 blue-green, 37 green, 1 prasinophycean, 80 brown and 169 red) and their lists incorporate previous records. Since then, a few significant additions have been made including the gametophyte form of *Asparogopsis armata* (recorded only once in September 1973) and 11 others noted in Hiscock & Maggs (1984). The flora is rich and includes many southern species seldom encountered in British waters and some universally rare species. Several lichen species occur in the littoral zone and are listed by Noon & Hawksworth (1973).

Animal species have been collected to prepare marine fauna lists for Lundy (various authors cited in the reference list). Seven hundred and fifty three macrofaunal species are recorded in those lists which lack only nemerteans, barnacles (about nine species) and mammals (about four species).

Both flora and fauna are southern in character and Lundy represents the northern recorded limits for several species.

Origins, longevity and change

This title, taken from a paper describing observations of change in marine communities and species at Lundy (Hiscock 1994), expresses one of the most important aspects of marine ecology we need to understand if we are to ensure that the beauty and richness of the marine life on Lundy is to be maintained. A formal monitoring scheme for the features of special nature conservation importance was commenced in 1984 and sites have been re-surveyed at irregular intervals since then (Fowler & Pilley 1992; Fowler & Laffoley 1993). Although there is an overall impression of constancy in the types of marine communities present at particular locations, there have been notable declines in abundance. Groups such as sea slugs may be expected to show marked fluctuations in abundance and the virtual loss of what were in the 1970s very large numbers of the spectacular orange and blue *Greilada elegans*, may be reversed in the future. Similarly, the high populations of the red band fish off the east coast in the 1970s may have been a chance or particularly successful recruitment which may not happen again for many years. Other species, for instance, the corals *Leptopsammia pruvoti* and *Hoplangia durotrix* appear not to have reproduced since monitoring commenced and numbers of *Leptopsammia* have declined significantly. Similarly, the branching axinellid sponges which may be up to 250 mm high have been found to grow at a rate of no more than 2 mm a year. Some monitored individuals were lost and others damaged during prolonged easterly gales in 1986 although a great deal more damage might have been rendered during scientific collecting in the 1970s when examples were collected to demonstrate the range of growth forms – of course, at a time when the slowness of growth was not realised.

The past and the future

Much remains unpublished from work on Lundy. The lists of fauna from kelp holdfasts and *Corallina* turf collected by Professor Harvey could not be published in full. The detailed studies of vertical zonation on underwater rocks including the quantitative samples of smaller fauna and the sampling from the wreck of the MV *Robert* have not been published. Nevertheless, the records are held by the author (those from Professor Harvey lent to me to copy many years ago) and, particularly those studies of sublittoral zonation and sampling, might one day see publication. The *Annual Report of the Lundy Field Society* has provided an important and a comprehensive vehicle for the publication of results of work on and around Lundy and, even where work has been published elsewhere, it should be noted in that *Report*.

There continue to be many gaps and opportunities in the study of marine ecology around Lundy. We know little of the fauna of sediments and this should be addressed by a programme of sampling. It is important to continue studies which will help us to better understand variability (including recruitment, longevity and growth) and its causes in marine communities and species. Such studies will especially help to manage the marine nature reserve to ensure the continued presence of its special features. Recent developments in using video cameras on remotely operated underwater vehicles may open-up exploration of underwater areas to a larger audience and allow exploration of deeper areas than by diving.

Lundy is a fabulous place to explore marine wildlife. There are doubtless new discoveries to be made by both amateur and professional naturalist and some of the species and scenery are a photographers dream. Enabling the pursuit of fisheries, recreation, educational activities and scientific study in ways which do not damage the diversity and special features of marine ecosystems around Lundy requires careful management underpinned by sound science.

References

Anonymous. 1949, Marine ecology. *Annual Report of the Lundy Field Society*, 2, 28-33.

Anonymous. 1952, *Flora of Devon. Volume II, Part I. The marine algae*. Torquay.

Atkinson, R J A 1976, Studies of a *Goneplax rhomboides* population off Quarry Bay. *Annual Report of the Lundy Field Society* 26, 55-60.

Atkinson, R J A and Pullin, R S V 1977. The red band-fish *Cepola rubescens* at Lundy. *Annual Report of the Lundy Field Society* 27, 58-63.

Atkinson, R J A; Pullin, R S V and Dipper, F A 1977, Studies on the red band-fish *Cepola rubescens*. *Journal of Zoology*, London, 182, 369-384.

Atkinson, R J A & Schembri, P J 1982, The marine fauna of Lundy. Crustacea: Euphausiacea and Decapoda. *Annual Report of the Lundy Field Society* 31, 35-63.

Brown, G H and Hunnam, P J 1977, The marine fauna of Lundy. Opisthobranchia. *Annual Report of the Lundy Field Society* 27, 37-47.

Cole, K R, 1991, An introductory survey of the periwinkle species found around the shores of Lundy. *Annual Report of the Lundy Field Society* 41, 67-72.

Collins, N R and Williams, R, 1982, Zooplankton communities in the Bristol Channel and Severn Estuary. *Marine Ecology Progress Series* 9, 1-11.

Forbes, E, 1851, Report on the investigation of British marine zoology by means of the dredge. Part 1. The infralittoral distribution of marine invertebrata on the southern, western and northern coasts of Great Britain. *Report of the British Association for the Advancement of Science*, 20, 192-263.

Fowler, S & Laffoley, D, 1993, Stability in Mediterranean-Atlantic sessile epifaunal communities at the northern limits of their range. *Journal of Experimental Marine Biology and Ecology*, 172, 109-127.

Fowler, S L and Pilley, G M, 1992, Report on the Lundy and Isles of Scilly marine monitoring programmes 1984 to 1991. (Contractor: The Nature Conservation Bureau Ltd.). Unpublished report to English Nature, Peterborough.

George, J D 1975. The marine fauna of Lundy. Polychaeta (marine bristleworms). 25th *Annual Report of the Lundy Field Society* 25, 33-48.

Gosse, P H, 1865, *Land and sea*. London: James Nisbet.

Harvey, L A, 1951, The granite shores of Lundy. *Annual Report of the Lundy Field Society* 4, 34-40.

Harvey, L A, 1952, The slate shores of Lundy. *Annual Report of the Lundy Field Society* 5, 25-33.

Hawkins, S J and Hiscock, K, 1983, Anomalies in the abundance of common eulittoral gastropods with planktonic larvae on Lundy Island, Bristol Channel. *Journal of Molluscan Studies* 49, 86-88.

Hayward, P J, 1977, The marine fauna of Lundy. Bryozoa. *Annual Report of the Lundy Field Society* 27, 16-34.

Heath, J, 1994, Marine archaeological fieldwork 1993: a pre-disturbance survey of the Gull Rock site. *Annual Report of the Lundy Field Society* 44, 52-55.

Heyes, M J, 1995, A preliminary survey of wrecks within the Lundy Marine Nature Reserve and their importance to the nature conservation resource. *Annual Report of the Lundy Field Society* 45, 77-85.

Hiscock, K, 1971, Observations on the fauna of submerged rocks around Lundy. *Report of the Lundy Field Society* 21, 20-21 & 24-33.

Hiscock, K, 1975, The marine fauna of Lundy. General introduction. *Annual Report of the Lundy Field Society* 25, 16-19.

Hiscock, K, 1975, The marine fauna of Lundy. Coelenterata. *Annual Report of the Lundy Field Society* 25, 20-32.

Hiscock, K, 1976, *The effects of water movement on the ecology of sublittoral rocky areas.* PhD Thesis, University of Wales.

Hiscock, K, 1981, South-West Britain Sublittoral Survey. Final Report. (Contractor: Field Studies Council Oil Pollution Research Unit, Pembroke.) *Nature Conservancy Council, CSD Report, No. 326.*

Hiscock, K, 1982, Marine life on the wreck of the M.V. 'Robert'. *Annual Report of the Lundy Field Society* 32, 40-44.

Hiscock, K, 1983, Water movement. In R. Earll & D G Erwin (eds). *Sublittoral ecology* 58-96. Oxford University Press.

Hiscock, K, 1985, Aspects of the ecology of rocky sublittoral areas. In P G Moore and R Seed (eds). *The ecology of rocky coasts* 290-328. London, Hodder and Stoughton.

Hiscock, K, 1994, Marine communities at Lundy – origins, longevity and change. *Biological Journal of the Linnean Society* 51, 183-188.

Hiscock, K and Hiscock, S, 1980, Rocky shore communities on Lundy. Vertical zonation at four sites. *Annual Report of the Lundy Field Society* 30, 40-48.

Hiscock, K & Mitchell, R, 1980, The description and classification of sublittoral epibenthic ecosystems. In W.F. Farnham, D E G Irvine and J H Price (eds) *The shore environment. Vol. 2. Ecosystems* 323-370. London: Academic Press.

Hiscock, K, Stone, S M K and George, J 1984, The marine fauna of Lundy. Porifera (sponges): a preliminary study. *Annual Report of the Lundy Field Society* 34, 16-35.

Hiscock, S & Maggs, CA 1984, Notes on the distribution and ecology of some new and interesting seaweeds from south-west Britain. *British Phycological Journal* 19, 73-87.

Hoare, R and Wilson, J, 1977, The macrofauna of soft substrates off the coast of Lundy. *Annual Report of the Lundy Field Society*, 27, 53-58.

Holme, N A, 1966, The bottom fauna of the English Channel, Part II. *Journal of the Marine Biological Association of the United Kingdom* 46, 401-493.

Howson, C M and Picton B E (eds). In prep. *The species directory of the marine fauna and flora of the British Isles and surrounding seas*. London, IMMEL, for the Marine Conservation Society and Ulster Museum.

Irvine, D E G, Smith, R M, Tittley, I Fletcher, R L and Farnham, W F, 1972, A survey of the marine algae of Lundy. *British Phycological Journal* 7, 119-135.

King, P E, 1977, The marine fauna of Lundy. Pycnogonida (sea spiders). *Annual Report of the Lundy Field Society* 27, 35-37.

Lane, D J W, 1977, The marine fauna of Lundy. Ascidiacea (sea squirts). *Annual Report of the Lundy Field Society* 27, 48-52.

Moore, P G, 1982, The marine fauna of Lundy. Crustacea: Amphipoda. *Annual Report of the Lundy Field Society* 32, 52-63.

Noon, R A and Hawksworth, D L, 1973, The lichen flora of Lundy. *Annual Report of the Lundy Field Society* 23, 52-58.

Picton, B E, 1979, The marine fauna of Lundy. Prosobranchia. *Annual Report of the Lundy Field Society* 29, 38-45.

Pullin, R S V, 1978, The marine fauna of Lundy. Pisces (fishes). *Annual Report of the Lundy Field Society* 28, 45-54.

Townley, M and King, P E, 1980, The marine fauna of Lundy – Ichthyoplankton (fish plankton). *Annual Report of the Lundy Field Society* 30, 49-55.

Tregelles, G F, 1937, An introduction to the seaweeds of Lundy. *Report of the Transactions of the Devonshire Association for the Advancement of Science* 69, 359-363.

Tregelles, G F, Palmer, M G and Brokenshaw, E A 1946, Seaweeds of the Ilfracombe district. In M.G. Palmer (ed). *The fauna and flora of the Ilfracombe district of North Devon.* Exeter: Townsend & Sons, for the Ilfracombe Field Club.
Tugwell, G, 1856, *A manual of the sea-anemones commonly found on the English coast.* London: Van Voorst.
Tyler, P A, 1979, The marine fauna of Lundy. Echinodermata. *Annual Report of the Lundy Field Society* 29, 34-37.
Warwick, R M and Davies, J R, 1977, The distribution of sublittoral macrofauna communities in the Bristol Channel in relation to substrate. *Estuarine & Coastal Marine Science* 5, 267-288.
Williams, R and Collins, N R, 1985, *Zooplankton atlas of the Bristol Channel and Severn Estuary.* Plymouth, Institute for Marine Environmental Research.
Wilson, J G, 1982, The marine fauna of Lundy. Bivalvia. *Annual Report of the Lundy Field Society* 32, 29-37.

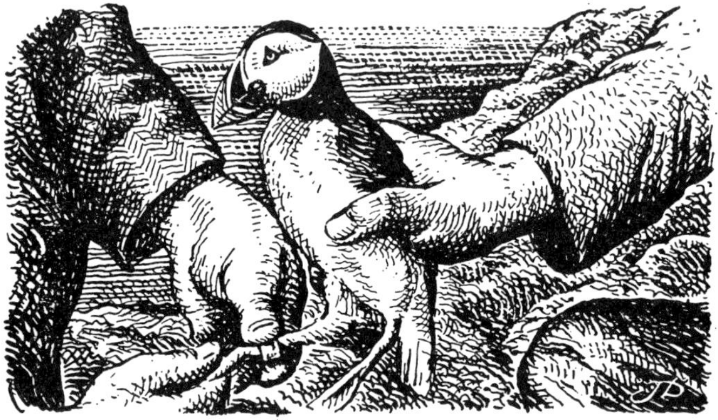

Lundy's Marine Nature Reserve – a short history

Robert Irving and Paul Gilliland

Introduction

When placed in the context of marine conservation worldwide, Britain may seem to have been relatively slow off the mark in establishing protected areas off its coasts. The fact that the waters which bathe much of our coastline are rather turbid and uninviting, especially when compared to the crystal clear waters of tropical coral reefs, could well have something to do with this. A paucity of the sort of imagery which enthuses film-makers and a strong terrestrial bias by the founding fathers of nature conservation, has resulted in a lack of awareness of the wealth of marine life that can be found in British waters, and hence any need to conserve it.

It was not until the advent of SCUBA diving that a full appreciation of our underwater wildlife started to be pieced together. The popularity of diving as a sport gradually grew during the 1960s when many of what are now recognised as being this country's best dive sites were visited for the first time. Lundy was one such place, and in the mid-1960s, sports divers visited the island for the first time. However, it was more for the clear waters, spectacular underwater scenery, wrecks and the edible or souvenir wildlife that the island was at first attractive.

The impressive array of marine wildlife at Lundy, however, would soon be liable to threat from several quarters. Spearfishing using aqualungs was popular with many of those early underwater explorers, leading to near-shore fish populations, particularly of territorial species which tend to remain in the one area, losing their largest individuals. This activity would also lead to many fish becoming wary of divers such that the fish would keep their distance when divers were in the water. Souvenir hunting for shells, urchins and sea fans also became popular, doubtless leading to a significant reduction in certain populations. It was soon realised by those who appreciated the need for conservation that measures to safeguard Lundy's underwater wealth were urgently needed.

In the late 1960s, there was a worldwide movement to establish marine parks and reserves. Lundy was an obvious candidate. Fortunately, through the hard work and persistence of a small number of individuals, Lundy became Britain's first voluntary marine nature reserve, and later had the distinction of also becoming the first statutory reserve. Indeed, it has remained England's sole Marine Nature Reserve (MNR) for ten years now, and it looks likely to remain so for some time to come, given the existing difficulties in the legislation and the process used to establish its status.

This paper summarises the background to how both the voluntary marine nature reserve and the statutory one around Lundy were established, and how the current MNR is being managed by English Nature (the Government's advisor on nature conservation in England), with the help of the Landmark Trust and the Devon Sea Fisheries Committee, in order to safeguard its interest for future generations to enjoy.

The early days: pre-1973

Diving around the island began in earnest in the mid-1960s when Don and Jeanie Shiers, founders of the Aquatic Club, established a diving centre, with the main aim of diver training and a commercial interest in marine salvage. Many of the wrecks around Lundy still remain in the ownership of Mr Shiers' company, Bristol Channel Divers. Bristol Channel Divers had negotiated the concession to run diving from the island with the Harman family and, with a well-equipped shore base, they were able to exert some control over the diving around the island. In an effort to supplement income, various marine 'souvenirs' were collected, including sea fans and sea urchins. Shellfish, particularly crawfish, were also greatly prized for their commercial value and as delicious meals. However, as the importance of Lundy's marine wildlife became apparent in the early 1970s, Bristol Channel Divers became collaborators in survey projects and in helping to protect the vulnerable wildlife.

The remoteness of Lundy was one of the main reasons for suggesting that it would be an excellent site at which to establish the first underwater nature reserve in Britain. Articles promoting the idea were published in the Journal of the Devon Trust for Nature Conservation by John Lamerton, Assistant Regional Officer for the Nature Conservancy (Lamerton 1969); and Heather Machin, working for the Devon Trust for Nature Conservation (Machin 1969). However, a number of questions immediately presented themselves. Should such an area be termed a 'marine nature reserve', a 'marine conservation area', a 'marine sanctuary' or even a 'marine park'? What was the legal position regarding ownership and/or leasing of the sea bed from the Crown Estate? Should all collecting by divers be banned within a reserve, or just collecting on a commercial scale? And should commercial fishing still be allowed?

In the same year that these articles were published, some of Lundy's underwater treasures began to be revealed, when Keith Hiscock and some student friends dived the island for the first time. He discovered a population of the rare cup coral *Leptopsammia pruvoti* (though it took him a year to put a name to it) – the first time it had been recorded in British waters. With ownership of the island passing to the National Trust, and the commitment of the Landmark Trust to manage and improve the island, both organisations dedicated to conservation, the proposal gained additional justification.

In March 1971, a group of conservationists and marine biologists, led by Keith Hiscock (at that time

1. The richness of the marine life and the variety of habitats and environmental conditions within a limited area isolated from local sources of pollution are outstanding.
2. The clear waters around the island and the spectacular underwater scenery are attractive to the diving public, the more discerning members of which require unspoilt scenery and interesting marine life.
3. Diving conditions are good and it is possible to dive somewhere around the island in most weather conditions.
4. The island's size, isolation and limited development has resulted in there having been little exploitation or collecting in the past.
5. Lundy is therefore an ideal locality for the study of marine ecology and for monitoring changes in the structure of marine communities.
6. Unless protected, the valuable asset of Lundy's marine life is threatened by the collecting activities of divers for souvenirs, for the curio market, and in the course of research.
7. Policing to protect the area is feasible as a result of the island's isolation and small size. Visitors either have to stay on the island or have substantial boat facilities to remain independent of shore based facilities. Visitors are easily seen, approached and informed of the status of the island's shore and sea bed.
8. Laboratory and reference facilities are or can be made available for the scientist. Interpretative and educational literature is available for the amateur diver on Lundy: e.g. a diving field guide.
9. Lundy is owned and managed by organisations wishing to conserve the best parts of man's environment. A marine reserve policy to control activities on the shore and sea bed complements and is compatible with the terrestrial management programme.

Table 1   Reasons presented for the establishment of a (voluntary) marine nature reserve at Lundy (taken from Hiscock *et al.*, 1972).

undertaking postgraduate research at the marine laboratories in Menai Bridge), put forward the proposal that a marine nature reserve be established around Lundy (Hiscock 1971a). The foreshore and sea bed up to 1 km around the island should be managed for the purposes of research, education and recreation. Details of the proposals were published in several journals, including *Nature*, *Triton* (the journal of the British Sub-Aqua Club) (Hiscock 1971b), the *Underwater Association Newsletter* and the *Journal of the Devon Trust for Nature Conservation*. From opinions expressed and correspondence received, it was apparent that there was a great deal of interest in these proposals. At the same time, the Natural Environment Research Council was also considering the practical and legal problems involved in setting up marine reserves in Britain, so they followed the Lundy project with interest.

In 1972, an Advisory Committee was formed which included representatives of the Landmark Trust, the Nature Conservancy, Lundy Field Society, Bristol Channel Divers Ltd. and marine biologists. Although it was originally envisaged that this committee would meet occasionally, it met only once to discuss the establishment of a voluntary reserve: most matters thereafter did not require decisions to be taken by a full committee. A Management Policy was drawn up which included a Code of Conduct (see Table 2), incorporated into a leaflet distributed to all divers visiting the island.

The voluntary marine nature reserve: 1973 – 1981

The voluntary marine nature reserve was formally identified in 1973, after the publication of the management policy (Hiscock *et al.* 1972). It covered the foreshore and sea bed around the island, from high water mark to 1 km offshore (Fig. 1). Its extent was determined by the following factors:

1. Inclusion of habitats, communities and species of high scientific interest. These are predominantly on rock substrata which extend to about 1 km offshore on the west and south coasts; and on/in sediments, rarely encountered on the open coast, which extend to about 1 km off the east coast.
2. Inclusion of an area which is reasonably small from the point of view of control.
3. Exclusion of fishing banks and areas of substrata which occur commonly in the Bristol Channel and its approaches.

During the mid-1970s, a major programme of research was embarked upon, aimed at describing the littoral and sublittoral ecology of the island and listing the marine fauna and flora (see also the paper by Keith Hiscock elsewhere in this volume). Additionally, two courses were run from the island, one in sublittoral ecology and the other in methods for studying underwater habitats using diving. There were also plans for the proposed island museum to feature a major marine display, but as we know, plans for a museum have never reached fruition.

As a pilot project, aimed mainly to assess the work of a warden, a marine warden (Nigel Thomas), was appointed on a six-month contract during the summer of 1978. The post was jointly funded by the Nature Conservancy Council, the World Wildlife Fund, the Lundy Field Society, the Browne Fund of the Royal Society, the Natural Environment Research Council and individual workers. As part of his brief he was asked to:

1. ensure the Code of Conduct was abided by; provide guidance and information to visiting divers;
3. assist field workers in carrying out their studies;
4. assist in organising and running field courses in sublittoral ecology; and to prepare illustrated guides for the reserve.

At the end of the six months, the project was deemed to have been a success, with all the above requirements being met (Thomas & Hiscock 1979). However, a further eight years had to pass before the next marine warden was appointed.

While the day-to-day management of the voluntary reserve required minimal interference, there was concern over two matters in particular: the commercial collection of sea urchins *Echinus esculentus*; and dredging/trawling over the area of sea bed occupied by the red band fish *Cepola rubescens* and other species of nature conservation interest off the east coast. In order to resolve these problems, a meeting was held with the Devon Sea Fisheries Committee (DSFC) in March 1979 (Hiscock 1983). While it was felt that the collection of sea urchins could not be considered under the jurisdiction of the DSFC, a "gentleman's" agreement was reached that no dredging/trawling should take place west of a line between the Knoll Pins and Surf Point, the area inhabited by red band fish and where one of the richest, most scientifically interesting sediment habitats was present.

Proposals to establish a statutory MNR, 1982 – 1986

The introduction of the Wildlife and Countryside Act in November 1981 allowed, for the first time, for statutory Marine Nature Reserves (MNRs) to be set up in UK territorial waters. The Nature Conservancy Council (NCC), who were given the task of selecting proposed sites, drew up an initial list of 26 sites of known outstanding scientific interest, with 7 being put forward in the first tranche. These were Lundy and the Isles of Scilly (in England); Skomer, Bardsey and the Menai Strait (in Wales); and Loch Sween and St Abbs (in Scotland).

The reasons for changing the voluntary status of the reserve around Lundy are set out in Table 3. One of the main stipulations of the Act was that all parties concerned were obliged to be fully consulted by the

Lundy (Voluntary) Marine Nature Reserve: Code Of Conduct

The variety of marine habitats, communities and species around Lundy is of outstanding conservation importance. Respect of this Code of Conduct will help to ensure that these special features remain as undisturbed as possible, thereby helping to maintain the present interest for all to enjoy.

Species other than fish or shellfish

1. Many vulnerable species and communities occur within the Reserve and to ensure their protection no destructive sampling of marine wildlife should be undertaken unless a permit allowing such sampling has been issued following consultation and agreement with the Nature Conservancy Council.

2. To minimise the impact of collecting, only single specimens of marine wildlife should be collected for the purpose of identification. Any other collection may only take place after issue of a permit following consultation with the Nature Conservancy Council. Permission may be withheld for some species of coral, soft coral and sea fans in particular.

3. When looking for examples of marine wildlife, you are requested to replace boulders in their original positions if they have been overturned for examination. Please limit this activity as every time a boulder is disturbed the associated communities are damaged.

4. There are large numbers of rare or unusual species growing on the Knoll Pins many of which are delicate and particularly vulnerable to damage from certain activities. To minimise the risk of such damage to the communities found here, there should be no anchoring within 100m of these pinnacles, not should fishing gear be deployed with in this area.

Fish and shellfish

5. The towing of trawls and dredges over the seabed can cause considerable damage to soft sediment habitats and communities, many of which are of high scientific interest. For this reason, trawling and dredging within the Reserve boundary is prohibited.

6. Tangle and gill nets can break free from their set positions and may ensnare divers, seals, diving seabirds and other marine wildlife. To minimise the risk of this happening, such nets should only be deployed within the Reserve after agreement with the Devon Sea Fisheries Committee.

7. There should be no collection of shellfish by any means within 100 m of the Knoll Pins.

8. To protect populations of nearshore territorial fish (many of which are long-lived and remain or return to the same area over many years), anglers are asked to return to the sea any wrasse caught.

9. The use of spearguns within the Reserve is prohibited.

Seals

10. Intertidal caves and inaccessible boulder beaches are used by grey seals for pupping during September and October. To minimise disturbance to seals at this time, do not approach nearer than 100 m by sea or land to these areas between 1 September and 1 November, except by agreement with the Nature Conservancy Council.

Seabirds

11. Boats operated close to sea bird colonies, especially at speed, may disturb breeding birds. Please therefore proceed slowly (max. 8 knots) and quietly when within 100 m of such areas, between 1 April and 1 August.

Rubbish

12. To avoid littering the beach or seabed with unsightly rubbish, boat operators and others visiting Lundy should not deposit rubbish within the Reserve.

Wrecks and Archaeology

13. Owners of wrecks or anyone else planning salvage operations using explosives within the Reserve should consult the Nature Conservancy Council, so that adverse effects on wildlife can be minimised.

14. Persons intending to use underwater excavation equipment for archaeological or other purposes should likewise consult the Nature Conservancy Council before such equipment is used.

Divers

15. When under water, divers are asked to disturb as little as possible. Thoughtless finning close to delicate species, such as sea fans and Ross coral, can easily cause damage. It can also stir up sediment, adversely affecting sediment communities in very sheltered areas and hindering other divers (especially photographers) from seeing what you've just seen. Also remember your bubbles can lodge in caves and can kill marine life there. When diving on the wreck of the MV *Robert* off the east coast (which is of considerable scientific interest), divers are requested not to disturb the marine life growing on the wreck.

Table 2 The voluntary marine nature reserve's Code of Conduct (from Hiscock 1983)

NCC and that a submission to the Secretary of State for the Environment (for proposed MNRs in England) could only take place once the agreement of all had been reached. This presented the NCC with quite a challenge as initially there was a considerable amount of opposition to the proposals by local fishermen and also scepticism from the DSFC. The NCC stressed that the *status quo* for activities within the waters around the island would be maintained, with the exception of certain vulnerable areas which would acquire additional protection (in the form of byelaws). For their part, the DSFC were reluctant to introduce any byelaw which would be seen to discriminate against any one type of fishing. Even spearfishing was included within this proviso. Eventually, however, they were persuaded to introduce a limited number of fisheries byelaws designed to protect the sea bed and open water communities within the proposed MNR.

In order to try to allay some of the fears which had arisen, largely through insufficient explanation or misunderstanding, a meeting was held at Braunton Community College in February 1982, open to all interested parties. The meeting was organised by Dr Keith Hiscock (at that time co-ordinating the drafting of the marine reserve management plan for Lundy) and Heather Booker (North Devon Secretary of the Devon Trust for Nature Conservation). About 70 people attended the meeting and it proved a good opportunity to explain the procedures involved in establishing an MNR, whilst at the same time inviting comments on the proposals.

It soon became evident to the NCC that the establishment of the statutory MNR was by no means a foregone conclusion. There was much opposition amongst the fishing community (the phrase 'this is just the thin edge of the wedge' was heard on several occasions) and even some divers did not take kindly to being informed that their activities would be restricted to some extent. In an effort to explain the situation better, as well as to assess local opinion on the proposals, the NCC appointed a Marine Liaison Officer (Robert Irving) to Lundy in June 1983. He spent the summers of 1983 and 1984 on the island, talking about the proposals to visiting divers, fishermen and the islanders themselves (Irving 1984).

In August 1984, an 'informal meeting' was held in Bideford, organised by the NCC for all interested parties. These included representatives of the DSFC, the Landmark Trust, the Lundy Field Society, the Marine Conservation Society, scientific research interests, Aquaserve Diving Ltd. (who had taken over the diving concession from BCD Ltd. in 1983), British Sub-Aqua Club, South-West Federation of Diving Clubs, and the Royal Yachting Association. This group was to form the core of the Lundy Marine Consultation Group, which held its first meeting in February 1985. At that meeting, the aims of the Consultation Group were agreed (Irving 1991).

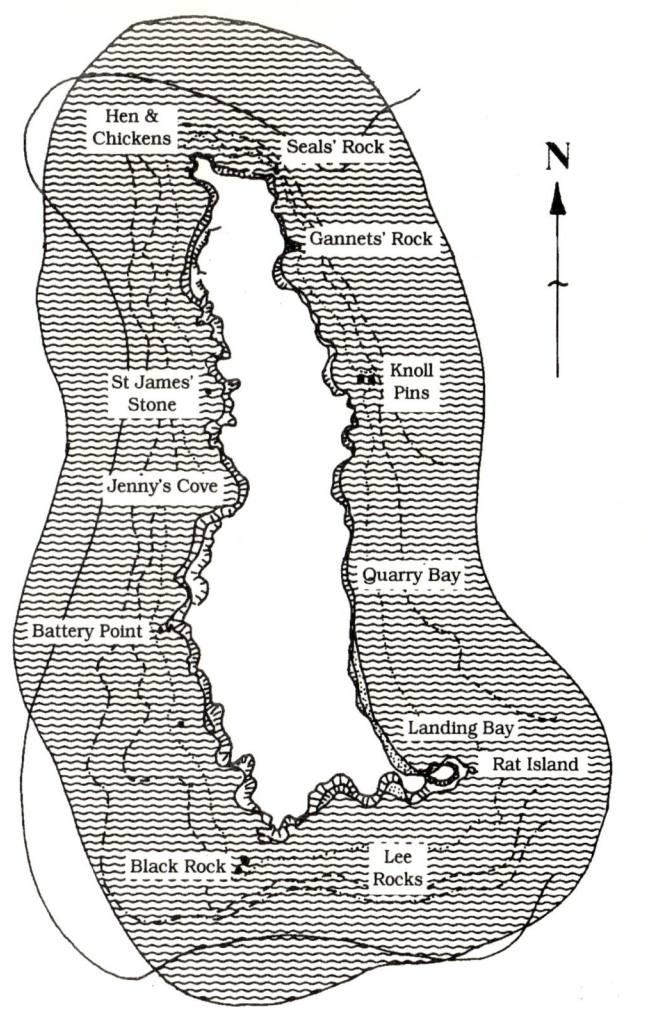

Fig. 1.

The seaward boundary of the voluntary marine nature reserve was approximately 1 km from the low water mark.

These were:
1. to provide a nucleus of expertise on the marine habitats and waters surrounding Lundy;
2. to provide a forum for exchanging views on present and proposed activities around Lundy; and
3. to safeguard the interests of all those who use the waters around Lundy and its natural resources.

After several further meetings between the NCC and the DSFC during a period of formal consultation, the proposal to establish a statutory MNR around Lundy was put before the Secretary of State in early 1986. After a three month period of public notification, it was then declared Britain's first MNR on 21 November 1986.

The Statutory Marine Nature Reserve: 1986 onwards

One of the most important benefits that designation as a statutory MNR brought with it was the provision of an on-site warden, who would have responsibility for the day-to-day management of the MNR, as well as spending some time looking after the island's Site of Special Scientific Interest. In February 1986, Neil Willcox was the first such marine warden in the country to be appointed. Two years later Andrew Gibson took over and had to face many challenges which confronted the MNR during his six years in post (Parkes this volume). Emma Parkes then took on the position of warden in early 1995, leaving at the end of 1996. At the time of going to press, Liza Cole has just been appointed to the post. It should also be noted here that the Wardens have been helped in their work by a variety of volunteers over the years, especially in the guise of working parties from the Lundy Field Society and the Marine Conservation Society.

Initially, much of the NCC's financial commitment to the MNR was directed towards a monitoring programme (begun in 1984), which they were obliged to undertake as part of the active management of the site (since 1991 this duty continues with English Nature). In particular, the study of certain marine communities and species of high nature conservation interest, but about which relatively little was known, was seen as a priority. If the MNR was to be managed effectively to ensure the protection of these, there was a need for a better understanding of the ecology and life history of each species: for example, how long do they live; what is their potential for recruitment; and are they particularly sensitive to changes or impacts? To tackle these questions, a regular (in most cases annual) photographic monitoring programme was established covering a variety of subjects including changes in: rockpools; the main shore cover organisms; sublittoral rock communities; and some Mediterranean-Atlantic species such as sea fans and solitary cup corals at sites both on the shore (e.g. Devil's Kitchen) and in the sublittoral (e.g. the Knoll Pins). This work continued from 1984 to 1991 (Fowler & Pilley 1992).

Much of the monitoring work ceased in 1991 for

	Reasons for a change to statutory status		**Reasons against**
1	Increased (national) recognition of the importance of the marine wildlife and habitats around Lundy.	1	By creating a reserve, more divers will be attracted to the area, thereby increasing the chances of damaging the very species that the reserve should be protecting.
2	Greater protection of marine life and habitats through introduction of byelaws limiting or prohibiting certain destructive activities from taking place. Codes of Conduct give no protection against 'cowboys' who can quite legally clean out a resource which has been carefully preserved by the self-restraint of everyone else.	2	Introduction of controls on commercial fishing activities around the island, which would be unpopular with fishermen. [A]
3	Provision of a warden to ensure compliance with the regulations, oversee management of the MNR and to act as a source of information.	3	Access to island expensive and reliant on reasonable weather conditions, thereby limiting the numbers who may wish to visit the reserve. No threat to marine life due largely to isolation of island.
4	Provision of educational materials, in the form of display panels and leaflets, promoting interest in the reserve and respect for its marine life.	4	More officialdom restricting an individual's rights to do what he/she wants. [B]
5	Greater 'say' in limiting activities outside the reserve's boundary (such as gravel extraction or sewage dumping), which may affect marine life and/or habitats within the reserve.		

Responses

A Any new byelaws affecting fishing practices which are thought necessary can only be introduced through the DSFC.

B The creation of an MNR may not remove the rights of commercial fishermen or restrict them in any way. The byelaws may not interfere with the right of passage by a vessel other than a pleasure boat; or of a pleasure boat except with respect to specific parts of the MNR and/or during specific periods.

Table 3. Reasons for and against Lundy becoming a statutory Marine Nature Reserve.

two reasons (although some work has continued every year, such as fixed viewpoint photography of the shores). Firstly, some of the main questions originally posed had been answered, i.e. some of the species are extremely slow growing, reproduce infrequently and are particularly sensitive to disturbance. Secondly, it was felt that there were other aspects of the MNR which merited greater consideration, bearing in mind that the monitoring programme was very demanding on resources.

More recently, monitoring within the MNR has again come to the fore. In 1995, English Nature re-investigated the sublittoral sites and assessed future monitoring prospects (Munro 1995); in addition, a group of Marine Conservation Society volunteer divers, part-funded by English Nature, tackled a number of projects within the reserve (Irving *et al.* 1995); and in 1996, the entire sea bed of the MNR was mapped using RoxAnn remote echo sounding equipment. Consideration is now being given to putting all the monitoring of the MNR on a more strategic basis, to include a range of topics from physical parameters (particularly of water temperature) to the uses of the reserve, and the ways in which these might be studied.

The change in emphasis to considering other aspects of the MNR (besides monitoring) partly reflected the changes in the organisation of the country's statutory nature conservation body, when in April 1991, the NCC split into country agencies including English Nature. Whilst continuing the work of the former organisation, English Nature placed an increasing emphasis on aspects other than science, including promotion and interpretation as well as management. After the restructure had settled down, the marine section within English Nature set out their marine strategy (English Nature 1993). This placed Lundy clearly at the centre of their work as a 'flagship' and recognised the need to consider the profile of, and work at, Lundy and its benefit to marine conservation as a whole. Two major developments flowed from this and from other changes, such as the increased interest in all aspects of managing coastal areas.

The first of these developments was to look more critically at the management set up for the MNR. English Nature had continued the funding begun by the NCC for a Warden employed by the Landmark Trust and, together with the DSFC, these bodies met from time to time to discuss management issues. However, there was obviously a need to put the management on a more strategic basis particularly as the management plan drafted in 1983 had 'remained on the shelf'. This was given impetus by negotiations over the contract for employing the Warden and the need to agree a properly set out work programme. As a result of these deliberations a new Management Plan was drafted in 1993 covering all aspects of the MNR and SSSI, including a register of projects from which the Warden's work programme is derived. Following a wide consultation, the Management Plan was published in May 1994 (English Nature 1994) and signed up to by

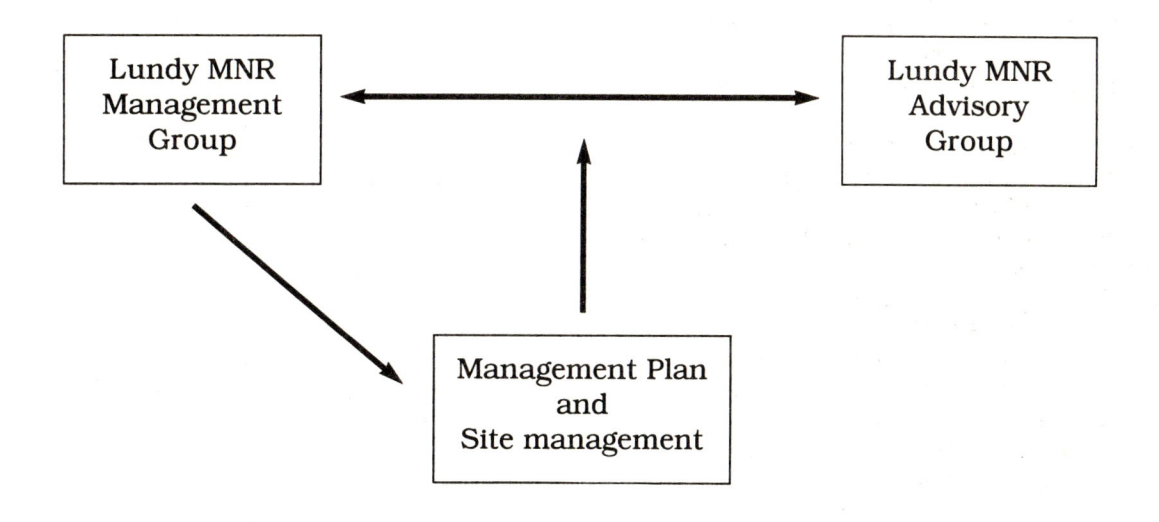

Fig. 2. Administrative structure for the management of the MNR.
Both groups currently meet twice a year.

the relevant statutory and management bodies (English Nature, Devon Sea Fisheries Committee, the Landmark Trust and the National Trust). This is a 5-year plan although the project register is reviewed annually. The Plan includes agreed objectives which inform the decisions and work that go into the running of the reserve.

The Plan has led to new ways of working and to new areas of work. One of the objectives was to establish an effective structure for overseeing the management of the reserve. This led to the Consultation Group taking on a more formal role as an Advisory Group whilst the statutory bodies formed a Management Group. The former discuss relevant issues and provide advice or raise concerns to the latter, who in turn are responsible for taking decisions about the reserve (Fig. 3).

The plan brought a number of new initiatives with it, for example in forming links with maritime archaeology. It was recognised that there was a need to integrate nature conservation and archaeological interests, as, in 1990, two of the wrecks around the island (*Iona II* and the Gull Rock wreck) had also acquired statutory protection under the Protection of Wrecks Act 1973. This led to English Nature holding meetings with a variety of maritime archaeological bodies in order to investigate the nature conservation importance of the wrecks (Heyes 1995); and to the inclusion of the Warden in the licensing system for visits to the protected wrecks. This trend is set to continue and is another good example of Lundy being at the forefront of developments in managing marine areas.

Other initiatives on the MNR are also leading the way. In conjunction with the Management Plan, it was decided to consult on a new idea, that of a zoning scheme for the reserve. This is a useful 'tool' pioneered in marine reserves abroad for summarising byelaws and other regulations, thereby presenting a wealth of sometimes confusing management information in an easy to understand way. This information is interpreted as an overlay on a navigation chart making effective use of colour to indicate differing levels of protection or regulation. The scheme for Lundy, which contained no new regulation but simply summarised existing information, was put out to public consultation in 1993 and generated a lot of interest nationally as well as locally. A revised scheme, incorporating many comments, was launched in early 1995 (Plates 38 & 39). This will be revised every couple of years to take account of changes and further comments starting in 1997.

The second major development referred to above was to take a considered look at the interpretation and promotion of the MNR. To this end, English Nature carried out an Interpretative Review to assess the effectiveness of existing facilities, using some market research on day visitors to the Island (Fowler 1993). Some interpretative material already existed, including various leaflets produced by the Lundy Field Society, a colour booklet about the MNR produced in 1988, and information boards on the quays at Bideford and

Lundy Marine Nature Reserve
Animals and plants of the snorkel trail

Shanny dark brown/green, up to 16cm, single dorsal fin.

Pollack silver green, up to 40cm.

Ballan wrasse brown to red, 30-40cm, single dorsal fin, thick lips.

Common hermit crab usually found in whelk shells, up to 10cm.

Cushion star grey green, 3cm.

Spiny spider crab pink body up to 15cm, well camouflaged.

Beadlet anemone red, brown, orange or green, 2cm, common.

Grey mullet striped grey body, 30-50cm, thick upper lip.

Spiny starfish grey/purple tips to arms, up to 20cm.

Lesser spotted dogfish grey, many small spots, up to 1m, blunt head, sharklike.

© English Nature

ENGLISH NATURE

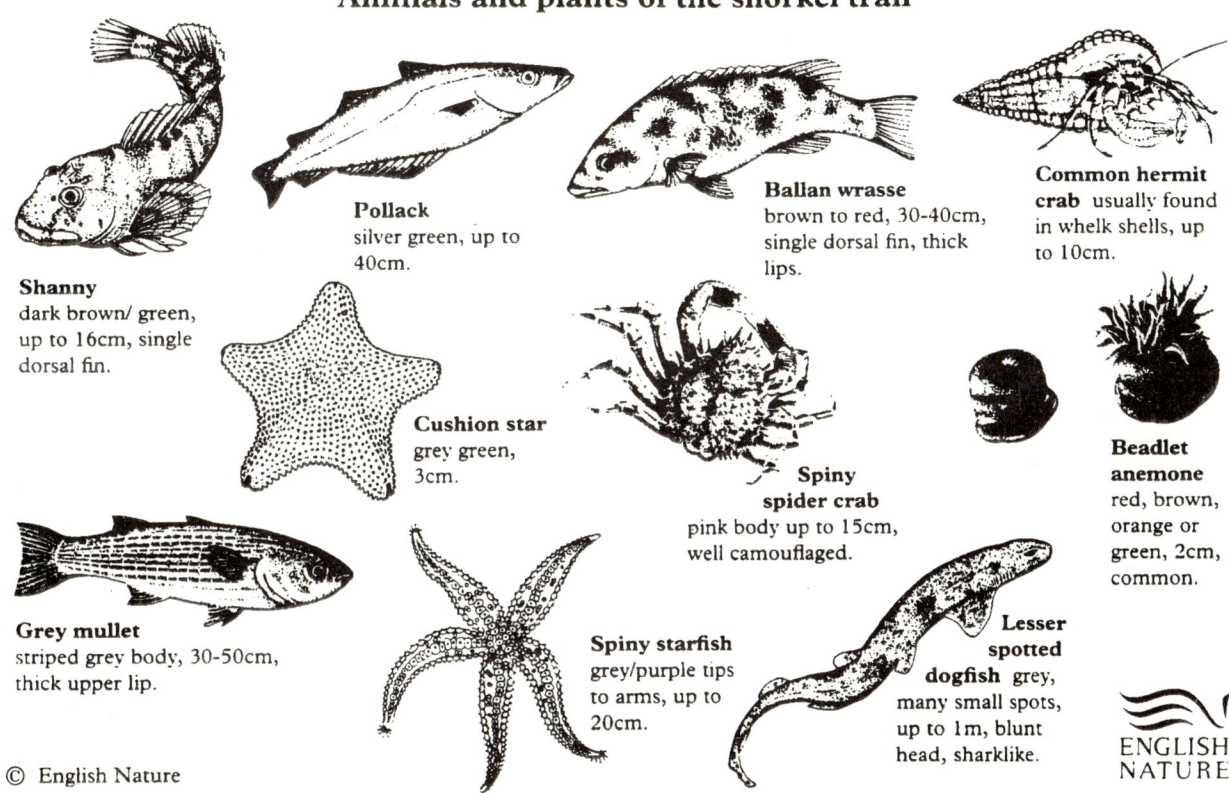

Fig. 3. Part of the guide produced for use on the snorkel trail. It is waterproof and can be attached to the snorkeller's wrist.

Ilfracombe, each with a map and a list of the byelaws. However, it was apparent from the review that much more could be done. As a consequence a number of projects were instigated all aimed at improving the appreciation of the MNR by the 20,000 or so casual visitors per year to Lundy (Table 4).

Now visitors travelling to the island aboard the MS *Oldenburg* start their journey at the quayside with a colourful vision of why Lundy is a special marine site. On board they can learn about the reserve and its inhabitants (without getting wet!) from a 14 minute video made by English Nature; and various leaflets are available on the ship (as well as on the shore and in the island's shop) which can help visitors to get more out of their trip to the MNR. For those staying on the island there are opportunities to get even closer to the MNR's wildlife through guided walks on the shore provided by the Warden and taking to the snorkel trail. The latter was set up by the then Warden Andrew Gibson in 1993, with funding from a variety of bodies to provide appropriate equipment. The trail has proved very successful – particularly on a hot summer's day – and provides a wonderful opportunity for non-divers to come face to face with the MNR and its underwater inhabitants.

The MNR in a wider context

The Lundy MNR continues to be a 'flagship' in English Nature's marine conservation work and as such is discussed and promoted at a national level. It has now been provisionally recognised at a European level as a candidate Special Area of Conservation (a recent conservation designation) for certain of its marine habitats. As an important marine site, Lundy is also on the world map with the video being widely circulated in the marine conservation community and Lundy also being discussed at relevant conferences at the forefront of the field. This role is likely to continue.

The experience gained in the long history of the MNR and the other MNRs in the UK are of great value in considering the future progress of marine protected areas. Progress has been slow for a number of reasons including perhaps the requirement to secure unanimous agreement for designation, under the terms of the 1981 Wildlife and Countryside Act. However, it should be noted that the designation of marine reserves in other countries can also be very slow: in New Zealand for instance, regarded as being very 'progressive' on this front, only two reserves had been declared 10 years after the relevant legislation came into being. The UK legislation requires that many of the protection measures at Lundy have to be arrived at through discussion and voluntary agreement with other bodies. Both of these issues, however, point up the lessons of needing to consult effectively, ensuring full involvement of local groups and individuals, and communicating information clearly and positively. English Nature will continue to put these lessons into practice at Lundy to the benefit of the MNR and marine protected areas elsewhere.

Summer 1993	Interpretative Review (Fowler 1993).
Autumn 1993	New all-weather promotional panels for the MNR at Bideford and Ilfracombe.
Spring 1994	Series of leaflets published aimed at day visitors including ones on the MNR, Shore Walk at Devil's Kitchen, seals and seabirds.
Summer 1994	Underwater guide to the plants and animals of the snorkel trail.
Autumn 1994	Video: *Lundy Marine Reserve – a special place*.
1995	New information centre on the MS *Oldenburg*.
Spring 1995	Portable information and leaflet board on Lundy.
Summer 1995	Repeat of visitor questionnaire.
Spring 1996	New information board for display in the Church.
Winter 1996	New information panel on board MS *Oldenburg*.

Table 4. Recent developments in interpretation and promotion.

Acknowledgement

Many people have been involved in promoting the conservation of Lundy's marine habitats and species over the years. However, one person, more than anyone else, was instrumental in setting up the voluntary marine nature reserve around Lundy, and still remains deeply committed to the well-being of the MNR. He is Dr Keith Hiscock of the Joint Nature Conservation Committee. His dogged persistence and enthusiasm have helped to ensure that the marine life which makes Lundy so special has been duly recognised and protected, and he is to be warmly applauded for so doing.

Landing Beach & Rat Island

References

English Nature, 1993, *Conserving England's marine heritage – a strategy.* , Peterborough: English Nature.
English Nature, 1994, *Managing Lundy's Wildlife – A Management Plan for the Marine Nature Reserve and the SSSI.* English Nature, Peterborough.
Fowler, S L 1993, *Interpretative review of Lundy Marine Nature Reserve.* Unpublished report to English Nature from the Nature Conservation Bureau Ltd, Newbury.
Fowler, S L and Pilley, G M 1992, *Report on the Lundy and Isles of Scilly marine monitoring programmes 1984 to 1991.* English Nature Research Report No. 10, Peterborough.
Heyes, M J 1995, A preliminary survey of wrecks within the Lundy Marine Nature Reserve and their importance to the nature conservation resource. *Annual Report of the Lundy Field Society*, 45, 77-85.
Hiscock, K 1971a, The proposal to establish a marine nature reserve around Lundy – progress. *Annual Report of the Lundy Field Society* 22, 31-34.
Hiscock, K 1971b, Lundy – Underwater Nature Reserve? *Triton* 16, (5), 186-187.
Hiscock, K Grainger, I G, Lamerton, J F, Dawkins, H D and Langham, A F 1972, Lundy Marine Nature Reserve. A policy for the management of the shore and seabed around Lundy. *Annual Report of the Lundy Field Society* 23, 39-45.
Hiscock, K 1983, *Lundy Marine Nature Reserve Draft Management Plan.* Huntingdon: Nature Conservancy Council iv and 87 pp.
Irving, R A 1984, 1984 report of NCC's marine liaison officer. *Annual Report of the Lundy Field Society* 35, 28.
Irving, R A 1991, Lundy's Marine Nature Reserve – Five years On. *Annual Report of the Lundy Field Society* 42, 85-89.
Irving, R A; Holt, R and Moss, D 1995, Selected reports from the Marine Conservation Society's diving working party to Lundy, 3-10 June 1995. *Annual Report of the Lundy Field Society* 46, 54-65.
Lamerton, J 1969, Coastal Conservation. *Journal of the Devon Trust for Nature Conservation* 20, 880.
Machin, H 1969, Conservation in the Sea. *Journal of the Devon Trust for Nature Conservation* 23, 992-994.
Munro, C 1995, *Lundy Marine Nature Reserve: sublittoral monitoring site assessment.* (Contractor: C. Munro, Marine Biological Surveys). Unpublished report to English Nature. (ENRR No. 155).
Thomas, N and Hiscock, K 1979, *Lundy marine nature reserve. Report of the marine warden. May 6th to October 31st 1978.* Unpublished report to the Nature Conservancy Council and the World Wildlife Fund. vii & 44 pp.

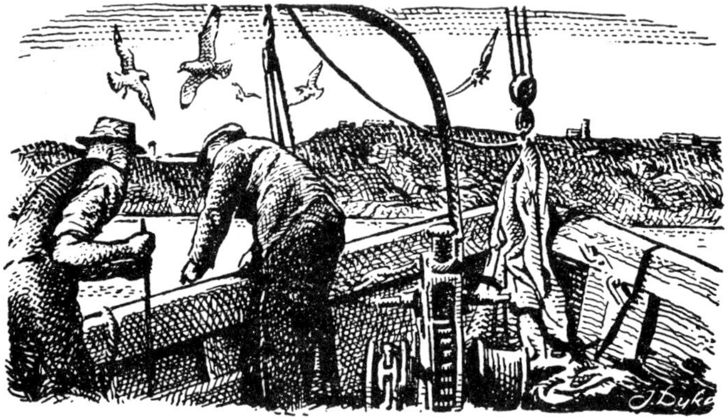

Lundy Wardens

Emma Parkes

Introduction
The first Lundy warden took up residence in the Old Light in the summer of 1947, and began formally recording observations of Lundy's wildlife. This was an exciting start for what was to be a continually developing post. Field Society wardens were followed by Nature Conservancy Council (now English Nature) funded wardens as the post developed and diversified into its present form. Lundy now boasts a Site of Special Scientific Interest, a Marine Nature Reserve and a full time warden employed by Landmark Trust to ensure these special areas are continually protected. Over the years a wealth of information has been recorded, survey projects have been set up and continued and many visitors to the island have benefited from and enjoyed the help of a resident warden. What follows is a brief account of the changing role of the Lundy warden.

Lundy Field Society wardens
Looking after nature conservation on Lundy has always been a shared task. Throughout the last fifty years the Field Society has supported and assisted Lundy's wardens both practically and financially. Indeed, the Field Society were responsible for setting up the first wardens on the island and sponsored the post for several years from 1947 onwards.

Initially the warden's responsibilities included the upkeep and maintenance of the accommodation and facilities that visiting Field Society observers and survey teams would use during the summer (Fig.1). The Old Light buildings were, at this time, set aside for Field Society use and housed a very active group of, amongst others, ornithologists, botanists, entomologists and marine biologists. The warden was present to make observations and to coordinate ongoing research projects undertaken by other visitors. Summer visitors to the Old Light had a range of expertise and took on varying duties. Mary Lee accompanied her brother David who was warden during the summer of 1950 to act as sub-warden, cook and cleaner (Fig.2). The season of observations was at this time limited to the summer months with the first volunteers arriving in March and the last leaving in September.

Gradually the warden's season of stay on the island was increased so that observations were continually carried out over most of the year. Peter Davis (Warden 1951-53) was the first warden to see out all the seasons, arriving in January and departing the following December (Fig.3). This greatly improved the scope of observations particularly with regard to ornithology as both spring and autumn migration movements could be recorded.

The bulk of the warden's work was concerned with

ornithological observations and bird ringing and of course domestic duties in the continual battle to improve accommodation in the Old Light. A daily walk known as the "cruise" was undertaken; this consistent route allowed for daily bird counts and migration observations to be made, and gave a clear picture of bird movement around the island.

Each warden in these early years had an extremely high level of ornithological knowledge. Records were gradually built up and added to, and Lundy gained standing as an important bird observatory and a useful site at which to study migration. With the development of the station at the Old Light, facilities for bird ringing were improved and an emphasis was placed on ringing activities. Heligoland traps were constructed and maintained by the resident warden and the wealth of ringing data began to be compiled. By the early 1950s coverage was such that a comprehensive Lundy bird list could be produced. This then became an annual feature in the Field Society's Annual Report. Ornithological work was at this stage greatly advanced in comparison to other ecological observations and an active effort was therefore made to build up a collection of reference material on all Lundy's ecological aspects, to provide information and baseline data for future reference. The warden's task here was to collate results to ensure the wealth of work carried out was put to good use (Fig.4).

The first annual seabird counts were carried out in June 1949. Checking seabird nesting sites and counting visiting seabirds during the breeding season continues to be an important part of the warden's summer work. Information gathered from seabird counts was originally collated by the RSPB; this task now falls to the Joint Nature Conservancy Council Seabirds Team who take a very active interest in Lundy's breeding seabird populations. Seabird surveys provide just one of several examples of long term research work on Lundy which has provided reliable data over many years and now contributes to make Lundy such a special site.

Fig.1. Lundy Field Society quarters in the Old Light, 1948 – basic but comfortable accommodation (John Dyke).

Volunteer helpers and research workers

Summer volunteers were initially involved in survey and monitoring work rather than in practical conservation tasks. The first call for practical assistance with conservation work was made when the alarming rate of spread of the rhododendron was noted. Volunteers since then have been called upon again and again to assist with what is probably one of the warden's main headaches – the control and containment of rhododendron along the east sidelands. These days Lundy has the help of up to eight volunteer weeks a year with work parties from the Lundy Field Society, the National Trust, British Trust for Conservation Volunteers and Hartland Heritage Coast, gallantly tackling a range of tasks from dry stone walling to tree planting. Tree planting and maintenance has always been a favourite task of Field Society groups, but in Lundy's harsh conditions it is not an easy one (Fig.5).

The early 1960s saw the first visit of a university group to the island – a tradition which continues to this day. This first group carried out ornithological research, producing a contribution for the Field Society's Annual Report. Today Lundy welcomes more university groups each year to carry out a number of research tasks, many of which overlap the warden's remit, assisting with such things as counts of the Soay sheep and estimates of kittiwake breeding success. Lundy has developed strong links with Leeds University biology and ecology students who are being encouraged to conduct honours research projects on the island. With guidance, these projects can be valuable both to Lundy and to the students who certainly benefit from a spell on the island.

Development of the warden's role

In the late 1960s the Field Society had to cut back on expenditure: the warden's period of stay was at first reduced to a summer season and then in 1968 lack of funding made it impossible to directly employ a warden. Volunteers were however unstoppable in their enthusiasm for unravelling Lundy's natural history. To a certain extent the lack of a warden inspired the recording and reporting systems which remain so successful today. A visitor log book was drawn up and made available for all those staying on the island to record their daily observations. At the end of the year the data from the log was then used to compile the annual bird report.

1969 was a time of change, with the Landmark Trust taking Lundy on a long-term lease with the aim of opening up properties on the island to visitors whilst still keeping it beautiful and accessible. Landmark were keen to appoint a warden and Nick Dymond, previously working as a migrations officer for the British Trust for Ornithology, took up post in 1971. He was able to devote a large amount of his time to Field Society duties and natural history observations, and the Field Society were once again able to join the Bird Observations Council. Although a full time warden had returned to the island, the log book, which had proved

Fig 2. David Lee (centre boat) and Mary Lee (stern right) arriving at the Landing Bay, June 1950. David Lee stayed as warden from March to November 1950; his sister Mary was his assistant responsible for cooking and cleaning in the Old Light. (Photo: by kind permission of Mary Percy.)

both popular and effective, still remained in the Tavern to allow visitors to assist with observations.

Although Nick's work was proving very successful, the Landmark Trust were suffering financial difficulties which sadly meant the post of warden was again lacking funding. It can, however, be said that Lundy was continually wardened both by Field Society representatives visiting the island and by knowledgeable members of permanent staff, who, when not working as barmen, were either out observing or bird ringing. And what better place to inform people of Lundy's wildlife than from over the bar! So although there was no formally-employed warden there was no break in the amount of research being carried out on the island. Naturalists continued to visit and the Annual Report continued to record their findings. Experienced naturalists amongst the staff carried out the traditional observation duties and were able to provide visitors with information as well.

An important step forward for the future protection of the island's terrestrial habitats was achieved in 1976 with the designation of much of the island as a Site of Special Scientific Interest. This designation aims to guard the land by guiding management techniques and practices used. Site of Special Scientific Interest designation has recently been reinforced by proposals to include the island as a Special Area of Conservation under the EU Habitats and Species Directive.

Marine Wardens

During the 1970s work began in earnest to try and establish the sea around Lundy as a Marine Nature Reserve (MNR). A comprehensive picture of the marine environment around Lundy was gradually being built up: the area was found to be extremely special and after designation as a Voluntary Marine Nature Reserve in 1973 the case for Lundy's designation as England's first Marine Nature Reserve was pushed forward (see Irving and Gilliland, this volume).

With designation of a Voluntary Marine Nature Reserve (VMNR) the first marine warden (Nigel Thomas) spent five summer months on the island. This was seen as a pilot project to assess whether the marine reserve message was getting across to users of the reserve. A code of conduct was distributed to visitors and the warden helped to explain this and tried to encourage users of the reserve and particularly divers to adhere to it. There was a great deal of interest from visiting divers and an increase in diving activity.

Although marine research continued at a fierce pace, the sea was without a warden until the early 1980s. In 1983 and 1984 a Marine Liaison Officer (Robert Irving) was posted over the summer, acting as the Nature Conservancy Council's representative on the island with the remit of working towards statutory MNR designation. The lack of a warden on the island at this time meant that the Marine Liaison Officer worked to fill this role as well as pushing forward MNR proposals. The warden's tasks diversified to include guided walks, slide shows, preparation of interpretive materials and dissemination of information to users of the reserve. The more traditional survey and monitoring tasks were also continually carried out. A visitor centre was set up in the Linhay with wildlife displays and information. This set the ground work for the way the warden's tasks would develop to encompass a large element of interpretation and visitor liaison.

Developments in recent years

Lundy entered the 1980s as an important site for bird observation; an area of heather moorland protected by SSSI designation; a VMNR; and an area for which a wealth of natural history information had been collected. During the early 1980s the Field Society were as active as ever on the island, bi-annual field study holidays were run as well as practical conservation weeks to carry out tasks such as tree planting and the ever-necessary rhododendron work.

Although the island was still without a warden, events were continuing apace. In 1985 the Lundy Marine Consultation Group was formed to coordinate and support the MNR proposals. This forum for all parties interested in and concerned with the establishment of the MNR continues to guide the progress of the reserve and coordinate the warden's work today. The designation of England's first MNR in 1986 followed many years of hard work and was a great achievement for Lundy and all those involved. The reserve brought with it the financial help of Nature

Fig. 3 Peter Davis, warden 1951-1953. All the early wardens were chosen for their extensive ornithological knowledge, and they recorded bird observations daily. (Photo: by kind permission of Jennifer Langham.)

Conservancy Council (now English Nature) funding which now makes the warden's post secure for the future.

The new warden (Neil Wilcox 1986-1988) started to prepare a management plan concerning mainly terrestrial aspects of management such as tree planting and rhododendron control. Several projects that had previously been carried out by Field Society members came into the warden's remit such as seal surveys, seabird counts and the production of leaflets. The warden's time was shared between practical conservation (with an emphasis on rhododendron control and tree planting), and interpretation, including the production of display materials, guided walks, talks and slide shows. Survey work and monitoring were still of great importance, as of course was continually joining in with other island duties as necessary. The log book still had its place in the Tavern and the bird report continued to feature in the Field Society's Annual Report.

Today the warden works to a management plan produced by English Nature in close consultation with the Landmark Trust and the Devon Sea Fisheries Committee. Although still heavily involved in terrestrial conservation, a large part of the warden's work is now marine based. A zoning scheme has been produced for the MNR, which develops the original code of conduct, providing clear information on the restrictions within the reserve. It is the warden's job to ensure users of the reserve comply with and understand the importance of this code of conduct, as well as other restrictions, to protect both seabird and seal populations during their breeding seasons.

Each summer season Lundy greets an increasing number of staying and day visitors; the warden is their primary contact for information and advice about the island's wildlife and how best to spend time on the island. Regular guided walks are conducted on a range of topics from seabirds to seashore. Would the first Lundy wardens ever have foreseen leading snorkelling sessions or designing underwater viewers for use in rock pools!

Conclusion

Throughout the years each warden on Lundy will no doubt have found conflicting demands on their time and energies. It can often be a very demanding balancing act between survey work, visitor activities, practical work and helping to keep the island running smoothly. Over the years there has been considerable commitment from each warden, and to list their individual achievements would require a volume in itself. Although the warden's duties have changed over the years, there has always been a continuity of purpose to protect Lundy's natural environment and improve our understanding of this special island and the sea surrounding it.

Fig.4. Barbara Whitaker (warden 1954-1957) at the head of the table in the Old Light common room. Each evening the log book would be filled in with records of the day's observations. Barbara was an excellent ornithologist and rock climber, well known for climbing in bare feet (John Dyke 1957).

APPENDIX : List of Lundy Wardens

Warden's name	Date
Rowland Barker	1947
Hugh Boyd	1948-9
David Lea	1950
Peter Davis	1951-3
Barbara Whitaker	1954-7
Bill Workman	1958
Michael Jones	1959-64
Jonathon Sparrow (died in post)	1965
Clifford Waller	1965-7

1968-71: *No resident warden on the island; the log book system for residents and visitors to record their observations is set up and proves very successful.*

Nick Dymond	1972-3

1974-85: *No warden on the island; the log book system continues to work well. Observations and ringing records were kept by the following island representatives:*

Mike Rogers	1975-7
Richard Campey	1978-80
Keith Mortimer	1980-3
Mary Gade	1984-5

Warden's name	Date
Neil Willcox	1986-8
Andrew Gibson	1989-94
Emma Parkes	1995-6
Liza Cole	1996—

Fig 5   Tree planting above Millcombe 1978

The Contributors

Dr Paul Gilliland is the Marine Protected Areas Officer of English Nature, based with their Maritime Team in Peterborough. He deals with a variety of issues in relation to marine protected areas and coastal zone management. Since he took up his position in 1993 he has been closely involved in the development and management of the Lundy Marine Nature Reserve because of its importance nationally (and now internationally). He has seen the reserve first hand on several visits and his work has taken him into a range of areas including interpretation, monitoring and survey, site management, policy development, publicity and promotion.

Professor Jennifer J George, the Chairman of the Lundy Field Society since 1990, has carried out research in the Lundy ponds and streams since the mid 1970s. Jennifer is Head of the Department of Biosciences at the University of Westminster.

Clive Harfield read Archaeology and History at Southampton University, and Criminal Justice at Portsmouth University. A Lundy Field Society member, he first visited Lundy in 1989 as part of John Schofield's survey team. He has published a number of papers on various archaeological and historical subjects

John Heath has been diving the waters around Lundy for many years. He continues to monitor and photograph the Gull Rock site and is also carrying out a long term photographic survey of the Seal population.

Dr Keith Hiscock frequently visited Lundy as a child and first dived around the island in 1969. That trip provided a glimpse of the outstanding quality and variety of marine wildlife which drew him back to the island with a wide range of colleagues over the next twenty two years to document and understand better the marine ecology of Lundy. In the course of that period, he was instrumental in establishing the voluntary marine reserve around the island and undertook much of the work which now underpins the management of the statutory Marine Nature Reserve. Keith is a past Chairman of the Lundy Field Society and now an Honarary Vice-President. He is head of the Marine Nature Conservation Review team of the Joint Nature Conservation Committee in Peterborough.

Elizabeth Hubbard's training and wartime work were in physics and chemistry, but after the war she began a lifetime interest in education, first as a teacher and then as a school governor. From childhood, however, she had an interest also in natural history – especially wild flowers. She first visited Lundy in 1951 and then began a study of its flora which was pursued during the many years she stayed on the island. Based in Taunton, she is an active member of the Lundy Field

Society and has served on the Committee. Her husband and two children have shared in her interest.

Robert Irving first went to Lundy as the Nature Conservancy Council's Marine Liaison Officer in the summer of 1983. His job was to help smooth the way for the establishment of the statutory Marine Nature Reserve around the island, which involved speaking with many divers, fishermen, visitors, and the islanders themselves of course. He was involved with the diving monitoring work within the MNR during the late 1980s and has recently taken over working parties of divers to carry out a variety of underwater conservation tasks. Robert joined the Committee of the Lundy Field Society in 1988 and became Secretary of the Lundy MNR Advisory Group in 1990. He works as a marine biological consultant based in West Sussex.

Dr Ian Linn joined the Lundy Field Society in the early 1950s when assisting Professor LA Harvey, the society's first Secretary, with student field courses on the island. A retired university teacher, he has studied the ecology and behaviour of mammals, birds and snakes in Britain, Africa and Arabia.

Emma Parkes was warden on Lundy from 1994-6. A marine biology graduate from Birmingham, Emma worked as warden in a coastal country park near Aberdeen before moving to Lundy. She now lives in Australia.

Tony Parsons is a senior partner in a large veterinary practice based in Somerset. He has been visiting Lundy since 1957 and has been studying the invertebrates, in particular, during the past fifteen years. In 1996, he published the results of a twenty year study of the invertebrates of another island in the Bristol Channel: Steep Holm. Being President of the Somerset Ornithological Society, a registered bird ringer for nearly thirty years and a member of the International Society of Hymenopterists, Tony's life revolves around all aspects of natural history. He has served as a Committee member of the Lundy Field Society.

Dr Hayley Randle is a lecturer in Quantitative Methods and Animal Behaviour at Seal-Hayne Faculty of the University of Plymouth. Since first going to Lundy in 1991 she has spent many hours involved in behaviour studies of the animals living on Lundy, particularly the farm animals.

Clive Roberts is a part-time PhD student at the Open University and a Lecturer in Environmental Sciences at Wolverhampton University. He has a particular interest in geophysics and has worked on the magnetic mapping of Lundy.

Philip Robertson studied marine archaeology at Bristol and St. Andrews Universities, specialising in resource management and interpretation. Since graduating in 1992, he has worked as a marine warden in Sussex and has carried out numerous archaeological assessments, on land and under water. Trained as a commercial diver, Philip has spent three seasons running underwater archaeological projects and field courses based on Lundy and elsewhere, on behalf of the Nautical Archaeology Society (NAS). He now lives at Lochaline on the Sound of Mull, Scotland, where he runs the Lochaline Dive Centre.

Dr John Schofield has been a regular visitor to Lundy since 1985, has undertaken archaeological fieldwork on the island and, since 1989, has edited the Field Society's Annual Report. John works as an Inspector of Ancient Monuments with English Heritage. His research interests include cultural development amongst island communities.

Julia Abel Smith was the Landmark Trust's Information officer from 1987 until 1990. She spent much of this time writing about and promoting holidays on Lundy, where she has made frequent visits both for work and her own holiday purposes.

Dr Sandy Smith is a marine geophysicist working at the Open University, Department of Earth Sciences. She has led three field trips to the island with Open University Geological Society members, who carried out much of the recent research on which the geology chapter was based.

Tony Taylor spent four summers on Lundy in the 1970s studying seabird breeding behaviour. He is now a biology teacher, continuing to visit the island regularly. He organises bird-ringing on Lundy and compiles the bird and ringing reports for the Lundy Field Society's Annual Report.

Caroline Thackray is an archaeological research assistant for the National Trust, who has undertaken project work thoughout the West Country. She co-ordinated the archaeological survey of Lundy from 1990-1994 which is currently being prepared for publication.

Professor Charles Thomas, formerly Director of the Institute of Cornish Studies, is concerned with the history, archaeology and languages of Britain and Ireland AD and is author of numerous textbooks. He claims to have explored more islands than he has fingers and toes.

Chris Webster is an archaeologist working for Somerset County Council. He has worked in many areas of the country, including on Lundy with John Schofield. In 1994 he was 'persuaded' to become the Honorary Secretary of the LFS.

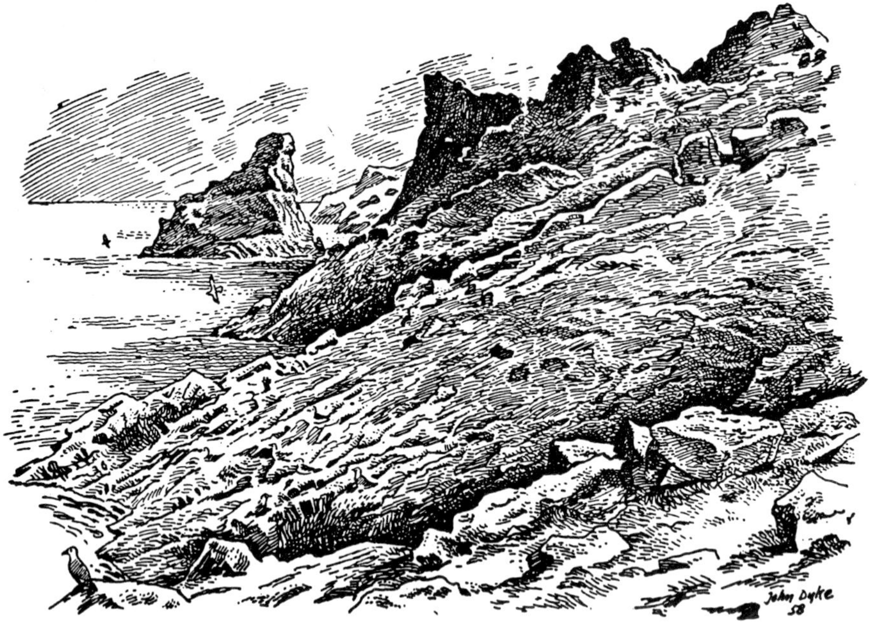
John Dyke
58

LUNDY FIELD SOCIETY

Constitution

FOUNDED 1946

1. The name of the Society shall be The Lundy Field Society.

2. The objects of the Society shall be:
    a) To further the study of Lundy and in particular its history, natural history and archaeology;
    b) To undertake investigations in these fields;
    c) To further the conservation of wildlife and antiquities of the island.

3. The Society shall consist of a President, Vice-President(s), Chairman, Honorary Secretary, Honorary Treasurer, Honorary Editor, a Committee and ordinary members. The Officers shall be elected at the Annual General Meeting and shall be eligible for re-election. Nominations for Officers, if any change is proposed, should be sent to the Hon. Secretary at least 14 days before the meeting.

4. The Society shall appoint a committee consisting of the Officers, and not more than six other members who shall be elected for a period of three years. The duty of this committee shall be to organise and supervise the field work on the island. Members shall retire after serving for three years. They may offer themselves for re-election for one further term of three years, providing that only one member may be so re-elected in any one year, but on retirement after two consecutive terms shall not be eligible for re-election until the lapse of one year. The Committee shall have the power to co-opt. The Committee shall have the power to appoint sub-committees, each of not more than three members who will advise the Committee on particular matters.

5. Persons desiring membership must observe the Constitution of the Society and their application must be approved by the Committee. Annual subscriptions are as decided by the Society from time to time in accordance with the Constitution and are set out in the current Application for Membership form.

6. Members will be required when visiting Lundy to conform to the customs of the Island and to respect its rights and privileges. Any member behaving in a manner prejudicial to the interests and work of the Society is liable to summary expulsion at the discretion of the Committee.

7. An Annual General Meeting shall be held, normally on the first Saturday in March. The Committee shall, at any time, upon the requisition in writing of not less than fifteen members stating the motion or motions to be brought forward, call an Extraordinary General Meeting of the Society. Such a meeting may also be

called at the discretion of the Committee. At all meetings the decisions shall be taken on a majority of those members present and voting.

8. Any proposed alteration or addition to the Constitution must be notified to the Hon. Secretary at least 28 days before a meeting and communicated by him in not less than 14 days to all members and must be carried by a two-thirds majority of those members present, but no amendment may be made which would have the effect of the Society ceasing to be a charity at law.

9. Should the Society be dissolved and any property remain after the satisfaction of all debts and liabilities, such property shall not be paid to or distributed among the members of the Society but shall be given or transferred to such charitable institution or institutions having objects similar to some or all of the objects of the Society as the Society determine.

The LUNDY FIELD SOCIETY is registered charity No. 258294.

For information about the Lundy Field Society, contact:

Mr C J Webster, Hon Sec LFS,
38 Greenway Avenue
Taunton
Somerset TA2 6HY

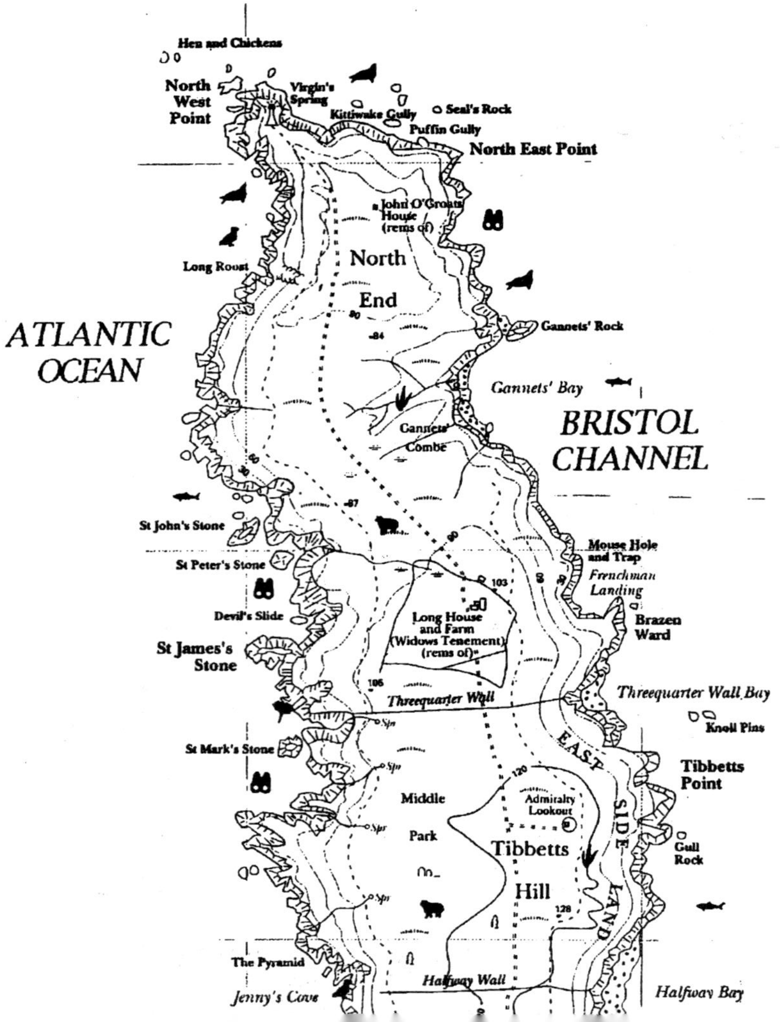
Hen and Chickens
North West Point
Virgin's Spring
Kittiwake Gully
Seal's Rock
Puffin Gully
North East Point
John O'Groats House (rems of)
North End
Long Roost
ATLANTIC OCEAN
Gannets' Rock
Gannets' Bay
BRISTOL CHANNEL
Gannets' Combe
St John's Stone
St Peter's Stone
Mouse Hole and Trap
Frenchman Landing
Devil's Slide
Long House and Farm (Widows Tenement) (rems of)
Brazen Ward
St James's Stone
Threequarter Wall
Threequarter Wall Bay
Knoll Pins
St Mark's Stone
EAST SIDE LAND
Tibbetts Point
Middle Park
Admiralty Lookout
Tibbetts Hill
Gull Rock
The Pyramid
Halfway Wall
Jenny's Cove
Halfway Bay